EXTRA- AND NON-DOCUMENTARY WRITING IN THE CANON OF FORMATIVE JUDAISM

VOLUME THREE

PERIPATETIC PARALLELS

EXTRA- AND NON-DOCUMENTARY WRITING IN THE CANON OF FORMATIVE JUDAISM

VOLUME THREE

PERIPATETIC PARALLELS

Jacob Neusner

Academic Studies in the History of Judaism
Global Publications, Binghamton University
2001

Copyright © 2001 by Jacob Neusner

All rights reserved. No portion of this publication may be duplicated in any way without the expressed written consent of the publisher, except in the form of brief excerpts or quotations for review purposes.

Library of Congress Cataloging-in-Publication Data

Neusner, Jacob, 1932-
  Extra- and non-documentary writing in the canon of formative Judaism / Jacob Neusner.
      p. cm. -- (Academic studies in the history of Judaism)
  Includes bibliographical references.
  ISBN 1-58684-106-8 (pbk : alk. paper) -- ISBN 1-58684-107-6 -- ISBN 1-58684-113-0
  1. Midrash--History and criticism--Theory, etc. 2. Talmud--Criticism, Form. 3. Rabbinical literature--History and criticism--Theory, etc. 4. Becker, Hans-Jürgen, 1956- Die großen rabbinischen Sammelwerke Palästinas. I. Title. II. Series.
  BM514 .N466 2001
  296.1'206--dc21
                                                                2001003604

Published and Distributed by:
Academic Studies in the History of Judaism
Global Publications, Binghamton University
LNG 99, Binghamton University
State University of New York at Binghamton
Binghamton, New York, USA 13902-6000
Phone: (607) 777-4495 or 777-6104; Fax: (607) 777-6132
E-mail: pmorewed@binghamton.edu
http://ssips.binghamton.edu

THE SERIES

Extra- and Non-Documentary Writing in the Canon of Formative Judaism. I. The Pointless Parallel: Hans-Jürgen Becker and the Myth of the Autonomous Tradition in Rabbinic Documents

Extra- and Non-Documentary Writing in the Canon of Formative Judaism. II. Paltry Parallels. The Negligible Proportion and Peripheral Role of Free-Standing Compositions in Rabbinic Documents

Extra- and Non-Documentary Writing in the Canon of Formative Judaism. III. Peripatetic Parallels

TABLE OF CONTENTS

ANNOTATED PREFACE TO THE FIRST EDITION, 1985 xv

PREFACE TO THE SECOND EDITION, 2001 xxxi

I
THE BAVLI AT THE END

I. THE BAVLI AT THE END. A CANONICAL PERSPECTIVE ON THE PROBLEM OF THE PERIPATETIC SAYING 3

    i. Introduction 3
    ii. From the Yerushalmi to the Fathers According to Rabbi Nathan to the Bavli 23
    iii. From the Sifré on Deuteronomy to the Bavli 29
    iv. From the Yerushalmi to the Bavli. Two Cases 30
    v. From Josephus to the Bavli 35
    vi. The Bavli at the End 43

II
THE THRICE-TOLD TALE IN RABBINIC STORIES ABOUT PHARISEES BEFORE 70

II. SIMEON THE JUST 49

III. ANTIGONOS OF SOKHO. YOSÉ B. YOEZER AND YOSÉ B. YOHANAN 73

IV. JOSHUA B. PERAHIAH AND NITTAI THE ARBELITE. JUDAH B. TABBAI AND SIMEON B. SHETAH 81

V. SHEMAIAH AND ABTALION 111

VI.   YOHANAN THE HIGH PRIEST 119

VII. MENAHEM. SHAMMAI 127

VIII. HILLEL 133

IX.   SHAMMAI AND HILLEL 159

X.   GAMALIEL 169

XI.   SIMEON B. GAMALIEL 177

XII. YOHANAN B. ZAKKAI 181

III
THREE THEORIES OF THE PERIPATETIC SAYING

XIII. "HE OFTEN USED TO SAY" 205

XIV. IN SEARCH OF THE "ORIGINAL" "TRADITION" 219

XV. INCREMENTAL HISTORY: "WHEN HE WAS A STUDENT… AND WHEN HE GREW UP…" 239

IV
TOWARD A GENERAL THEORY OF THE RABBINICAL LITERATURE:
THE DOCUMENTARY PICTURE OF THE FORMATIVE AGE

XVI. A DOCUMENTARY-HISTORICAL THEORY 249

Appendices

1. Autonomy, Connection, Continuity: The Three Dimensions of a Text of Formative Judaism 271

2. The Bavli at the End: The Judgment of Menachem Fish 283

Bibliography

Bibliography 307

EXTRA- AND NON-DOCUMENTARY WRITING IN THE CANON OF FORMATIVE JUDAISM

VOLUME ONE

THE POINTLESS PARALLEL

HANS-JÜRGEN BECKER AND THE MYTH OF THE AUTONOMOUS TRADITION IN RABBINIC DOCUMENTS

TABLE OF CONTENTS

PREFACE

PART ONE

SHOWING THAT, IN INDICATIVE TRAITS, ONE DOCUMENT IS DIFFERENT FROM ANOTHER DOCUMENT

1. DIFFERENTIATING KINDRED DOCUMENTS: GENESIS RABBAH AND LEVITICUS RABBAH

    i. The Documentary Reading of the Rabbinic Canon in the Formative Age
    ii. The Program of Genesis Rabbah
    iii. The Program of Leviticus Rabbah
    iv. Comparing the Programs of Genesis Rabbah and Leviticus Rabbah
    v. The Centrality of Redaction in the Formulation and Selection of Exegeses of Scripture

PART TWO

SHOWING THAT A SHARED PERICOPE IS PRIMARY TO
ONE DOCUMENT, SECONDARY TO ANOTHER

2. THE SHARED PERICOPE AND THE PRIOR CLAIM OF LEVITICUS RABBAH: THE RELATIONSHIP BETWEEN LEVITICUS RABBAH AND PESIQTA DERAB KAHANA. THE FORM-ANALYTICAL PERSPECTIVE

   i. Literary Structures of Pesiqta deRab Kahana Pisqa' 6
   ii. Literary Structures of Pesiqta deRab Kahana Pisqa'ot 14 and 22
   iii. Pesiqta deRab Kahana 27 = Leviticus Rabbah 30
   iv. The Shared Pisqa'/Parashah: Where Does It Belong?

3. THE SHARED PISQA' IN PESIQTA DERAB KAHANA AND PESIQTA RABBATI

   i. Introduction
   ii. The literary Structures of Pesiqta Rabbati
   iii. Pesiqta Rabbati Pisqa One
   iv. The Forms of Pesiqta Rabbati Pisqa One
   v. The Thematic Program and Proposition of Pesiqta Rabbati Pisqa One: Syllogism, Collage, or Scrapbook?
   vi. The Order of the Forms of Pisqa' One
   vii. Recurrent Literary Structures: Types of Units of Discourse, their Order, and their Cogency
   viii. The Rhetorical Plan of Pesiqta deRab Kahana

ix. Comparative Midrash [1]: The Rhetorical, Logical, and Topical Aspect. The Plan and Program of Pesiqta deRab Kahana and Pesiqta Rabbati
x. Comparative Midrash [2]: The Two Pesiqtas side by Side
xi. Leviticus Rabbah, Pesiqta deRab Kahana, and Pesiqta Rabbati: The Three Kindred Compilations and the Documentary Reading of the Rabbinic Canon

PART THREE

SHOWING THAT SHARED TRADITIONS, PRIOR TO AND AUTONOMOUS OF THE TWO TALMUDS DO NOT LINK THE BAVLI TO THE YERUSHALMI

4. DO THE YERUSHALMI AND THE BAVLI POINT TOWARD AN AUTONOMOUS TRADITION?

   i. A Null-Hypothesis: The Yerushalmi and the Bavli Draw on Common Sources Other than the Mishnah, the Tosefta, and Counterpart Canonical Documents
   ii. A Common Source Utilized by both Talmuds
   iii. Do the Bavli and Yerushalmi Draw on (a) "Q"? And Does a Topical Protocol Define the Talmuds' Mishnah-Exegesis?
   iv. Does a Topical Protocol Define the Talmuds' Mishnah-Exegesis?
   v. Does a Shared Program of Questions Dictate the Shape of the Talmuds' Mishnah-exegesis?
   vi. Does a Common Exegetical Program Dictate the Talmuds' Reading of the Same Tosefta-Pericope

vii. Do the Yerushalmi and the Bavli Form Distinct Expressions of a Single Tradition? The Null-Hypothesis Revisited

PART FOUR

TOWARD A GENERAL THEORY OF
THE FORMATION OF THE RABBINIC TRADITION

5. THE PRIOR RABBINIC TRADITION AND THE AUTONOMOUS TRADITION: THE THREE STAGES IN THE FORMATION OF CANONICAL DOCUMENTS

   i. A Theory of the Formation of the Rabbinic Documents: Accounting for Different Kinds of Writing
   ii. The Three Stages in the literary History of the Rabbinic Canonical Documents and How We Discern Them
      1. The Latest Stage in the literary History of the Rabbinic Documents: Writings that Conform to the Particular Document's Indicative Traits
      2. An Intermediate Earlier Stage in the literary History of the Rabbinic Documents: Writings That Can Have Served Redactors of Documents but that Did not Serve the Redactors of the Particular Documents that we Now Have
      3. A Still Earlier Stage in the Literary History of the Rabbinic Documents: Writings Autonomous of a Particular Document's Indicative Traits. The Peripatetic Composition
      4. Classes of Writing, Stages of Formation

- iii. The Correct Starting Point
- iv. Redaction and Writing. The Extreme Case of the Mishnah
- v. When the Document Does Not Define the Literary Protocol: Stories Told But Not Compiled and the Autonomous Tradition
- vi. Pericopes Framed for the Purposes of the Particular Document in which They Occur
- vii. Pericopes Framed for the purposes of a Particular Document But Not of a Type We Now Possess
- viii. Pericopes Framed for a Purpose Not Particular to, or Realized in, a Type of Document Now in Our Hands
- ix. The Three Stages of Literary Formation

APPENDICES

A. POINTLESS PARALLELS AND SUPERFICIAL FRAMING OF ISSUES: HANS-JUERGEN BECKER, *DIE GROSSEN RABBINISCHEN SAMMELWERKE PALAESTINAS. ZUR LITERARISCHEN GENESE VON TALMUD YERUSHALMI UND MIDRASH BERESHIT RABBA*

B. BUT WHAT IF WE HAVE NO DOCUMENTS? THE PROBLEM OF ESTABLISHING THE TEXT AND THE SOLUTION OF FORM-ANALYSIS. THE DEBATE WITH ARNOLD GOLDBERG AND PETER SCHAEFER

BIBLIOGRAPHY

EXTRA- AND NON-DOCUMENTARY WRITING IN THE CANON OF FORMATIVE JUDAISM

VOLUME TWO

PALTRY PARALLELS

THE NEGLIGIBLE PROPORTION AND PERIPHERAL ROLE OF FREE-STANDING COMPOSITIONS IN RABBINIC DOCUMENTS

TABLE OF CONTENTS

PREFACE

PART ONE

EXTRA- AND NON-DOCUMENTARY WRITING

1. THE BAVLI'S MASSIVE MISCELLANIES

    i. Extra- and Non-Documentary Writing and the Bavli
    ii. Differentiating the Types of Writing in the Bavli
    iii. The Bavli's Paramount Mode of Discourse: The Propositional, Analytical Composite
    iv. The Composition and the Composite
    v. The Rationality of a Major Massive Miscellany: Bavli Abodah Zarah Chapter One
    vi. The Problem of Agglutinative Discourse
    vii. Traits of Agglutinative Discourse in the Bavli

PART TWO

EXTRA- AND NON-DOCUMENTARY WRITING IN PROPORTION AND POSITION

QUANTITATIVE:
SHOWING THAT A MINISCULE PROPORTION OF RABBINIC DOCUMENTS IS COMPRISED BY FREE-STANDING STORIES

AND

QUALITATIVE:
SHOWING THAT THESE FEW FREE-STANDING STORIES ARE TANGENTIAL IN THE COMPOSITIONS WHERE THEY DO OCCUR

2. PROPORTION AND POSITION: EVIDENCE OF SHARED, AUTONOMOUS TRADITIONS IN A SAMPLE OF THE MISHNAH AND THE TOSEFTA

   i. When a Later Document Cites an Earlier One
   ii. The Special Situation of the Mishnah
   iii. The Free-Standing Composition in the Tosefta. Tosefta Hullin 2:21-24
   iv. The Negligible Proportion and Peripheral Role of Free-Standing Stories: Tosefta Moed Qatan Chapter Two
   v. The Reception by the Yerushalmi and the Bavli of the Non-Documentary Composite of Tosefta Moed Qatan Chapter Two

3. PROPORTION AND POSITION: EVIDENCE OF SHARED, AUTONOMOUS TRADITIONS IN A SAMPLE OF SIFRA

- i. The Documentary Traits of Sifra
- ii. The Sample: Sifra Parashat Tazriʻa 122-124
- iii. The Negligible Proportion of Free-standing Stories
- iv. The Peripheral Role of Free-Standing Stories

4. PROPORTION AND POSITION: EVIDENCE OF SHARED, AUTONOMOUS TRADITIONS IN A SAMPLE OF GENESIS RABBAH

- i. The Documentary Traits of Genesis Rabbah
- ii. The Sample: Genesis Rabbah Parashah One
- iii. The Considerable Proportion of Free-standing Stories
- iv. The Peripheral Role of Free-Standing Stories
- v. Documentary, Non-Documentary, and Extra-Documentary Writing: The Case of Genesis Rabbah
    1. Documentary Writing
    2. Non-Documentary Writing
    3. Extra-Documentary Writing
- vi. The Documentary Complex

CONCLUSION

- i. Summary
- ii. Pointless Parallels, Paltry Parallels
- iii. Imagining the Rabbinic Canon: Toward a General Theory
- iv. The Two Theories of the Rabbinic Canon: Documents *versus* Scrapbooks — And Why They Matter

BIBLIOGRAPHY

Annotated Preface to the First Addition, 1985

I

This is the third and last part of a trilogy on three principal methodological problems in the analysis of the literature of the canon of Judaism that began with the Mishnah, ca. A.D. 200, and concluded with the Talmud of Babylonia ("Bavli"), ca. A.D. 600: [1] attributed sayings, [2] unattributed sayings, and [3] peripatetic sayings.[1]

The first of the three problems occupied [1] *In Search of Talmudic Biography. The Problem of the Attributed Saying* (Chico, 1984: Scholars Press for Brown Judaic Studies [now: Lanham, MD., 2000: University Press of America]),

[2] *From Mishnah to Scripture. The Problem of the Unattributed Saying* (Chico, 1984: Scholars Press for Brown Judaic Studies [now: Lanham, MD., 2000: University Press of America]),

and [3] the present volume [originally: *The Peripatetic Saying: The Problem of the Thrice-Told Tale in Talmudic Literature* (Chico, 1985: Scholars Press for Brown Judaic Studies)].

In all three books I make use of completed research to point up main lines of inquiry into a methodological issue transcending the limits of that earlier research. *In Search of Talmudic Biography* rested on my *Eliezer ben Hyrcanus: The Tradition and the Man* (Leiden, 1973: E.J. Brill [now: Binghamton, 2001: Global Publications. Classics in Judaic

---

[1] [I gloss the original preface with footnotes placed in square brackets. Written for the second edition, these update this account of what, in my view, was then at issue and what now is at stake in the topics under discussion.]

Studies series]) I-II. *From Mishnah to Scripture* stood in the same relationship to my *History of the Mishnaic Law of Purities* (Leiden, 1974-1977: E.J. Brill [now: Binghamton, 2001: Global Publications. Classics in Judaic Studies series]), I-XXII. This book absorbs and revises parts of my *Development of a Legend. Studies on the Traditions Concerning Yohanan ben Zakkai* (Leiden, 1970: E.J. Brill [now: Binghamton, 2001: Global Publications. Classics in Judaic Studies series]), a chapter of *Judaism in Conclusion. The Evidence of the Bavli* (planned for publication later on)[2], and, mainly, completed synoptic exercises of my *Rabbinic Traditions about the Pharisees before 70* (Leiden, 1971 [now: Binghamton, 2001: Global Publications. Classics in Judaic Studies series]) 1. *The Masters.* As will be clear, the tables of comparisons of versions of stories given in that book form the shank of the present work. Here I amplify and vastly extend the discussion of the problem at hand in the chapter of *Judaism in Conclusion* devoted to the relationship of the Bavli's to the Yerushalmi's versions of the same materials.

In this way I wish to make available some of the results of inquiries originally conducted for quite separate purposes. After fifteen years [1970-1985], I realize that those earlier inquiries, devoted as much to methodological as to substantive problems, made their appropriate contribution principally to the substantive discussion of their topics. The larger methodological implications of the exercises demanded articulation and explanation, which I failed to supply. In restating the results in the present context of the trilogy at hand, I aim to correct that error in the presentation of my results. In this way I hope to call attention to the methodological implications of facts uncovered long ago and in a distant setting.

---

[2] [It was published as *Judaism: The Classical Statement. The Evidence of the Bavli.* Chicago, 1986: University of Chicago Press.]

Preface to the First Edition, 1985 xvii

For the issue remains present and vivid: what, really, can we know about the formation of Judaism in late antiquity from the canon of Judaism of that age?[3] How, actually, do we know it?[4]

To state the matter simply, I wish to explain what we are to do with attributions of sayings and stories to particular sages. I propose to show how we may deal with unattributed sayings and unassigned stories. Here I begin the work of sorting out which lessons we learn, and which we reject, from the fact that the compilers of successive documents include, in diverse versions, the same saying and the same story.[5] The

---

[3] [As is clear, I was still preoccupied with historical facticity and debating with a scholarly consensus that focused on history as self-evidently worthy. The shift to problems of religion, theology, and culture had begun but not run its course as of that writing. The recapitulation, "to state the matter simply...," continues to insist that what we want to know about the texts is, did the person really say it? Did the event really happen? So did the received tradition dictate the course of my learning at that time.]

[4] [I framed the apothegm, "what we cannot show, we do not know," and that captured the issue that struck me as critical in that time. The other side was quite explicit in claiming access to a "historical a priori," in the words of one of my critics, as in, "Neusner does not realize that there are historical facts that we know a priori." So the issue was joined exactly as I defined it.]

[5] [When I wrote these words, in 1984, I was not yet cognizant of the challenge to the documentary reading of the canonical writings that is represented by sayings and stories that travel from document to document. I saw the traveling sayings and stories as a problem in documentary interpretation: why does a given document persistently make changes of one sort, rather than another, in stories that circulate among several documents? Can we identify a bias that is effected in variations of one kind or another? That was the burden of *Development of a Legend. Studies on the Traditions Concerning Yohanan ben Zakkai.* Leiden, 1970: Brill. In retrospect, I do not regard the results as a success. In any event the claim that stories that circulate call into question the integrity of documentary boundaries did not enter my mind. I owe to Hans-Jürgen Becker the recognition of the matter of variant textual readings of stories and sayings that travel from document to document as worth systematic examination,

guidelines of future research flow from the answers, based on facts, we find to these problems in the limited exercises already accomplished. Here at last we confront the bedrock questions of the formation not of the documents alone, but of large segments of the prior compositions drawn together and included in those documents. So we move deeper than we have been before into the formation of the raw materials of the system — if not to the depths of the matter.

The idea for this book came to me as I worked on Chapter Eight of *Judaism in Conclusion: The Evidence of the Bavli*.[6] I realized that the issue of that chapter — Yerushalmi-Bavli relationships — required systematic treatment in a much broader setting than defined there.[7] I debated with myself on

---

such as I carry on in this part of the present project. But the present volume shows how I had been working within the documentary hypothesis without realizing its implications, and the rest of this preface shows how oblivious I was to what was implicit.]

[6] [That is, *Judaism: The Classical Statement. The Evidence of the Bavli*. But that turned out to be only the first glimmerings of what would have to unfold.]

[7] [I ultimately outlined each Talmud and set the outlines side by side for the divisions of the Mishnah treated by both Talmuds. This is in print in *The Two Talmuds Compared*. Atlanta, 1995-6: Scholars Press for USF Academic Commentary Series. I.A *Tractate Berakhot and the Division of Appointed Times in the Talmud of the Land of Israel and the Talmud of Babylonia. Yerushalmi Tractate Berakhot*. I.B *Tractate Berakhot and the Division of Appointed Times in the Talmud of the Land of Israel and the Talmud of Babylonia. Tractate Shabbat.*. I.C *Tractate Berakhot and the Division of Appointed Times in the Talmud of the Land of Israel and the Talmud of Babylonia. Tractate Erubin*. I.D *Tractate Berakhot and the Division of Appointed Times in the Talmud of the Land of Israel and the Talmud of Babylonia. Tractates Yoma and Sukkah*. I.E *Tractate Berakhot and the Division of Appointed Times in the Talmud of the Land of Israel and the Talmud of Babylonia. Tractate Pesahim*. I.F *Tractate Berakhot and the Division of Appointed Times in the Talmud of the Land of Israel and the Talmud of Babylonia. Tractates Besah, Taanit, and Megillah*. I.G *Tractate Berakhot and the Division of Appointed Times in the Talmud of the Land of Israel and the Talmud of Babylonia. Tractates Rosh Hashanah, Hagigah, and Moed Qatan*. II.A *The Division of Women in the Talmud of the Land of Israel and the Talmud of Babylonia. Tractates Yebamot and Ketubot.*. II.B *The Division of Women in the Talmud of the Land of Israel and*

whether or not to present, once more, a sizable array of facts already in hand.[8] I persuaded myself to take time out for such a project. First, the passage of a decade and a half in which the facts at hand had attracted no [discerning] attention and made no [constructive] contribution seemed to me to justify restating them, but with appropriate emphasis. Second, my original failure to spell out precisely the implications I saw in these facts seemed to me the principal error demanding correction. So in restating the matter, I mean to spell out more clearly both my theory of what things mean and the facts upon which any theory will have to rest.

So far as the primitives and the Israeli Talmudists[9] continue to do historical work (and they have given us

---

the *Talmud of Babylonia. Tractates Nedarim, Nazir, and Sotah..* II.C *The Division of Women in the Talmud of the Land of Israel and the Talmud of Babylonia. Tractates Qiddushin and Gittin..* III.A *The Division of Damages and Tractate Niddah in the Talmud of the Land of Israel and the Talmud of Babylonia. Tractates Baba Qamma and Baba Mesia.* III.B *The Division of Damages and Tractate Niddah in the Talmud of the Land of Israel and the Talmud of Babylonia. Baba Batra and Niddah..* III.C *The Division of Damages and Tractate Niddah. Sanhedrin and Makkot..* III.D *The Division of Damages and Tractate Niddah. Shebuot, Abodah Zarah, and Horayot..*]

[8] [For reasons stated in the Preface to the Second Edition, I had to explain to myself why, after a decade and a half, the charts that form the shank of this book required restatement. When I examined the most recent monograph on the problem of variant readings and their implications and found yet another beginning scholar, this time Professor Becker of Goettingen, once more ignoring published results and so reinventing the wheel, I decided to present the materials yet again.]

[9] [It was unfair on my part to limit my indictment to Israeli Talmudists, since counterpart in the USA, including scholars whom I served as *Doktorvater*, at that time continued to cite sayings as verbatim recordings of things determinate persons had said, and continued to paraphrase Talmudic stories and to call the paraphrase "history." Since writing these words, I have observed that excellent, critical historical work has begun to emerge from the Israeli universities (if not from their Talmud departments), and the discipline of religious studies also has begun to take root. So matters are not so grim as they then seemed to me. But still, the

remarkably little in a decade and a half), [when we have multiple versions of a story spread over three or more documents] we shall continue to hear about "once.... and then again... and on yet a third occasion...."[10] Works on the history of the law, on the one side, and on the history of the "mystical tradition" (that is, the chariot-vision and similar matters), on the other, have shamelessly assumed the incremental-historical theory of the literature which I explain in the introduction and illustrate in Chapter Fifteen. The premises of that theory are expressed as best I can and measured against data.

These facts, as I here amply demonstrate, point to a continuous literary history. It is a history of people making changes, ordinarily additions but sometimes deletions, to stories and revisions, some major, some minor, to sayings. This they did for reasons we do not know, in settings we cannot identify, and for a larger purpose, program, and system, we cannot specify. To impute reasons made up for the occasion, to claim to specify settings and context, to allege we know what they were thinking and why —these theses demand sustained argument, analysis, even evidence. [Merely announcing one's opinion hardly suffices.] Exercises of verification and falsification cannot be made up *ad hoc* for the occasion, item by item, merely as the author's larger

---

principal journals, e.g., Tarbiz and Zion, remain museums of obsolete methods and discredited approaches. And much of the work in this canon that does go on continues the tradition of collecting and arranging, hunting and gathering, that takes the place of rigorous, reasoned learning in those settings.]

[10] [An articulate debate between Israeli Talmudic historians and American critics took place in *Judaism in Late Antiquity*. Volume Three. *Where We Stand: Issues and Debates*. Part One. In the series, *Handbuch der Orientalistik. Judaistik*. Leiden, 1999: E. J. Brill, which I edited with Alan J. Avery-Peck. The exchange proved illuminating, and showed that I do not exaggerate the retrograde character of Israeli "talmudic history."]

purpose demands. They have to confront the whole in its entirety.¹¹

I insist we see the literature as a canon, the stories as they flow, not hither and yon but from document to document. What this means I explain in the appendix.¹² Hence all facts to begin with demand interpretation in the context of specific documents and their larger traits. That is a sizable program, and, in my view, until it has yielded viable generalizations of an encompassing character, all work resting on the incremental-historical method will have to await its appropriate hearing. For I see no point to argue about details when the main premises demand rigorous definition, analysis, and demonstration. To make matters specific, — and I state with emphasis —

*if we do not know what a given document ordinarily does with a received saying or story, for instance, what the authors of the Yerushalmi are likely in general to wish to do to any saying or story they receive from the Tosefta or from Sifra or one of the Sifrés, then we also do not know how to evaluate what they have done with a specific received saying or story.*¹³

---

¹¹ [As is clear from the Preface to the Second Edition, the issues have shifted. The use of Talmudic sayings and stories for historical purposes no longer defines much of a debate; only a few carry forward the received agenda of "historical" study, with diminishing returns at best. But the implications of textual variations for the description of the canonical documents are now subject to debate, as the Preface to the Second Edition indicates.]

¹² [Here I do make explicit the first principles of the documentary reading of the Rabbinic canon. But it was only with the articulated opposition of Professor Schaefer in his 1986 published lecture in *the Journal of Jewish Studies* that I began to realize these ideas are not self-evident, as in my oblivion I assumed they were.]

¹³ [Note that for me, at this point, the issues were still principally historical in the simplest sense: finding out what really happened. Only in the later 1980s and earlier 1990s did I give up on the notion that the texts can tell us more than what the writers and compilers of those texts imagined; that we could describe a realm of reality beyond the texts. In cultural terms, we

Clearly, in moving so far as the present phrasing of matters,[14] I have gone some distance from the discourse with the primitives and Israeli Talmudic historians.[15] But no one who does not say what they want to hear can enter into discourse with them. They tell us that they will not listen [or

---

surely can, for there, the texts constituted irreducible facts: what people imagined. But in historical terms, I do not know how to move from what a text claims to what actually happened, except via the material culture of archaeology. Everything else ends up as paraphrase of the sources, plus or minus contemporary opinion-passing.]

[14] That "present phrasing of matters" extends to 2001, as Hans-Jürgen Becker's unfortunate dissertation shows. I did not find in it a sustained effort consistently to interpret variant readings. Becker did a good job of collecting and arranging variant readings, but did not succeed in making sense of them. That is what led him to the nihilistic position that he took in the book. See my review in Volume One of this project. The Goldberg-Schaefer-Becker school excels at computer-collations of variant readings, but has yet to show the capacity to translate them into useful theories of the phenomena under study. Uninterpreted facts do not contribute to learning.]

[15] [But that is not to suggest all work on Rabbinic literature in the state of Israel is retrograde. Nothing could be further from the truth. Scholars in Tanakh who extend their interest to Rabbinic writings, scholars in literature and in folklore, produce important, vital research. In this connection, Professor Guenter Stemberger comments: "As to Israeli work on Rabbinic literature, there is not just textual criticism and historicist readings of the sources, but there are also some attempts at dealing with these sources as literature which are worth reading, e.g. Ofra Meir, *Rabbi Judah the Patriarch. Palestinian and Babylonian Portrait of a Leader* (Hebrew), Tel Aviv 1999' Galit Hasan-Rokem, *Web of life: folklore and Midrash in Rabbinic literature*, Stanford, Cal., 2000 (Hebrew Tel Aviv 1996) — a folkloristic reading of the popular stories in Ekha Rabbati. You might consider it as characteristic that both authors are not in departments of Talmud or Rabbinic Literature - Meir teaches in a department of comparative literature (Haifa), Hasan-Rokem was a student of Dov Noy and teaches in the department of folklore (Jerusalem)." So the sociology of knowledge — the departmental setting and tradition in which a given source is studied — governs, and takes over from logic and interior discipline the presentation of that source.]

read],¹⁶ so we need not try any more. In any event the issue before us does not interest them. Why not? The primitives already "know" that whatever a story says happened really happened, and whatever people impute to a given sage really was said by him. So on the basis of perfect faith we can do history straight out, without the intervention of the considerations so troubling to this world of doubters and disbelievers. So be it. We shall do our work and watch them try to do theirs.¹⁷

---

¹⁶ [That is a new low. I am informed by Professor Ithamar Gruenwald, Tel Aviv University, of a conference organized by Dr. Alon Goshen-Gottstein in Jerusalem last year, 1999, at which paper after paper explained why the author simply would not open a book of mine and actually read it. The Jerusalem scholars knew *a priori* that the work was wholly worthless, and this without any direct knowledge whatsoever. The conference concerned the periodization of Rabbinic Judaism, a subject on which I have worked for upwards of four decades now; A summary volume was in print before the conference was announced, see *The Four Stages of Rabbinic Judaism*. London, 2000: Routledge Nonetheless, no one will be astonished to know that I was not invited to participate. Nor did the reports reaching me suggest that those who resolutely refuse to open a book of mine on a subject on which they are working misrepresent themselves. If they had answers to my questions, which call into question their fundamental methods and premises, they would give those answers. Since they do not, they are left to make a public demonstration of how they do not notice me. The history of scholarship is littered with the failures of boycott, and campaigns of Todschweigen rarely accomplish their goal of suppressing critical thought. Even Jerusalem ultimately surrendered. Until the death of Ephraim Urbach, my books were kept under lock and key, along with the pornography, by the Hebrew University Library. After he died, they were liberated and placed in the appropriate reading room. But it was too late for an entire generation of students to engage with ideas coming from a source outside of Jerusalem and broadly circulating in the world at large.]

¹⁷ [Nearly every issue of *Tarbiz* contains an article of one sort or another that proves I do not exaggerate the retrograde character of Jerusalem scholarship in this area. They even publish articles on whether a given talmudic rabbi was nasty or nice. Indeed!]

II

Readers who follow the current polemical literature will have wondered where and how I propose to reply to three remarkable [and then current] discussions of books of mine.[18]

1. Where, as in *Journal of the American Oriental Society* 104, 2, 1984, a critic, Saul Lieberman, supplies valued corrections of mistakes, I ignore the violent language and take over the criticisms as rapidly as possible. Lieberman's diverse observations[19] concerning my a few paragraphs of my *Talmud of the Land of Israel. A Preliminary Translation and Explanation* have been worked into a list of corrections to be made, and these are printed in *Talmud of the Land of Israel. A Preliminary Translation and Explanation.* 23. Nedarim (Chicago, 1985: University of Chicago Press).[20] When we ignore, as all scholars must, the *obiter dicta* that Lieberman left as his testament of his character,[21] we come up with about a page

---

[18] [The occasion of recapitulating the results reviewed here and in the companion works cited in the opening paragraphs was the debate I had precipitated with *Judaism: The Evidence of the Mishnah* and the then-beginning Yerushalmi translation. Hence it seemed only proper to deal with other views of the same matter, hence Lieberman, Maccoby, and Cohen. In retrospect, they diminish in importance, but at the time it seemed an appropriate reply was called for. Of the three, only Maccoby went on to constructive work of his own, but that remained amateurish and impressionistic to the end.]

[19] [Delivered posthumously; the "review" was found in his papers after he died. But I have no doubt he would have printed it at his own initiative, had he lived to do so. I do not question that these were sincerely-held views.]

[20] [I further collected other corrigenda in *In the Margins of the Yerushalmi. Notes on the English Translation.* Chico, 1983: Scholars Press for Brown Judaic Studies.]

[21] [The brutality of his Parthian shot at me is what people outside of the circle of his *hasidim* remember about him — if indeed, they remember anything at all.]

and a half of minor corrigenda. But all of them are valuable, though none of them makes much material difference to the main point of even the handful of paragraphs in which they occur. [Nor does any of them materially change our grasp of the composition at hand.] Would that we had a better text, dictionary,[22] and commentary on which to base a preliminary translation. What Lieberman really reviewed and found wanting was his generation's accomplishments in Yerushalmi-studies. Had he provided the dictionary, the text, and the commentary, he would have found no reason to complain about my translation.[23]

2. Where, as in *Midstream*, May 1984, an amateur, Hyam Maccoby, a librarian and learned journalist, has his say, and, as it happens, his say turns out to concern not the issues of method and substance that occupy true scholars, but contemporary theological and publicistic concerns of Reform Judaic apologetics, there is nothing to be learned, therefore nothing to be said in reply.[24]

---

[22] But I hasten to add, for the Aramaic of the Yerushalmi we now have Michael Sokoloff, *A Dictionary of Jewish Palestinian Aramaic of the Byzantine Period*, Ramat Gan 1990.

[23] My Tosefta-translation into English depended on his text and commentary, and Lieberman never objected to the result. It has been reprinted and now comes out in a two-volume edition, *The Tosefta in English*. I. *Zeraim, Moed, and Nashim*. Peabody, 2001: Hendrickson Publications. With a new introduction. *The Tosefta in English*. II. *Neziqin, Qodoshim, and Toharot*. Peabody, 2001: Hendrickson Publications. With a new introduction.

[24] [But *Midstream* accorded a full right of reply, which I exercised. Alas, that was not the case with the *Journal of the American Oriental Society* and *Conservative Judaism*. Nor did Dr Morna Hooker, editor of *the Journal of Theological Studies* allow me to answer even the gross errors of fact in Maccoby's ignorant treatment of my *Uniting the Dual Torah: Sifra and the Problem of the Mishnah*. Cambridge and New York, 1989: Cambridge University Press. These journals do not advance the cause of learning when they suppress *Auseinandersetzungen*, as they routinely do. They make themselves sectarian and partisan, traits that mark them and their editors

3. Where, as in *Conservative Judaism*, Vol. 37, 1, 1983 (which appeared in November, 1984), a [then] rank beginner, Shaye J. D. Cohen, decides to turn scholarship into a blood sport, there is nothing to be said. Scholarly issues really are interesting when they can be discussed with mutual dignity and respect. But where the issues are framed, as in the Conservative-Judaic theological setting, in brutal and vile language, no serious interchange of ideas is possible. It is a pity. There really are issues worth pursuing.

Lieberman, whatever else he was, was still a scholar, who accomplished a considerable labor of talmudic exegesis.[25] My other critics have nothing to teach the world.[26] I accept this abuse in a spirit of humility and cheerfully confront slander and libel, because it is in the cause of learning. And at least now it is public. I am glad that the defamation carried on in an other-than-public form for twenty-five years [1960-1985] has now come to the public forum. The time has now arrived in which the nature of criticism and of the critics is there for all to see and assess. So we can get on with the task at hand. No one any longer needs to pay attention to *ad hominem* comments that prove, in the full light of day, to be deranged, or ignorant, or stupid, or

---

as fundamentally lacking in scholarly integrity. Surely Maccoby had a right to a debate. But not engaged by me in a forum open to us both, he simply went on to repeat the same mistakes in his own book on the subject dealt with in those of mine that he reviewed. So others, in their reviews, now dismiss his work as ignorant; it did not have to end up that way.]

[25] [His *Tosefet Rishonim* will endure as his most original and perspicacious work. Unhappily, the Hebrew University did not tenure him in consequence of that superlative achievement, so he had to go into exile for the rest of his career. What he did in his second go-around on Tosefta is amplify and expand and repeat ideas originally expressed in the masterpiece of the 1930s.]

[26] [Since 1985, apart from edited books, Cohen produced a textbook, which rapidly went out of print, and a collection of essays, of dubious value. So these remarks in my view are entirely a propos.]

merely silly. If truth be told, no scholar with a serious program of inquiry ever did pay much attention to political and theological side-shows.

The main event remains what it always was, the description, analysis, and interpretation of the formative age of Judaism [through its canonical writings]. When the critics have something to say about that problem, they will have their hearing and appropriate answers. I envy Rudolph Bultmann many things, but above all, I envy him Karl Barth. He had a critic worth serious discourse, and so far in the circle of Judaic learning I have not. But I remain confident that the future will hold for me and for the issues I address that serious and sustained, rigorous criticism, that I believe appropriate to the issues at hand and to the methodological and substantive dimensions of the debate.

The scholarly world in any event knows how to assess political, *ad hominem* attacks.[27] Scholars nearly everywhere respect those canons of civil discourse that permit free interchange of differing opinions. To engage in public in this labor of description, analysis, and interpretation, we all accept risks of libel and slander. To respond to discourse of such unilluminating character as has recently soured scholarly exchange serves no constructive purpose. It merely demeans the dignity of learning. Were any of us who are engaged in investigating the formative history of Judaism to invest energies in defense against slander and murderous personal attacks, the work would suffer, but nothing would be gained. Anyhow, the witless editors of the *Journal of the American Oriental Society* and *Midstream* and *Conservative Judaism* did

---

[27] [I take as the judgment of the academic world the nine honorary degrees and fourteen academic medals I have received, not to mention the innumerable endowed lectures I have been invited to give and the like. These degrees, medals, and invitations of honor come from people who have been reading — and working on their own as well.]

manage to spell my name right.[28] And the honorary degrees and academic medals that were awarded to me after these denunciations conveyed the general response of the academy to them: they were dismissed as wide of the mark.[29]

III

I owe to my co-worker, William Scott Green, and to my students of the present, Howard Eilberg-Schwartz, and Paul Flesher, thanks for the encouragement to undertake this book and the opportunity to discuss problems in its contents and composition.

Jacob Neusner

Program in Judaic Studies
Brown University
Providence, Rhode Island 02912-1826 U.S.A.

Ereb Sukkot 5745
October 10, 1984

---

[28] [As I said above, *Midstream* accorded me the right to reply, which I exercised. *The Journal of the American Oriental Society* does not permit scholarly debate, publishing only one side of any given issue, and *Conservative Judaism* is not a scholarly journal and can be judged only by the criteria of the political tracts of religious sects. I did not choose to reply in their columns to what was a contemptible screed. So the scholarly issues were obscured by the scholarly politics.]

[29] [In the footnote at the end of Appendix One I review a specific incident, the reception of the plenary lecture, reprinted as Appendix One, that I gave at a national meeting of the Society of Biblical Literature, at which Morton Smith disgraced himself in public.]

Preface to the Second Edition, 2001

This second edition of my Peripatetic Saying[1] completes the trilogy begun with *Extra- and Non-Documentary Writing in the Canon of Formative Judaism. Volume I. The Pointless Parallel: Hans-Jürgen Becker and the Myth of the Autonomous Tradition in Rabbinic Documents,* and continued in the sequel, *Extra- and Non-Documentary Writing in the Canon of Formative Judaism. Volume II. Paltry Parallels. The Negligible Proportion and Peripheral Role of Free-Standing Compositions in Rabbinic Documents.*

In the first part of this trilogy, Pointless Parallels, I reviewed the affirmative evidence for the hypothesis that the canonical compilations, respectively, exhibit determinate traits of rhetoric, topic, and logic — thus the "pointless" of the title. In the second part, Paltry Parallels, I amass the negative evidence that other-than-documentary writing plays no material part in the canonical documents — thus the "paltry" of the title. And, in this part, as I have already explained, I deal with the Peripatetic Parallels and variations in their wording from document to document. In these ways I sample the documents to meet the challenge of the critics of the documentary hypothesis.

Let me explain why familiar data assembled long ago require attention in this new context.

I

---

[1] *The Peripatetic Saying: The Problem of the Thrice-Told Tale in Talmudic Literature.* Chico, 1985: Scholars Press for Brown Judaic Studies. Reprise and reworking of materials in *Development of a Legend; Rabbinic Traditions about the Pharisees before 70* I-III.

Since the manuscript evidence for the ancient texts of Rabbinic Judaism and their sayings and stories proves diverse, the question arises: just how diverse are the versions of stories and sayings that occur in more than one document, and with what implication for the integrity of the texts? Some maintain that the variant readings of documents and their contents exhibit such fluidity in wording as to call into question the notion of a cogent document altogether. All we have in the inclusive category of a given text then are kindred accounts, each with its own autonomy of all the others. To state the matter in extreme form, as has been stated just now, we have not a single Genesis Rabbah or Tosefta but as many Genesis Rabbahs and Toseftas as we have manuscript variants. Others hold that because a saying or story that comes to us in several versions out of as many documents is represented in more than a uniform wording, we must abandon the notion of a cogent version of said saying or story altogether. All we have are differently-worded examples of we know not what. Here I take a sizable sample of parallel versions of stories and sayings and examine the range of diversity of wording. As I have shown that the parallels in my sample proved pointless and paltry, so here my sample yields no proposition of interest. The variant readings attest to a sturdy text-tradition.

In what context and with what outcome? Critics of the documentary reading of the canonical documents of Rabbinic Judaism in the formative age make much of the variations in manuscript readings of sayings and stories. These variations are so different from one another that — so the critics maintain — they call into question the very conception of a document. Each manuscript has its own representation of a given compilation; there are no determinate documents. That is because the documentary program of rhetoric, topic, and logic of coherent discourse makes no impact on sayings or stories that circulate beyond the limits of any one document. All we have are diverse versions of we know not what. Then what we do have are not at all the coherent and crafted statements, possessed of cogency and integrity that I claim to describe, analyze, and interpret. How, indeed, the proponents of this view ask, can we speak of something coherent, reaching us to be sure in closely aligned versions, such as Leviticus Rabbah or Genesis Rabbah or the Yerushalmi? How indeed — when we have such diversity in the manuscript versions of those writings?

In these pages, sampling a variety of sayings and stories that circulate from document to document, I set forth my response. It may be simply stated. For the sample covered in these pages, these objections based on variant readings of stories and sayings as they move from document to document vastly exaggerate the range of variation. The variant readings are paltry and pointless, just like the parallels to which Volumes One and Two are devoted. That is the burden of this book.

What I show for the sample at hand, and it is sizable, is that these critics make much out of little. This I show by sampling not two or more versions of the same story occurring in the same document, where the sample should favor coherent readings, but versions of the same story spread over several documents in sequence. There the sample is more likely to produce diverse readings. So I ask not about manuscript variations of the same document, e.g., the Tosefta or the Yerushalmi, which have been or even now are being collated. Rather I choose sayings that move from the Mishnah or the Tosefta to one or another of the Midrash-compilations, and thence into one or another of the Talmuds. Here we should find manifest diversity of wording. But we do not. The differences in later documents' wordings are minor and represent on the whole rational improvements on a version in earlier documents.

That is not always so in ancient Judaic writings. But it is the case for most of the Rabbinic compilations. I recognize that the critics of the documentary hypothesis have solid foundations for their perspective on matters. For some documents come to us in wildly divergent versions, e.g., the Hekhalot writings, as Schaefer has shown. But the principal parts of the Rabbinic canon in particular rest on a text tradition that confirms the main lines of the representation of sayings and stories. That is not an opinion but a fact established here for the sample involving principal figures, their sayings and stories. Thus, when we follow a story as it moves from one document to another, as it gains or loses details, we shall find ourselves in a very different text-situation from that presented by the Hekhalot-MSS. Take the comparison of the text-traditions of the Mishnah with those of Schaefer's Hekhalot-writings, for example. No one can imagine that the range of variation of the latter compares with that of the former! The Mishnah's manuscript tradition is surely the tightest, some of the Midrash-compilations come to us in varying statements. But, over all, the collated textual variants have not been shown to call into question our access to a cogent version of the several canonical writings, though no one would deny the value of collecting and correlating the documents' diverse manuscript readings.

So I ask the more difficult question of textual variants. I inquire, specifically, about the diverse versions of sayings and stories as these make their way through the Rabbinic compilations. What occupies me in these pages is a simple question:

Do these diverse versions call into question the conception of a fundamentally stable text tradition, not only of the given document as a whole, but of a story preserved by a document?

Preface to the Second Edition, 2001 xxxv

In chapter after chapter, I lay out the variations in wording that occur as the story or saying travels from document to document and form a judgment on the weight and extent of those variations. Specifically, for the sample before us I show a striking fact. It is that when we take a close look at the versions of stories that travel from one document to another, we find paltry differences. The saying or story moves along, not intact, but fundamentally unimpaired. The variations of the text tradition affect minor details, the main lines preserve the basic structure of the story, the fixed character of the saying.

That is not the impression that critics of the documentary hypothesis wish us to form for ourselves. But for the sample before it is the fact, shown in huge detail, that where we have a story that moves from a document that attained closure earlier in the canonical process to another that was concluded later on, the story gains and loses bits and pieces of its complex but never loses its basic message or changes the character of its statement. So, to repeat, it is rarely intact. But it travels fundamentally unimpaired. And that fact attests to the stability of the story as it moves from one compilation to another, the reluctance of those responsible for the telling and retelling of a story vastly to revise what they had received. Through a sample, I cannot prove more than the plausibility of a working hypothesis, which awaits systematic examination. It is that the peripatetic staying or story, external to the documentary discipline of one or another formed statement in the canonical corpus, nonetheless circulates in a fundamentally stable textual formulation.

The shank of the book therefore is not new. All I have done is add some remarks to highlight the evidence as it pertains to the issue raised for the documentary reading of the Rabbinic canon by the fact that stories come to us in diverse wordings. This demonstration was published more than fifteen years ago. I reprint it for a new generation, because the critics of the documentary reading of the Rabbinic canon have not yet grasped, and I do not think they even knew about, the facts here assembled. They do not contend with the probability I had established many years ago. So most recently, and most deplorably, in the case of Hans-Jürgen Becker, they proceed to recapitulate procedures in which I pioneered, without even citing my work in their bibliographies. But in collating diverse versions of sayings and stories, the critics willy-nilly replicate my results for the sample that they examine. That is, they show some diversity in readings. That diversity they then exaggerate beyond all plausibility, and the importance thereof, beyond all reason.

II

Why do these facts matter? Let me now recapitulate the issues addressed in this project. At stake is the character of the literary representation of Rabbinic Judaism in its formative age and canon. Do the compilations that come down to us form purposive statements or random collections? Two theories of the formation of the Rabbinic canon presently contend. One, broadly held, regards documentary boundaries as null. The other deems them consequential. At stake is the possibility of the characterization of Rabbinic Judaism as a cogent structure and system, a contextual description based on coherent canonical documents. These are matters that require considerable amplification.

The former theory sees the Rabbinic tradition as a vast corpus of disorganized bits and pieces — a mass of contradictory opinions about we know not what. These yield no category-formations, let alone temporal aggregates of focused opinion. The compilations of Rabbinic writing within this theory begin with the smallest whole units of discourse, sayings, sentences, perhaps paragraphs, but nothing grander. And these are random and unformed. No wonder, then, that within the compilations are stories and sayings that circulate from one collection to another. These free-standing stories and other composites form a body of evidence that points to an extra-documentary origin of the compositions and composites of the Rabbinic compilations of late antiquity.

I mean something very simple. First — so the critics of the documentary hypothesis maintain — came the bits and pieces, and only later on the agglutination of these bits and pieces into the compilations we now have. Everything floated free in its day. Then, for reasons we know not, in some arbitrary manner, people collected and arranged this ready-made writing in the posterior collections now in our hands. On that theory of agglutination, we cannot hope to discern cogent category-formations of coherent opinion, building blocks of a religious structure, components of a religious system: Judaism. By definition, the formal building blocks and components are null, mere accidents and random composites, not purposive statements of a propositional character.

The contrary theory — the documentary reading of the Rabbinic canon of the formative age — maintains the opposite. The compilations begin with large-scale, cogent conceptions and reveal determinate traits of rhetoric (form), topic (proposition), and logic of coherent discourse. They precipitated a fair amount of writing intended for inclusion in the planned document. They also accommodate writing that is not documentary in origin or focus. The upshot may be simply stated. The canonical compilations are purposive. Rabbinic writing begins in the whole units formed by documents with their definition of distinctive rhetoric, topic, and logic of coherent discourse. The consequent documents register convictions, prove propositions, speak to a particular time and place and in behalf of a determinate corporate body. This characterization of the canonical writings adopts for itself a historical-temporal model of a determinate character. First — to summarize — came the program of forming a document with determinate qualities of rhetoric (form), topic (proposition), and logic of coherent discourse (how matters form coherent statements). Then came the preparation of compositions and composites exhibiting the determinate traits of the document. And out of a mass of non-documentary writing, other materials were selected, or found their way, into the document, always in a subordinated position.

    This contrary theory thus contains an important qualification. It recognizes that a variable proportion of the Rabbinic documents is comprised by non- and extra-documentary writing. By no means do all of the units of coherent thought and expression ("paragraphs") in the several canonical writings adhere to the indicative traits of the documents in which they appear. The documentary reading of the canonical compilations accommodates that fact without difficulty. In accord with its theory of the formation of the Rabbinic tradition, along the way, perhaps before writing *for* documents, *within the rules of* particular documents, began — so this theory maintains — writings of a non- and extra-documentary character were undertaken. Then these too found their way into the nascent documents.[2] The non-

---

[2] In Chapter Five of *Pointless Parallel*, the companion of the present work, entitled "The Prior Rabbinic Tradition and the Autonomous Tradition: The Three Stages in the Formation of Canonical Documents," I have elaborated on this general theory of the formation of the Rabbinic tradition in writing. This brief summary suffices for the present purpose. Chapter Sixteen of the present work goes over the same ground.

and extra-documentary compositions generally supplement the expositions to which they are tacked. They do not take a primary part in the documentary exposition of propositions.

One way or another, the parties to the debate take up the same data. But they evaluate it differently. Specifically, advocates of the documentary reading of the canonical writings must address the free-standing components of the documents — the other-than-documentary-writings, whether external to all documents or to a particular compilation. The advocates of an atomistic reading of the same compilations must deal with the distinctive traits of rhetoric and topic and logic of coherent discourse that, all together, define a given document and no other. Since they build upon the free-standing compositions, they have to account for the disciplined, rhetorically-formal and propositionally-purposive compositions and composites. Those who follow matters do not need to be told my position on this debate. And the contrary position has been set forth, most often casually and dismissively, but in some instances in a serious and weighty manner. The former may be passed over in silence. They have not yet done their home-work. Evidence for their views consists of pronouncements of their own opinions, and little more than that. Off-hand footnotes, casual dismissal in a sentence or so of massive bodies of data — these in the end cannot prevail. The latter, however, are best represented by the Goldberg-Schaefer-Becker school, which has the dignity of a fully-expounded and worked out position.

As the source and author of the documentary, form-analytical reading of the Rabbinic canon of late antiquity,[3] from the Mishnah through the Bavli, from Sifra and the two

---

[3] The main items that pertain are listed at the end of this book in the bibliography of some of my monographs and research reports and form-analytical translations and commentaries of the Rabbinic canon of the formative age.

Sifrés through Song of Songs Rabbah and the Fathers According to Rabbi Nathan, I have maintained that the canonical writings sustain distinctive definitions, each for itself. Each may be characterized with indicative, definitive traits of rhetoric (form), topic (proposition) and logic of coherent discourse. What of the acknowledged presence of the extra- and — more consequential still! — the non-documentary writing contained by every document except the Mishnah?[4] I face the challenge, to that characterization of matters, presented by those compositions and composites, now situated within the canonical compilations, that do not conform to a given document's distinctive traits. Because these demonstrably find a place in any document or in none, they call into question whether documentary boundaries govern — or even make a difference — in the formation of the Rabbinic canon. They call into question the identification, as the generative category-formation, of the several Rabbinic documents, from the Mishnah through the Bavli. That renders null any account of the religious structure and system, Rabbinic Judaism in the formative age, that identifies large-scale, coherent propositions represented by documentary statements. So the issues are not negligible.

III

The documentary reading of the Rabbinic canon rests on simple facts. These are readily summarized. First, the principal documents are subject to characterization by the

---

[4] The effort to identify in the Mishnah "sources" characterized by distinctive formal patterns yields some special cases, e.g., Eduyyot or Kelim Chapter Twenty-Four or Tamid-Middot. But documentary rules govern here too. No Rabbinic document is more successfully formatted than is the Mishnah, bearing in its wake the Tosefta and Sifra, as we see in these pages.

Preface to the Second Edition, 2001

criteria of the particular congeries of traits, distinctive to each document, indicated by rhetoric (form-analysis), topic (propositional program) and logic of coherent discourse. Second, each document exhibits its own particular qualities in combination, and no document is identical to any other in the union of the indicative traits of rhetoric, topic, and logic. But there are groups of kindred documents, e.g., the Mishnah and the Tosefta, Leviticus Rabbah and Pesiqta deRab Kahana, and the like. These are established facts.

These are not speculations as to what might be so, but statements of demonstrated facts. The constructive enterprise is now in print. In the works listed in the bibliography, I have shown how documents distinguish themselves. I have described each of the principal parts of the Rabbinic canon and compared and contrasted the major components thereof. The present project advances the argument. Now concomitantly, in the three volumes of this project I take up the extra- or non-documentary compositions and composites in those same documents. My position on extra- and non-documentary compositions, briefly stated, is very simple.

[1] The proportion of extra- or non-documentary writing in the canonical compilations in most of the sampled documents is negligible.

[2] The role of that writing in all of them is peripheral.

[3] The variation of wording in the extra- and non-documentary writing is minor; the text-traditions behind the extra- and non-documentary writing are as firm as those beyond the documentary writing.

So while the documentary hypothesis of the Rabbinic canon makes provision for other-than-documentary writing, it assigns to that classification of compositions and composites a subordinate role in the process of documentary-formation.

The model that I invoke is simple. Whatever the state of Rabbinic writing of compositions and composites, the canonical documents for their part begin whole. They commence in a definitive plan and program that form-analysis discerns. The several documents, respectively, originate in that initial decision on the part of a circle of Rabbinic sages

[1] to write a book on a given topic,

[2] to impose upon the writing particular traits of formalization, and

[3] to join the bits and pieces of composed writing into composites by appeal to one theory of logical coherence rather than some other.

The greater part by far of each of the several canonical documents is comprised by precisely that sort of documentary writing. But, as I said, circulating probably before but certainly at the time of the compilation of the canonical documents was a body of non- and extra-documentary writing. That writing rarely bears the principal burden of the document in which it is located. It commonly serves as a topical appendix, a footnote, a secondary amplification. Materials of that corpus were chosen for, or found their way into, the canonical documents. That was, I repeat, ordinarily in modest proportion, commonly in a peripheral role. That is what Volume Two of this research report proves for a sample of the several, principal documents.

IV

Perspective will illuminate matters. How did the debate, running on now for twenty years or more, get underway? The debate began before I had even enunciated the documentary reading of the Rabbinic canon. First I did the work, then I realized what I had done. The documentary hypothesis of the Rabbinic canon came to merely implicit expression in my work on the Mishnah (together with the Tosefta), *Judaism: The Evidence of the Mishnah*.[5] Willy-nilly, I precipitated a considerable row. I did so by writing on a single document in the context of the systemic description, analysis, and interpretation of a religious system. Reading a Rabbinic writing in such a way, which struck me as self-evidently required, represented an innovation, bearing implications of both a methodological and a theological sort.

But I did not at that time think through and articulate the implications of a work that read the Mishnah in its own terms and framework, in dialogue with the Tosefta. That is because it struck me as a self-evidently necessary first step: this text by itself, then that text by itself, then both, each in its consequent context established in a canon of documents continuous with one another.[6] Why not read the Mishnah in

---

[5] *Judaism. The Evidence of the Mishnah.* Chicago, 1981: University of Chicago Press. Paperback edition: 1984. Second printing, 1985. Third printing, 1986. Second edition, augmented: Atlanta, 1987: Scholars Press for Brown Judaic Studies. The work appeared also in Italian and in Hebrew.

[6] I backed into the entire matter. After *Development of a Legend, Rabbinic Traditions about the Pharisees before 70,* and *Eliezer ben Hyrcanus, The Tradition and the Man,* by which point I had given up on the established historical methods in studying the sources, I turned to the Mishnah because I realized historical work of a critical character could not be done as it was being done. That method was hopeless — ignoring the venue of the sayings and stories that at that time sustained historical study. After *Development, Pharisees,* and *Eliezer* I had come to the end of the line of form-criticism (as I then understood it), and the models of Tanakh and New Testament studies for historical research ceased to instruct me. I determined to start back at the beginning, taking as my problem the historical use of the Rabbinic documents, from the Mishnah, the first of them, onward. I quickly became absorbed by the Halakhic structure and system in its own terms — thus "Judaism: the evidence of the Mishnah" as a history and analysis of the Halakhic data. I was simply oblivious to the fact that one does not isolate a single document out of the corpus of the

its own terms, since it was, after all, the first document of Rabbinic Judaism beyond Scripture? Beyond Scripture, the Mishnah had no past. It marked the starting point. It therefore seemed to me self-evidently the right way to commence work on the documentary history of the ideas of Rabbinic Judaism. And that is what I contemplated, starting with the first writing. So I read the Mishnah (with the Tosefta) as an autonomous document. I understood that canonical documents also are connected one to another, and, further, that being formed into the canon of Judaism, they form a continuity from each to all.[7]

But the earliest reviewers, most of them, such as Eliezer Schweid, Hebrew University, benign and intellectual but some few of them memorably brutal and political, represented by Jakob J. Petuchowski and S. J. D. Cohen, immediately perceived and challenged the unacknowledged premise of my work. That was, that a given Rabbinic

---

oral Torah. All the documents — so people held — serve as mere utensils for the preservation of free-standing "traditions" about this and that, and the work of learning was to collect and arrange these "traditions" in new patterns. My documentary history of Rabbinic Judaism presented an unwanted alternative. But it took many years to reread the canonical writings one by one, describing, analyzing, and interpreting each in its own framework and context. And with the results now in hand, I am inclined to think a recapitulation of the work a productive project for the future. At the end point, new beginnings present themselves always.

[7] Not only so, but I had as my model the greatest exegete the Mishnah has ever had, that is, Maimonides, who not only re-founded the tradition of Mishnah-exegesis, but defined it for all time. His commentary to the Mishnah centers upon the Mishnah in its own terms, absorbing other Halakhic data within his representation of Mishnah-matters. His precursors in Mishnah-commentary hardly compare, and those that came later simply aped his model and paraphrased his results. With him in mind, I never imagined that I was doing other than an established procedure in Mishnah-exegesis, to be sure with my own program and generative problematic, which differed radically from Maimonides' but drew heavily upon his results to accomplish a new purpose.

document could be defined as autonomous of all other documents. With its distinctive traits of topic, rhetoric, and logic of coherent discourse, it could be studied in its own terms and framework. I took for granted that one could speak of "the Judaism," meaning, the religious structure, "of the Mishnah," that is, the system that the Mishnah and the Tosefta, which I treated as integral to Mishnah-commentary, the Mishnah's first talmud, set forth. I thought it self-evident that the Mishnah and the Tosefta provide their own first, best commentary: the very signals embodied in the rhetoric, topic, and logic of coherent discourse that characterize those compilations. That is what I expounded in *Judaism: The Evidence of the Mishnah*.

That work dictated its own succession: Could the other documents sustain the descriptive, analytical, and interpretative enterprise, one by one? Indeed so, for in subsequent studies, in a systematic way, I examined further documents, the Yerushalmi and Bavli in the line of the Mishnah, and Sifra, the two Sifrés and Mekhilta, and the Rabbah-Midrash-compilations of antiquity, in the line of Scripture, as well as Abot deRabbi Natan in the line of tractate Abot. So I did not neglect the other components of the ancient canon. So much for the autonomy of the canonical documents, each read on its own.

I further pursued the other two of the three dimensions of canonical context, connection and continuity. That is, I saw each document in succession as autonomous of all others, connected with some others, and continuous, by reason of canonical standing, with every other Rabbinic writing (inclusive of the liturgical documents, so far as these originate in late antiquity). I compared and contrasted two or more documents, e.g., two kindred Midrash-compilations, the two Talmuds, and the like.

Nonetheless, the possibility of describing a document as a systematic statement of a cogent system, not only as a component of a larger construction, was challenged. The challenge to what was implicit, in a variety of studies precipitated by my *Judaism: The Evidence of the Mishnah*, then, imposed on me the task of proceeding from the Mishnah to all the other documents of the Rabbinic canon, meaning, the Yerushalmi and Bavli, the several Midrash-compilations, and the like. That work of documentary description, analysis, and interpretation for the main part of the Rabbinic canon of late antiquity has required twenty years and is now complete, so far as I can accomplish it. Another generation will improve upon and refine the results. But I know of no assuredly-pre-Islamic, clearly-Rabbinic documents of any integrity, weight and consequence that await documentary description.

Now, as a matter of fact, the direction of criticism I scarcely anticipated proved the most engaging. I have already spelled it out, so a brief reprise suffices. That criticism held that the very conception of a document with a set of determinate traits, a document that is to be described, analyzed, and interpreted, in the Rabbinic canon cannot stand. Rabbinic writings are random, scrapbooks not documents of purpose.

That is for three reasons, which certainly require systematic attention.

[1] the indeterminacy of the readings of documents by reason of textual variants;

[2] the porous character of documentary boundaries by reason of the presence of a given composition or composite in two or more documents, thus the composition or composite autonomous of any single document; and

[3] the matter of intertextuality, the flow of thought from document to document, even when a particular passage is not explicitly cited by one document from another.

V

What about variant readings, addressed here for a limited purpose? Much excellent computer-work — self-evidently — goes forward, both in Germany and in the State of Israel, in collecting and collating variant manuscript-readings of the principal documents of the Rabbinic canon — and has for a hundred years and more. That excellent work carries forward the traditions of the classical Yeshivot, both in times past and in our own day, of identifying and interpreting the meaning of variant wordings of Halakhic and Aggadic writings alike. While computer-science has made easy the collection and collation of manuscript-variants, it has not innovated in material ways in the work of producing "critical editions," whatever people mean by that language.[8]

Collecting and collating variant readings of the several canonical documents represent a shibboleth in the contemporary scene of the study of ancient Judaism. For my part, I have relied on the best editions and commentaries available to me at the time I have done my work, e.g., of translation and form-analysis. But I have never made my task the provision of "critical" texts, meaning, texts that reproduce the variety of manuscript evidence of a given document. I have left that work to others and have used their results. I have always taken account of the possibilities of manuscript

---

[8] The variant readings collected and collated by Israeli scholarship, particularly in talmudic studies, is accompanied by a systematic effort at finding the intellectual foundations for the diverse ways of reading a given passage. That work is imaginative and constructive. German work, by contrast, is literal and heavy-handed, finding satisfaction in merely collecting and arranging uninterpreted data. The contrast between Peter Schaefer's Yerushalmi tractates and the counterpart editions, for the Bavli, of — to take two famous and justly admired examples — those of Haim Z. Dimitrovsky and Shimshon Rosenthal, suffice to make the point.

variation of a given text and never constructed an account of matters based on a single reading rather than some other reading. I have analyzed large aggregates of data and proposed characterizations that accommodate diversity of readings of those data. That is the very heart of form-analysis: recurrent patterns, exhibited by vast proportions of the document under analysis.

From my initial presentation of the Mishnah-Tosefta in my *History of the Mishnaic Law,* however, I failed to articulate the way in which I took account of variation in manuscript representation of documents. As a result, critics focused upon what I did not undertake to do — the collation of manuscript variations — and ignored how I framed matters in full cognizance of the state of the evidence at hand. Put simply, as I said, where text-scholars have produced superior editions and commentaries, I was among the first to build upon their work, and where I was left to depend upon the standard printed editions, I controlled for the range of uncertainty defined by the state of learning at that time.

Now, as a matter of fact, critics, represented in *Pointless Parallels* by H.-J. Becker[9] and his teacher Schaefer and *his* teacher Goldberg, have maintained that the variations in manuscript testimony are so vast as to deny cogency and coherence to any compilation. That may be so for the Qabbalah-documents that Schaefer studied, but it is not so for the Rabbinic ones on which I work. There the variations, however sizable, do not call into question the integrity of the documents that we know through diverse manuscript representations. Unfairly, I was accused of ignoring the matter of variant readings, even though my Mishnah- and

---

[9] I refer to *Die grossen rabbinischen Sammelwerke Palaestinas. Zur literarischen Genese von Talmud Yerushalmi und Midrash Bereshit Rabba* Tuebingen, 1999: J. C. B. Mohr (Paul Siebeck). 218 pp. My review of that dissertation is in Volume One of this project.

Tosefta-work systematically attended to them. That systematic work for the Mishnah and the Tosefta, the former by me and my students in the manuscript-representations of the Mishnah, the latter by Lieberman for most of the Tosefta and by overseas counterparts for the rest of it, yielded no grounds for denying the integrity of the Mishnah and the Tosefta, even in full recognition of variations among the manuscript representations of those documents. Where critical texts, collating variant readings, existed for the documents when I worked on those documents, I used those texts, Bernard Mandelbaum's for Pesiqta deRab Kahana, M. Margoliot's for Leviticus Rabbah, for example. My translations of both of those documents were the first to use the critical texts. My Yerushalmi translation was complete before Schaefer's collations of manuscript-variants began to appear, so I could not use them. I take note of these matters only to deal with the criticism that I ignore manuscript variants. I address them as required.

But still, I plead guilty. For, it is true that, in the framework of form-analysis, I am not paralyzed by the availability of two or more readings of a given passage or even representations of a given document. Variant readings do not pose a problem that, within the documentary hypothesis, requires intense engagement, because of what is claimed, and not claimed, by that hypothesis. Stated simply but with heavy emphasis:

at no point is the characterization of a document within the documentary reading of the canonical writings made to depend upon one reading rather than another, or on one MS version rather than another.

That is for a fundamental reason, which I do not think has been grasped by the critics of the documentary reading who base their criticism on the variations in manuscript-wording. It is this: the formal traits produced by documentary description repeat themselves throughout — that is the very point of form-analysis.

The form-analysis, the systematic description of the topical program, the characterization of the logic of coherent discourse — all three elements of documentary definition address large aggregates of data, not variant readings. We can define the documentary qualities of, e.g., Genesis Rabbah or the Mishnah, even though the wording of the documents — and even entire compositions — may vary from one manuscript to the next. Becker, for one, is so impressed by variant readings that he posits more than one Genesis Rabbah, each "version" defined by its own singular manuscript. The fact is, confronted by an unassigned variant, if the unassigned variant exhibits the indicative traits of a document, we are ordinarily quite able to identify the document to which it belongs, when we address the differentiating formal, topical, or logical traits of said variant.

That manuscript evidence provides us with diverse accounts of a given documents brings no news to me or anyone I know. Variant readings captured my interest early on. My initial encounter with textual variants came with the Mishnah and the Tosefta, and while cognizant of the findings of Y. N. Epstein in his monumental *Mevo lenussah hammishnah* (1954) and lesser works, I saw no variation so fundamental as to deny to the Mishnah all formal and intellectual cogency. It is one thing to recognize variations in wording of particular passages. It is another to deny that the Mishnah has distinctive and definitive traits that characterize the whole: no rhetorical patterns, no topical program, no logic of coherent discourse everywhere took charge of matters. But the variant readings rarely if ever call into question the indicative traits identified by form-analysis; forms are forms because they recur and define and dominate. In Saul Lieberman's Tosefta edition and the German counterpart, which I used for the first four and the sixth divisions, respectively, where the variants are carefully collated, variations in detail likewise left ample space for the recognition of something we may regard as a stable and coherent whole: *the* Tosefta, not merely this manuscript's version of the Tosefta and that manuscript's version of the same. Nothing in Lieberman's discussion suggested otherwise. And that is so, even though there are significant MSS variations, as everyone knows. Lieberman's apparatus articulates these variations; but he offers us a text, *the* Tosefta, and variants, not three or ten or fifty different Toseftas, as, by extension from what he says, Becker would maintain: each manuscript a document.

True, the relatively stable text-tradition of the Mishnah represents a particularly felicitous situation. Some of the Rabbinic compilations, as well as Judaic but not necessarily Rabbinic compilations, e.g., the Hekhalot texts, are represented in text-traditions of considerable diversity. Among them, indeed, are compilations with simply chaotic text-traditions. These are problems to be taken into account. Much depends on whether the definition of a given document — its rhetorical, topical, and logical program — can accommodate diverse textual representations of said document. When we invoke the three criteria of documentary definition, we define the document as a writings that conform to those indicative criteria and no others. That serves nicely for nearly the entire Rabbinic canon of late antiquity.

VI

What of compositions autonomous of documents? The matter of "parallels" — the "pointless parallels" and "paltry parallels" of the titles of the companion-studies, Volumes One and Two of this project — comes to the fore. Critics have argued that the occurrence of the same story or saying in two or more documents calls into question the conception that the compilers of documents exercised taste and judgment in selecting for their distinctive purpose the materials they present to us. The ubiquity of parallels shared by two or more documents bears a compelling implication, some have held. It is that compilers in no way carried out a systematic labor of composition, collection, and arrangement, a labor aimed at making a cogent statement of a systemic order. People made up compositions and even composites, and editors used these ready-made writings when they compiled their collections.

What is the upshot of the matter of variant readings, free-standing compositions, and the documentary hypothesis? It suffices to say, I concur entirely that variant readings are to be noted, especially where they represent a distinction that makes a difference; and that stories and sayings autonomous of particular documents require study in their own terms. Both approaches are necessary. But they are not sufficient. The full characterization of the canon requires the recognition of the simple fact that the Mishnah is different from Genesis Rabbah, which is different from the Yerushalmi, which is different from the Siddur and Mahzor; and that all the canonical documents participate in a single system in common.

VII

To summarize the two main points of debate: The critics thus have pursued two lines of attack on the documentary reading of the Rabbinic canon:

[1] textual variants vitiate the conception of a determinate document to begin with, and

[2] peripatetic sayings and stories demonstrate the irrelevance of documentary boundaries.

Both emphasize the diversity of documentary representations, both in the manuscript traditions and in the inclusion of the same story in more than one document. Each body of evidence is seen to invalidate the claim that the various compilations respond to distinctive programs and purposes, respectively. One approach is to compare and contrast versions of the same story as these occur in two or more Rabbinic documents. The other is to focus upon manuscript variations, some of them of a considerable order, that pertain to a single document. One manuscript represents the document in one way, another in quite a different way, the one including, the other omitting, sizable stretches of writing.

These two matters present no surprises to anybody who studies the canonical writings. They are commonplaces of learning. Differences arise only from diverse assessments of the matters' importance. From the early 1970s forward, I have addressed both matters, textual variations and multiple citations of a single story or saying.

As to the diverse manuscript testimonies to a given document, I addressed the question — important to me as much as to those who regard the canon as essentially chaotic — in two ways.

First, in my commentary to the Mishnah (*A History of the Mishnaic Law* [Leiden, 1974-1986: E. J. Brill, in forty three volumes]) I collated a fair portion of the variant readings of the Mishnah-text for some of the divisions; I found they yielded distinctions that rarely made much of a difference except as to Halakhic ruling, which did not concern me. And from the perspective of the description, analysis, and interpretation of free-standing documents, the variant readings made no difference at all. That is because, more important, I defined the documentary reading of the canonical documents in such a way as to take account of variations in manuscript representation of documents. The definition of a document — its description, analysis, and interpretation — never rests on one reading as against another, but on the indicative traits that everywhere characterize the whole and establish the paradigm that governs the parts. Within that definition, the inclusion or exclusion of one detail or another makes little difference.

Second, as to variant readings of a given document, I furthermore dealt with the matter explicitly in my debate with Schaefer. Since to my knowledge he has not replied in print, in systematic book, to my systematic response to his critique of 1986, I cannot guess at what he may be thinking. But there is evidence that suggests he lays heavy stress on variant MSS evidence of a given document. The evidence takes the form of a series of "books" comprised by computer printouts of collated variants. Alas, what difference the distinctions in readings make is difficult to assess. Schaefer's printouts do not encompass systematic reading and interpretation of what is collated. Specifically, Schaefer and his co-workers mechanically collate variant readings of the various Yerushalmi-tractates. But to my knowledge they have yet to interpret these variants. I have not seen their Yerushalmi-commentaries, based on their collation of variant readings, and I do not know how they interpret these variants in the context of the Halakhic issues to which, in general, they pertain.

There is another aspect of matters, the nihilism of the Goldberg-Schaefer-Becker school. That is shown by how they treats variant reading. It is as though they contained no implications for the exegesis of the document and for its contents. Anyone at home in the Rabbinic study of Rabbinic literature knows that a variant reading, e.g., of a Halakhic texts, commonly embodies a Halakhic theory of what is at stake in the text at hand. It is not a mere formality, it is a clue to the logical possibilities of the Halakhic issue before us. Everybody in the classical Yeshiva-world understands that fact. I do not think the Goldberg-Schaefer-Becker school does. That school exhibits remarkably faint interest in the contents of the texts they publish but keen devotion to problems of form. I find this superficial. Implicitly, their presentation of manuscript variants — a mere collation, without comment or interpretation, of the variants — treats the variations as formalities, lacking all meaning. That school explicitly does little to establish their cultural (e.g., logical or intellectual) consequence. I cannot overstress, in this context, that the Rabbinic tradition in the classical contexts of learning knows full well the meaning of diverse wordings and readings of Halakhic rulings. The received approach to Talmudic exegesis is able to discern the Halakhic theory that has generated one reading in preference to another. The freshest beginner in the authentic study of these texts is introduced to the problem of implications of variant wordings and readings, e.g., by Rashi and the Tosafists, among many. Schaefer and his co-workers have thus far declined to pursue the implications of their computer-collations. Accordingly, to date they have given us distinctions that make no difference to learning. But they have made much of that little.

Still, they owe it to themselves to make the effort. For the documentary reading of the Rabbinic canon concerns itself with precisely the matter of Rabbinic culture. Not only so, but the classical exegetical tradition of the Halakhic documents takes full account of not only the presence, but also the meaning, of variant readings of Halakhic rulings — the legal theory behind this version as against that — and of this fact, Schaefer and his co-workers exhibit remarkably slight appreciation. So the entire enterprise stands for little more than a formality of arid academicism: collecting and arranging information of no consequence to speak of. On that basis I characterize that school as nihilistic.

What, second, about the free-standing story or the peripatetic saying? As to the circulation of a given story or saying, complete with variations, over two or more compilations, I dealt with that phenomenon systematically between 1969 and 1974. Specifically, I undertook such systematic studies in the comparison and contrast of the same saying or story in circulation in a number of compilations, e.g., *Development of a Legend. Studies on the Traditions about Yohanan ben Zakkai; Rabbinic Traditions about the Pharisees before 70;* and *Eliezer ben Hyrcanus: The Tradition and the Man.*[10] In a long sequence of charts of comparisons of stories common to two or more documents, I laid out the differences in detailed charts and proposed theories to explain them. Struck by the heavy emphasis on these stories autonomous of particular documents, I restated the main results of those studies as well as others in what appeared as *The Peripatetic Saying: The Problem of the Thrice-Told Tale in Talmudic Literature.*[11] That is the work reproduced here.

But I have never addressed the implications of the peripatetic saying or story for the documentary reading of Rabbinic literature. And that brings us, in the setting of three decades of critical work on the Rabbinic culture, to the present exercise. Specifically, just how important,

---

[10] *Development of a Legend. Studies on the Traditions Concerning Yohanan ben Zakkai.* Leiden, 1970: Brill; *The Rabbinic Traditions about the Pharisees before 70.* Leiden, 1971: Brill. I-III; I. *The Rabbinic Traditions about the Pharisees before 70. The Masters;* II. *The Rabbinic Traditions about the Pharisees before 70. The Houses'* III. *The Rabbinic Traditions about the Pharisees before 70. Conclusions' Eliezer ben Hyrcanus. The Tradition and the Man.* Leiden, 1973: Brill. I. *Eliezer ben Hyrcanus. The Tradition and the Man. The Tradition;'*II. *Eliezer ben Hyrcanus. The Tradition and the Man. The Man.*

[11] . Chico, 1985: Scholars Press for Brown Judaic Studies.

proportionately, are these peripatetic sayings and stories in the setting of the documents that preserve them? And just how weighty are the variant readings of the same story as it occurs in two or more documents?

VIII

My answer now is perfectly clear. I find the parallels pointless in function and paltry in proportion. I find the variant readings of peripatetic sayings and stories to allow for a cogent text-tradition, not a wildly diverse and fluid one. So the samples yield little data to support the criticism of the documentary hypothesis. To review: By "the pointless parallel," then, in the companion-volume I mean, the existence of parallels in two or more documents, stories that occur here and there but make a documentary difference no where. By "the paltry parallel," in the second companion volume, I mean, such parallels as we do have play no substantial role in the documents in which they occur. A documentary difference would impose variables upon the definitive traits of the document. Stated simply: traditions autonomous of particular documents are parachuted down into particular documents, ordinarily for purposes we can readily discern. Their presence never requires the redefinition of the documentary traits of rhetoric, topic, and logic of coherent discourse that prevail throughout the document. Their presence signifies the intent to draw upon extra-documentary data to amplify or illustrate a documentary point. Here we see that the extra-documentary data attest to a textual tradition that produces only limited variation in detail, but little variation in main structure.

One of the principal outcomes of the debate concerns the characterization of the Bavli. I see that document as coherent and creative. In these pages, particular in Chapter

One, I show how the compilers of the Bavli rework received stories and improve upon them. That work evinces an independent and critical spirit, as I explain. A contrary view of the Bavli is that of Menachem Fisch. I review his statement of the view that the Bavli's compilers do their work of editing in a servile and merely traditional spirit. I reprint my review of his book as Appendix Two. In that way I mean to underscore the larger issues that are contained within the debate on the position of the documentary hypothesis on the character of the Bavli as coherent, principled, and critical. The contrary view represents the document as incoherent, arbitrary, and subservient to the prior generations' authority. Even the literary evidence that occupies us here shows that I am right and Fisch and the many who take the same view as he does) are wrong.

IX

To Professor William S. Green, University of Rochester, I owe the formation of the title, therefore the clarification of the plan of the work. That is no negligible debt!

I consulted upwards of twenty-five colleagues on this project as I routinely do in my on-going research. I appreciate their patient interest in my research and the suggestions that they make in improving it.

Well-settled now at Bard College, I express my pleasure at this ideal situation for my research. My colleagues, particularly Professor Bruce D. Chilton, create a pleasant environment in every way, and, in his case, a stimulating one as well.

JACOB NEUSNER

RESEARCH PROFESSOR OF RELIGION AND THEOLOGY
SENIOR FELLOW, INSTITUTE OF ADVANCED THEOLOGY
BARD COLLEGE
ANNANDALE-ON-HUDSON, NEW YORK 12504 USA

neusner@webjogger.net

December 29, 2000/3 Tevet 5761
The Eighth Day of Hanukkah
Ereb Shabbat, Parashat Miqqes

I

THE BAVLI AT THE END

Chapter One

The Bavli at the End:
A Canonical Perspective on the Problem of the Peripatetic Saying

I. INTRODUCTION

Rabbinic writings make recurrent use, in document after document, with revision and alteration, of a single saying or story. What does it mean when a saying moves from one document in the canon to yet another in that same canon? And, second, how are we to interpret variations in wording, the shifts and changes in versions of a tale as it is told over and over again in its journeys from one piece of writing to the next? Third, do the variations of wording signal a fundamentally distinct, autonomous version of a story, or do we have a single story, circulating with minor revisions? These are the issues pursued in this book. As usual in my work, I begin with an overview of the problem and my simple approach to a solution to it. Then I present a sizable corpus of facts. Third I review theories adduced to explain how we are to sort out and make use of those facts. Finally, I place into context the (rather humble) proposal I wish to make to deal with the same facts.

We shall see how sayings and stories pass from one document to the next, gaining or losing weight as they make the journey. In part two of this book I give many scores of examples of what happens as a given saying or story makes the trip from, e.g., the Mishnah to the Tosefta to the Yerushalmi to the Bavli. What, then, is the status of the variations and their implications for the character of the compilations that present one version rather than another?

4 *Peripatetic Parallels*

Are the several wordings signs of several separate sayings or incidents ("he used to say..." "on that day that happened, on the other day it happened again, but differently"). The relationships signified by diverse wordings are more complex than the relationships of books of the Bible that go over the same matters, for instance, Deuteronomy as against parts of Genesis through Numbers, or Chronicles as against Samuel and Kings., Chronicles reworks Samuel and Kings. But the successive versions of, e.g., Hillel and the Passover clearly represent something other than a reworking, for some new purpose, of a received tale.

What, then, do the changes indicate, and what do they signify for the study of the canonical documents and the religious structure and system that they embody? We of the current generation are not the first to ask, but we are different from our predecessors by reason of the premises that we hold. In another age history was at stake. Then the problem of parallel versions of what we now think was a single event, or, more accurately, a single original tale, found an easy solution. If we have three versions, then we know about three events. Hence in the Gospels' scholarship comes the famous postulate that in addition to the Sermon on the Mount, Jesus preached a Sermon on the Plain. In the Hebrew Scriptures, the slightly diverse versions of the Ten Commandments kept gainfully employed long generations of preachers. The several versions of creation and of human and Israelite history supplied by J, E, P, and D challenged the wits of exegetes for many centuries. The theory of simultaneous enunciation of the Ten Commandments in Exodus and in Deuteronomy ("Keep" and "Remember" the Sabbath day being stated by a single voice at a single moment.) kept at bay inappropriate doubt for so long as people did not give way to doubt. But what began as a serious answer to a challenge to faith in the literal historicity of the biblical tale long ago had come to signify poetry and theology, no longer to write history.

In the Rabbinical canon, by contrast, historians (of a sort) imposed their program and discipline on the Rabbinic documents. But, in an uncritical time, they then took several versions of a story to indicate one of three possibilities. Either the sage at hand went around saying the same thing a lot. Thus if the same saying occurs in four passages but in the same sage's name, that sage said it four times. This yielded such results as, "he often used to say." If the same saying is placed into the mouths of two different sages, then "X and Y agreed that..." Or among the more critical practitioners, several versions of a saying or story would demand integration and harmonization to supply the single reliable and accurate account of what really happened. That is to say, when we can reduce the versions to their "original" form, we not only account for the later revisions. More important, we know pretty much accurately what had actually been said or done. As I shall show, an alternative approach, very commonly taken nowadays, accounts for the inclusion of each detail of a saying or story — among a variety of diverse details — by making up a theory on where and how, by whom and for what purpose, a given detail "might" or "would" have been added. This approach is characteristic of the last century of scholarship and stands as the (uncertain) foundation of much work even now. When we have a long sequence of versions of a single matter, for instance (as we shall see below) the vision of the chariot described by Ezekiel as that vision was interpreted by Eleazar b. Azariah to Yohanan b. Zakkai, each successive shift and change in the version appearing in the earliest document to contain it will demand, and receive, a manufactured explanation.

The first of these three theories of the meaning and historical significance of the peripatetic saying serves mainly among the yeshiva-primitives and the Israeli Talmudic historians. It hardly demands serious scrutiny. It falls into the class of marvels and wonders, along with "Keep" and "Remember" in a single act of speech in the Decalogue in Exodus and Deuteronomy. Theologians and deciders of law harmonize, drawing on all sources to make one point. Others do not have to do so and people interested in the formative history to which stories and sayings attest had best not do so. Our work demands studied description, analysis, and interpretation and not a leap of faith. But, I hasten to add, theologians rightly seek for the system, the cogency, of complex and diverse data; that is their métier. And, it goes without saying, their questions are not "historical" and their answers do not tell us precisely what happened that day — not at all. It is pseudo-theology masquerading as history that I deplore.

The second is a datum, mostly among the same circles. It hardly contradicts the first but depends on the same fundamentalism.

The third — the fabrication of a fresh context and a new history particular to each version, thus, the invention of a pre-history — proves popular among the more critical and up-to-date historians of the Jews in late antiquity and of the religion, Judaism, in that same period. It is imaginative. But it is also, to say the least, premature, because it rests on infirm foundations. How so? What we are given are merely good guesses, plausible hypotheses, lacking all corroborative evidence, let alone possibility of a null-hypothesis. The reason for dismissing the approach is contained by my apothegm, "what you cannot show, you do not know." Good guessers rarely sift evidence; they set out to *prove* propositions, not to examine and test them. But plausible guesses unsustained by evidence and untested by the imposition of a null-hypothesis cannot claim a reverential hearing and cannot ask for a reasoned argument.

The assumption that each detail testifies to a given historical occasion, event or moment, different from other details in the same literary construct, assumes two things. First, the details — it is postulated — represent things that really happened. So the premise reveals that same literalist fundamentalism that the allegedly modern historians reject. Second, it is assumed that the text at hand was preserved from the beginning exactly as it was written. Any change exhibited by a later version of a saying or story has, therefore, to find its explanation. Changes do not just happen; they are made for reason. The people who make them do so for reasons that the scholar can report (as we shall see, *with no evidence whatsoever*). Nothing lacks "significance" of the present sort, and everything demands its explanation. No explanation covers everything; each item demands an *ad hoc* interpretation of its own So the text is studded with histories, each supplied for its distinct occasion, none proposing to harmonize with or relate to the last or the next. Accordingly, it is theorize people took a text and rewrote it as new things happened. They then handed it on to others who did the same. This literary theory awaits any sort of sustained argumentation, not to mention documentation. But it generates such scholarship as now flourishes on the problem at hand, alas.

So what do I propose, and what question pertaining to stories and sayings that occur two or more times in diverse documents do I deem urgent? In this book I reenter the question at hand at a fundamental level. Specifically, I want to assemble and interpret a few facts about the thrice-told tale and the peripatetic saying. On the basis of these facts fresh approaches to the same long-standing problem will open before us.

Specifically, in this chapter, I point to the simple fact that when stories move from earlier documents to the Bavli, the final component of the canon, in that last appearance they take on a full and complete character that versions appearing in earlier documents lack. Whether the movement passes over two or more documents, e.g., from the Yerushalmi to The Fathers according to Rabbi Nathan to Bavli, or from the Mekhilta to the Tosefta to the Yerushalmi to the Bavli, or from the penultimate Talmud to the last, that is, from the Yerushalmi to the Bavli, the pattern is the same. The Bavli's authors persistently add details to what has gone before. A policy on receiving and revising stories characterizes the document as a whole, and the possibility of identifying that policy through hard data — numerous cases — provides validation for the documentary reading of the canonical compilations. It shows that the document exhibits persistent traits. The framers of the document always do the same thing with materials of the same classification. That is a formal demonstration of what the characterization of a writing's rhetoric, topical program, and logic of coherent discourse yields. Then how are we to proceed?

The way forward lies through the study of the literary characteristics and preferences exhibited by the successive documents, viewed one by one, as they receive and revise sayings and stories.[1]

We may state, as a theory based on substantial evidence, that the authors of the Bavli persistently exhibit a

---

[1] I wrote these words in 1985, and in the systematic studies summarized by them, e.g., *Development of a Legend*, I carried out what I propose here. The upshot is, the documentary hypothesis was in play before I articulated it. But I should criticize the concrete results of, e.g., *Development of a Legend*, from the same perspective as I criticize the invention of a history to match the movement of details from one version to another: how would I know that I was wrong in a given hypothesis? A consistent theory of the meaning of variant readings of the same saying or story as set forth in successive documents does emerge here and can be defended.

preference for completing tales by adding missing details. The hypothesis therefore presents itself that the authors, editors, and redactors of other documents along these same lines will exhibit equally persistent and definitive traits, characteristic of their treatment of a diversity of versions of sayings and stories as they fall into their hands. Thus the variations of wording and reading in a story or saying as it moves from document to document find significance in the larger documentary characteristics of a given compilation. What it does in one case should be replicated in what it does in most others.

What are these persistent documentary habits in the presentation of received stories or sayings? Precisely how to define these changes and what to make of them, first of all, demands collection and classification, by document, of *types* of shifts and changes in stories. Once we dismiss as simply unlikely the notion that, because a saying recurs, therefore the person to whom it is ascribed said the saying a lot, we begin this other and, I think, better-founded inquiry into the continuities and changes of the sayings as they wend their way from document to document. We assume only what the facts at hand dictate, which is that we have in fact one and the same saying. We then ask what comparison of what is like from document to document tells us about what is unlike among those same documents. Since the saying is our fixed point of reference, our variable must derive from recurrent traits of the diverse documents that receive and revise the saying.

What is to be done? That is the question answered in these pages. First, I state the hypothesis in its simplest form in Chapter One, with sole reference to the Bavli. In the shank of the present chapter I demonstrate that the Bavli consistently amplifies received stories and sayings by adding details or smoothing out problems or amplifying undeveloped points in versions of stories and sayings that occur in documents completed earlier.

In Chapters Two through Twelve, second, I then lay out a sequence of sayings and stories assigned to successive named authorities or told about them. My purpose is to show, with a large and substantial sample, *exactly* what types of changes persistently occur in the peripatetic sayings and stories. I do so by a sequence of synoptic tables. Here I compare in parallel, vertical columns, the way in which stories occur in several documents. I compare in horizontal lines the details of a saying, given item by item down the left side. Sometimes what shifts is wording. Other times what changes is the inclusion or exclusion of a detail. After each synoptic exercise, I say in my own words what I think the table indicates. As often as I can, I explain why I think the authors have made the changes that we discern. These synoptic tables derive from my *Rabbinic Traditions about the Pharisees before 70* (Leiden, 1971: E. J. Brill) I. *The Masters*, and from my *Development of a Legend. Studies on the Traditions Concerning Yohanan ben Zakkai* (Leiden, 1970: E. J. Brill). The cumulative effect of the synoptic studies, in my judgment, serves not to settle but only to underline the question at hand. It will not invalidate the hypothesis I propose in response to the question. Only detailed studies of documents one by one, then in comparison and contrast to one another, will yield a nuanced and well-grounded theory of the matter.

In part three I proceed to take up the three theories of the peripatetic saying outlined just now. I wish simply to show how and we each theory proves inadequate to the data at hand.

In the case of the theory that recurrence of a saying here and there means that the person to whom it is imputed said it a lot, I show that that theory is impossible in one striking and important case.

The Bavli at the End: A Canonical Perspective 11

In connection with the theory of an "original" "tradition" (at which point I explain the quotation marks used in the title of the chapter), I demonstrate that, if we recover what clearly is an "original' "tradition" we do not gain a great deal. That is to say, once we know what wording lies behind a set of parallel and probably interdependent compositions, which present their variations on the same set of words, we scarcely know more than we did when we recognize that the several versions do vary the same set of words. So the quest for an "original" "tradition" yields trivialities.

In connection with the third theory of how to interpret the shifts and turnings of a single story or saying in its movement across the canon, I take up a current example of "incremental history" and show how it actually works. The example derives from the newest generation, the work of an autodidact. So I cannot be accused of calling up ghosts or invoking long-repudiated approaches to refute an abandoned theory. What I think becomes clear is that the theory I call "incremental history," is "talmudic" in the worst sense. That is, it is *ad hoc* and made up, just as the Talmud itself fabricates history to explain several versions of one saying. Indeed, for all its claim to think in fresh and free ways, the more recently arrived generation, as represented here, botches the work. In its bungling, the latest Talmudic historians, as exemplified in Chapter Fifteen, do not outperform their direct precursors in the more credulous and more primitive age of learning.

So, in all, I insist that we begin with facts, appropriately classified and categorized, properly analyzed, explicitly and articulated interpreted. In the conclusion I simply point to what has now to be done. That, in a few words, is the thesis and method of this book.

To introduce the exercises that are to follow, let me begin with a comparison of a single passage as it makes its way from Mekhilta, in some circles thought to be an early composition of exegeses of Scripture,[2] to the Tosefta, thence to the Yerushalmi, and finally to the Bavli. Here we see precisely how the sages who received a piece of composition proposed to preserve the given but also to transmit something new. The passage at hand complements M. Hag. 2:1-2, which refers to a corpus of doctrine connected to Ezekiel's vision of the chariot (Ez. Ch. 1). In the left-hand column, I present the matter as it occurs in the Mekhilta attributed to R. Simeon. In the next, I give the Tosefta's version, in the third, the Yerushalmi's, and in the fourth, the Bavli's.

---

[2] For thirty years now I have been puzzled by the relative position of the Mekhilta in relationship to the other Rabbinic documents of the formative canon. I participated only casually in the debate precipitated by Professor Ben Zion Wacholder's article on the subject, in *Hebrew Union College Annual*, 1969, and then followed the debate as others, better equipped than I to pursue the question, engaged. But when I returned to the document, I kept finding it anomalous in context, as I point out in *Mekhilta Attributed to R. Ishmael. An Introduction to Judaism's First Scriptural Encyclopaedia*. Atlanta, 1988: Scholars Press for Brown Judaic Studies. In the present setting, I invoke the hypothesis that the document derives from the same stratum as Sifra and the two Sifrés, and the argument is composed on that basis. But if Mekhilta were decisively situated in medieval times (and I tend to think that it is more like the Yalqut-collections of that period than the purposive and pointed documents of late antiquity, the entire construction would have to be reworked, and all the hypothetical conclusions drawn here would be discarded. The larger issue of the "dating" or the relative positioning of the Rabbinic documents also requires attention. I think we have sound reason for positioning, e.g., Tosefta after the Mishnah, or Yerushalmi after the Tosefta. I do not know why the consensus of the moment concurs that the Yerushalmi dates to 400 and Genesis Rabbah to 450 — precisely or approximately.

The Bavli at the End: A Canonical Perspective   13

Mekhilta de R. Simeon	Tos. Hag 2:1-2	Y. Hag. 2:1	B. Hag. 14b
And the story is told that Yohanan was riding on an ass and going out of Jerusalem	*(see Mekhilta de R. Simeon)*	*(see Mekhilta de R. Simeon)* going on the way riding on an ass	Teno Rabbanan The story is told that Yohanan was riding on an ass and driving the ass
Eleazar b. Arakh his disciple was going behind him.	*Driving the ass*	going	
Eleazar: Teach me a chapter in the Merkabah	*(see Mekhilta de R. Simeon)*	*(see Mekhilta de R. Simeon)*	*(see Mekhilta de R. Simeon)*
Yohanan: Have I not taught you. Not of the Merkabah... understand of his own knowledge.	*told*	see Mekhilta de R. Simeon	taught
If not, give me permission to speak before you.	*(see Mekhilta de R. Simeon)*	*(see Mekhilta de R. Simeon)*	before you *something you taught me.*
	Yohanan descended from the ass, covered self with cloak; both sat on a stone under an olive tree.	Yohanan descended saying, It is not lawful that I should hear the glory of my creator and be riding on an ass. They went and sat under the tree.	Forthwith Yohanan descended from the ass, covered himself, and sat on the the *stone* under the olive-tree.

			He said to Him, Rabbi, Why did you descend.
			He said to him, Is it possible that you should expound the Chariot, and The *Shekhinah* be with us, and the ministering angels accompany us, and I should ride an ass?
Eleazar expounded Until flames licked around about.	He lectured before him.	Forthwith all the trees broke out in song and said Ps. 96.	Eleazar opened on the Chariot and expounded, and fire went down from heaven and encompassed all the trees roundabout. What song did the trees sing? Ps. 145.

The Bavli at the End: A Canonical Perspective   15

			An angel answered from the fire and said, These, these are the works of the chariot.
When Yohanan Saw the flames, he got off the ass, kissed him, and said.	He stood and kissed him and said, Blessed is the Lord God of Israel who gave a son to Abraham our Father who Knows how to understand and expound the glory of his father in heaven. Some expound the glory of his father in heaven. Some expound well but do not fulfill well,	When Eleazar finished the Works of the Chariot, Yohanan stood and kissed him on his head and said,	Yohanan stood up and kissed him on head and said, Blessed be the Lord, God *of Israel* who gave a son to Abraham our father who knows how to understand and *to investigate* and to expound the Chariot.
Eleazar, Happy She that bore you. Happy Abraham our father that such has come forth from his loins.		Blessed is the Lord, God of Abraham. Jacob who gave to Abraham a son wise and knowing how to expound the glory of our father in heaven. Some preach well… Eleazar does Well.	Some preach well, etc. Happy are you Abraham our father that Eleazar has come forth from your loins.
	Happy are you, Abraham our	Happy are you, Abraham our	

		father that Eleazar b. Arakh has come forth from your loins, who knows how to understand and expound the glory of his father in heaven.	father, that Eleazar has come forth from your loins.	
He would say, If all sages were on one side of scale and Eleazar on the other, he would outweigh them all.	R. Yose b. Judah: Joshua lectured before Yohanan, ᶜAqiba before Joshua, Hananiah b. Hakhinai before ᶜAqiba.		When Joseph the priest and Simeon b. Natanel heard, a discourse on the Chariot.	And when these things were told to Joshua, he and Yose the priest were walking on the way. They said Let us also expound the Chariot. Joshua
			They said, it was The first day of summer, and the earth trembled, and a rainbow appeared and an echo came and said to them, Behold the place is ready for you and your disciples are slated for the third class.	opened and expounded. That day was the first day of summer, but the heavens clouded over and a kind of a rainbow appeared, and the angels gathered and came to hear like men running to a wedding.

The Bavli at the End: A Canonical Perspective

Joshua and Yose the priest went and told these things to Yohanan, who said, Happy are you, and happy are those who bore you. Happy are my eyes who have seen such.

And also you and I in my dream were reclining on Mount Sinai and an echo came forth to us from heaven, "Come up hither, come up hither. Your disciples are slated for the third class.

Is this so? And is it not taught? (TNY'):

Joshua laid

out matters before Yohanan, Aqiba before Joshua, Hananiah b. Hakhinai Aqiba.

And Eleazar is not mentioned.

What, then do I think I have shown? It would be difficult to invent a better example of the development of a tradition from simplicity to complexity,³ from being relatively unadorned to being full articulated, and from earlier to later versions. In the earliest document the story is shortest, simplest. The Tosefta represents an obvious expansion. The Palestinian Talmudic account is still further enriched with details and entirely new components. And the Babylonian version, last of all and youngest in the age of the document in which it appears, clearly is most fully, carefully worked out. The Mekhilta's components are:

1. Yohanan riding an ass
2. Eleazar with him
3. Teach me — It is illegal.
4. Then let me speak.
5. Eleazar expounded and flames licked round about.

---

³ As I said in the preceding note, that is in the premise that Mekhilta is the first document in order. If it is last, then what we see is the streamlining of a tradition from complexity to simplicity. The facts remain the same, the interpretation of the facts will shift.

6. Then Yohanan blessed him, Your mother and Abraham are happy.
7. Scale

The concluding element (No. 7) is, as I said, a separate and unrelated saying. It plays no integral part in the *Merkabah* tradition.

The Tosefta's version is close to the foregoing, but it adds that Yohanan ceremoniously descended from the ass before the lecture began. Only then did Eleazar say his sermon. The detail about the flames, on the other hand, is absent. But the blessing is greatly expanded. The praise s now extended to Eleazar's ability to achieve a fully realized mystic experience; he does not merely describe the Merkabah, but presumably is able to go down in it. Then a second, and separate, blessing is repeated from Mekhilta, Happy are you... This clearly indicates dependence, for the first blessing would be sufficient in an independent account. But the second blessing is augmented with reference to the Mekhilta's: Abraham should be happy because you expound well and fulfill well. Thus the narrator tied in the duplicated blessing of the original version. The most important omission is the praise of Eleazar. This is replaced by the story that Joshua did the same before Yohanan, Aqiba afterward, and so forth. The later version thus emphasized that despite the excellence of Eleazar, which no one denied, the true line of transmission extended through Joshua, not through Eleazar. We may assume the first and simplest version derives from Eleazar's school, and the second has been altered, then handed on in the Joshua-Aqiba line.

The Palestinian version begins as do the early ones. But it adds a careful explanation of why Yohanan got off the ass. This explanation is itself rather fulsome. Only afterward do the master and disciple sit down — under a tree, the olive is lost. Then fire comes down, but this detail, from the Mekhilta version, is greatly embellished. Angels dance as at a wedding. They even praise Eleazar's sermon, before Yohanan has a chance to say anything. He plays no part in the proliferating details. Then the trees sing a Psalm. Only after the expanded element has been completed do we return to the matter of Yohanan. He then kisses Eleazar and gives the double blessing. Blessed is the Lord... Happy are you, Abraham. Then Joseph/Yosé the priest and Simeon are introduced, with further supernatural events accompanying their never-recorded sermon. The echo invites them to the third level of the heavens.

The Babylonian version is augmented in almost every detail. Eleazar is not merely walking, but driving the ass. He wants to teach something he has already heard. Not only does Yohanan descend, but Eleazar asks why he did so. This is clearly a point at which the Babylonian version has expanded on a mute detail in the immediately preceding account. Yohanan then develops his earlier saying. It is not merely the glory of the creator, but rather both the Shekhinah and the Ministering angels are present. Eleazar speaks, and fire pours from heaven. The trees sing a Psalm, this time Ps. 145. An angel repeats the message of the Palestinian version. The order of the trees' psalm and the angels message is therefore reversed. Then comes the kiss — now on his head — and the blessing is expanded to include to investigate after to understand and to expound. The "Some preach well"-formula comes verbatim, then the second blessing. Joshua is now the link. The story is drawn from the earlier version. The rainbow is not enough; now the angels come to a wedding — a detail presumably borrowed from the Palestinian dance of the ministering angels. Then Yosé told Yohanan, who expressed approval. The heavenly echo of the Palestinian version becomes the whole dream about the circle of Yohanan on Mount Sinai, with a direct invitation to heaven, both elements based upon and developments of Behold the place is ready for you.

As I said, *if* Mekhilta is the first of the Rabbinic documents, coming prior to Tosefta and Yerushalmi and so forth onward, then I can think of no better demonstration of the fact that versions of a single story appearing in documents of successive age normally proceed from the simpler to the more complex-formulation as they pass from an earlier document to a later one. Since they clearly depend on one another, there can be no question as to which comes first, which later, in time of formulation. If I may now generalize on the basis of the demonstration at hand: the framers of the Bavli clearly proposed to contribute their own, original ideas to a received tradition. What they wished to do, it further is clear, is to rewrite and revise to suit their tastes about what a full and conclusive account of the matter required.

The upshot is, the compilers of the Bavli served also as authors, imposing their own program on received stories and sayings, filling in gaps, amplifying and extending narratives. A single example does not constitute a proof, of course. I cannot say precisely what sort of sample of the whole would be required to establish the simple, but critical claim at hand concerning the Bavli's editorial policies and program. One important aspect is whether the same relationship that the Bavli's authors establish to the materials presented to them in the Yerushalmi characterizes their approach to other documents. A second is to see the somewhat more complex interplay among three documents, one of them the Bavli. A third is to ask whether the Bavli's authors find themselves constrained by the details of what the Yerushalmi's authors in particular set down or whether they were prepared to make fundamental changes in the received materials. A fourth is to inquire about whether attribution to Tannaite authority is one of the Talmuds means that a passage enjoyed more protection from the hands of the artists of the Bavli than the absence of such an attribution. We proceed to take up examples pertinent to each of these questions in turn.

How do these facts relate to our problem, the peripatetic parallels? We should not neglect the issue that draws us back to the data at hand: the documentary reading of the canonical compilations of the formative canon. Critics of the documentary hypothesis see in the diverse wording of the story ample evidence that each version, in each manuscript, represents an autonomous statement. It signals the nullity of documentary lines. But if we can show regular patterns of variation, as our case suggests that we can, then the documentary hypothesis finds confirmation from an unanticipated source. That is, the recurrence of a given story in two or more documents underscores the prevalence of traits that characterize a given document. A determinate authorship routinely treated stories received from other documents in one way, rather than in some other. In the present instance, the Bavli's compilers take over a story and greatly enrich it. But they have not told a new story. More to the point, they also have imposed upon the received story the traits that in general characterize their document. Since, for the Bavli, we can show persistent characteristics of a document in its reception of a story that has already occurred in an earlier compilation, the documentary hypothesis gains in plausibility.

That is because of the context in which the issue comes to bear. The critics make much of changing versions of the same story over a sequence of documents, or diverse wordings of a given story in the manuscript versions of a single document. These represent issues to be addressed in its own terms, case by case. Generalizations based on a couple of cases serve only to lay the foundations for research. They do not constitute research worthy of the name.[4]

II. FROM THE YERUSHALMI TO THE FATHERS ACCORDING TO RABBI NATHAN TO THE BAVLI

In the following exercise, we take up four versions of the death-scene of Yohanan ben Zakkai, two occurring in the Yerushalmi, one in the Fathers according to Rabbi Nathan, a document secondary to Mishnah-tractate Abot ("The Fathers"), and, finally, the Bavli's version of the same matter.

Y. A.Z. 3:1	Y. Sot. 9:16	AR Na Ch. 25	B. Ber. 28b
R. Jacob b. Idi in the name of R. Joshua b. Levi	(see y. A. Z. 3: 1)	---	Teno Rabbanan When Eleazar was dying, his disciples came to visit...
When Yohanan was dying, he said	commanded and said	---	And when Yohanan fell ill, his disciples came to visit.
---	---	When Yohanan was dying, he raised his voice and wept.	When he saw them, he wept.
---	---	Disciples said,	Disciples said

---

[4] In these sentences I dismiss as merely suggestive the claims of Hans-Jürgen Becker. See my review of his *Die grossen rabbinischen Sammelwerke Palaestinas. Zur literarischen Genese von Talmud Yerushalmi und Midrash Bereshit Rabba* Tuebingen, 1999: J. C. B. Mohr (Paul Siebeck).in *Extra- and Non-Documentary Writing in the Canon of Formative Judaism. I. The Pointless Parallel: Hans-Jürgen Becker and the Myth of the Autonomous Tradition in Rabbinic Documents.*

		Tall pillar, light of the world, mighty hammer why weep?	Light of Israel, Right-hand pillar, Mighty Hammer Why weep?
---	---	Do I go to judgment before a mortal kind, who dies and can be bribed? I go before king of kings and don't know his decision Ps. 22:30.	If I were going before mortal king who may be bribed, I'd weep. Now that I go before immortal God, and do not know his decision, should I not weep?
---	---	---	They said, Bless us. He said, May you fear heaven as much as you fear men.
Clear the house because of uncleanness	clear the courtyard	---	When he died, he said, Clear out the vessels and prepare a chair for Hezekiah who comes.
And give a chair for Hezekiah King of Judah	ordain		
Rabbi Eliezer when dying said	---	---	---

Clear the house because of uncleanness	---	---	---
And set a chair For Rabban Yohanan ben Zakkai	---	---	---

The two Palestinian Talmudic versions are simple and unadorned. That in y. A.Z. 3:1 includes the death scene of Eliezer, but in proper chronological order, that is, first Yohanan, then Eliezer. The reference to a chair for Yohanan is omitted in the corresponding death scene in Ber. 28b, which is as different for Eliezer as it is for Yohanan. Sot. 9:16 omits all reference to Eliezer's death scene. It is otherwise close to the account of Jacob b. Idi in Joshua's name in Y. A.Z., and is given the same attribution. The long baraita in b. Ber. 28b involves an extended account of Eliezer's death, followed by a similarly long version of Yohanan's. The "clear out the vessels," which is the point of the Palestinian versions, is rather awkwardly tacked on at the end by the device of having the long sermon introduced by "When he was sick," and the dying words by "In the hour of his death." The final blessing is included, parallel to that of Eliezer, but of different content The ARNA version omits all reference to Eliezer. It begins with Yohanan's weeping; the disciples play a less important role; and they do not get a blessing at the end. Light of Israel becomes of the world; right-hand pillar becomes tall pillar; that is, the Babylonian version is more specific alludes to concrete images. The actual homilies require closer comparison:

ARNa	B. Ber. 28b

Do I go before a king of flesh and blood
  - whose anger is of this world
  - whose punishment is of this world
  - whose death-penalty is of this world
  - who can be bribed with words or money?
 	
I go before King of Kings
  - whose anger is eternal
  - who cannot be bribed with words or money
Before me are two roads, one to Paradise, one to Gehenna
 	
And of this the verse says — Ps. 22:30.
	If I went before a king of flesh and blood, who is here today and in the grave tomorrow
	  - whose anger is not eternal
	  - whose imprisonment is not eternal
	  - whose death-penalty is not eternal
	And I can bribe him with words or money
	Even so would I weep
	I go before the eternal God
	  -whose anger is eternal
	  -whose imprisonment is eternal
	  -whose death-penalty is eternal
	
	And I do not know to which he will sentence me.
	
	They said to him, Master bless us? [As above.]

The homilies are practically identical, certainly close enough to show dependence on one another. It is therefore striking that the concluding blessing is absent in ARNA. I think the additional clause in the Bavli's version was added so that Yohanan's death-scene would be symmetrical to Eliezer's. The same factor accounts for the importance of the disciples in the baraita's death-scene, by contrast to their role as mere bystanders in ARNa.

It seems clear to me that the primary Palestinian version is y. A.Z. 3:1, for it is unlikely that Jacob b. Idi in Joshua's name would have handed on two separate versions, on long, the other short. Rather the Y. Sot. 9:16 version has merely been shortened by the emission of reference to

Eliezer. It is otherwise so close as to be completely dependent on the longer version. There can be no question of relative age. Both appear in the name of the same master and cannot be thought to come from different schools or periods.

The Babylonian and ARNa versions are another matter. I should imagine, following the former analogy, that b. Ber. 28b is the older, more complete version, shaped along the lines of Eliezer's death scene, as I said. ARNa afterward omits the details involving masters other than Yohanan, introduces the exegesis of Ps. 22:30, and concludes with the (probably) famous, "Clear the house..."

What are the primary elements of Yohanan's death scene? Clearly they began with "Clear the house... prepare a chair," which appears throughout, even to the point of being awkwardly tacked on in b. Ber. 28b and ARNa. In the Palestinian accounts, by contrast, the two-fold message fits together without strain. In the ARNa and B. Ber. versions, we thus find five further, certainly later elements:

1. He wept as he was sick/dying,
2. Disciples [came to visit and] asked why,
3. And heaped on him encomia,
4. He replied saying he was going to eternal judgment and did not know the likely decision,
5. [They asked to be blessed].

I see no reason to suppose all these elements are not late inventions, coming long after the very simple account of Joshua b. Levi. They cannot be called "expansions" of Joshua's account; indeed they bear little or no relationship to it. Rather they make use of some of the same materials as Joshua, particularly the Clear the house... set a chair... These may not have been original with Joshua. We do not have to imagine the Bavli's version was shaped by masters who had ever even heard Joshua's version. Indeed, I doubt they did.

To conclude: The death-scene went from the simple to the complex, and from the Palestinian Talmud's attribution by R. Jacob b. Idi to R. Joshua, on the other hand, to the fully articulated baraita-form (Teno Rabbanan) on the other. ARNa again seems closer to the Babylonian baraita than to the simpler Palestinian version. It seems to me possible that the question of the date of the ARNa will have to be restudied, for it sometimes conforms not to the earlier Palestinian versions, but to the substantially later Babylonian ones. Even though all authorities derive from the third century or earlier, the forms of important sayings which do exhibit Babylonian parallels normally adhere to those Babylonian parallels, hence to later, Babylonian developments of Palestinian materials or to materials invented to begin with in the Babylonian schools.

We once again see clearly that a passage frequently shows development and elaboration when it appears in later documents, with the Bavli at the end of the line more often than not. Details are added later on. As we follow stories through several recensions, we do find that passages are normally developed, details are added, and, as I said, the Bavli's version commonly is the fullest and best elaborated. The documentary hypothesis finds confirmation in the uniform characteristics of the several documents' respective modes of receiving and revising the same story.

III. FROM THE SIFRÉ ON DEUTERONOMY TO THE BAVLI

Sifré Deut. 144	B. San. 32b
Righteousness... shall pursue	Teno Rabbanan

The Bavli at the End: A Canonical Perspective 29

Go after a good court.	Go after a good court.
After the court of Yohanan.	After the court of Eliezer in Lud
After the court of Eliezer. Hayil	After the court Yohanan in Beror
	<u>Teno Rabbanan</u>
	Righteousness... shall pursue
	Go after the sages to the academy [*yeshivah*].
	After Eliezer to Lud
	After Yohanan to Beror Hayil
	After Joshua to Peqiin
	After Gamaliel to Yabneh
	After Aqiba to Bnei Beraq
	After Matthew to Rome
	After Hananiah b. Teradion to Sikhnin
	After Yosé to Sepphoris
	After Judah b. Bathyra to Nisibis
	After Hananiah nephew of R. Joshua to the Exile
	After Rabbi [Judah] to Bet Shearim
	After the sages to the Hewn Stone Chamber.

The two versions appear in sequence in the Babylonian Talmud. The latter of the two obviously is an expansion of the former, the brief and simple version of Sifré Deut. It adds the details of where their courts were. I think it unlikely that, had those details been at first included, they would later on have been suppressed. It would have deprived the disciples of useful information, and there was no good reason to do so. The third and longest entry cannot date from the earlier than the first third of the third century. We see the immense expansion of the one quoted just above. Eliezer and Yohanan keep their places. Then follows the first generation of Yabneh, that is, Joshua and Gamaliel; then the generation of Aqiba; then the one immediately following the Bar Kokhba war; finally Judah; and at the end, "the sages" to the (presumably eschatological) Hewn Stone chamber. It is again noteworthy that the versions appearing in later documents are elaborated and clearly later than the versions appearing in earlier documents.

IV. FROM THE YERUSHALMI TO BAVLI

We come now to two simple instances in which materials occur in the Yerushalmi and then in the Bavli, with no intervening stage (if that is what the Fathers according to Rabbi Nathan represents!) and little complexity.

The Mishnah states that if one is coming along the way and hears an outcry and says, "May it be his will that this does not come from my house," that is a false prayer. We then find the following:

> He was coming from the way, what does he say? "I am sure that these are not in my house."
> Hillel the Elder says, "From a bad report he does not fear." (Ps. 112:7).

The next version is attributed to Tannaim, with the redactional superscription. Our Rabbis taught (*Teno rabbanan*), then given a duplicated superscription, story about (*Ma'aseh b*). It follows:

> Hillel the Elder was coming from a journey, and he heard the sound of an outcry in the city. He said, "I am sure this is not my house."
> And of him Scripture says, "From a bad report he does not fear: his heart is steadfast, trusting in the Lord (Ps. 1 12:7)."

Hillel's "exegesis" of Ps. 112:7 thus is turned into a story. The verse of Scripture cited concerning Hillel is made to say in the second story what *anyone* is supposed to say according to the first version. I take it for granted that the Bavli's version comes later than, is and is based upon, the Palestinian Talmudic version (which is not given a Tannaitic attribution!). The word-for-word correspondences make this virtually certain, and the movement from an anonymous to a named teaching seems to me decisive evidence that the Babylonian version depends upon the Palestinian.

The second story bears attribution, in the Bavli's version, to Tannaite authority. While such an attribution is commonly interpreted to mean that the story derives from authorities who occur, also, in the Mishnah and hence from the second century or before, the example at hand will not sustain that theory of the matter. From the present perspective that is a tangential point. The main thing, once more, is simply to see what the Bavli is prepared to do with materials first used in the Yerushalmi. In the present exercise, however, I list the Bavli first, then the Yerushalmi, to show that the result remains the same, however we arrange the sources. We begin with the texts under study.

> A. Our Rabbis taught (TNW RBNN): The story is told about (M'SH B) a certain man whose sons did not conduct themselves in a proper manner. He arose and wrote his estate over to Jonathan b. Uzziel.

What did Jonathan b. Uzziel do? He sold a third, consecrated a third, and returned a third to his sons [of the man].

> B. Shammai came upon him with his staff and bag. He said to him, "Shammai, if you can take back what I have sold and what I have consecrated,

> you can also take back what I have returned. But if not, neither can you take back what I have returned."
>
> C. He exclaimed, "The son of Uzziel has confounded me, the son of Uzziel has confounded me."
>
> B. Baba Batra 133b-I 34a,
> (trans. I. W. Slotki, 562)

The setting is supplied by a saying of Samuel to Judah not to transfer inheritances even from bad sons to good ones. What is even more interesting is the following story, which concerns the disciples of Hillel: The greatest of them was Jonathan, the least was Yohanan ben Zakkai. So the framework is set of pericopae on the greatness of Jonathan b. Uzziel, and the above story is, with interruptions and glosses, in fact part of a little Jonathan b. Uzziel-tractate.

The story seems to be a unity, but only if it depends on Y. Ned. 5:6. Otherwise, part B is certainly separate, for we have no hint of Shammai's involvement in part A. Here is the Yerushalmi's version:

> A. Said Rabbi Yosé b. Rabbi Bun, "Thus was the case ['BD']: Jonathan b. Uzziel's father foreswore him from his property, and arose and wrote them over to Shammai.'
>
> B. "What did Shammai do? He sold part, sanctified part, and gave the rest to him [Jonathan] as a gift, and said, 'Whoever will come and complain against this gift, let him remove the hand of the purchasers and from the hand of the sanctuary and afterward he may remove from his hand.'"
>
> Y. Nedarim 5:6

The Palestinian version of the Jonathan-story is strikingly different from the Babylonian *baraita*. Here the gift is to Shammai, who acts in behalf of Jonathan by saving for him part of the father's property. Shammai's presence is now comprehensible. This is the whole pericope. The story certainly is a unitary composition. No element comes as a surprise; nothing is intruded. Now to the comparison:

B. B. L3. 1 3 3b- 1 3 4a	Y. Ned. 5:6
1. TNW RBNN	1. R. Yosé b. R. Bun said
2. Ma'aseh b- ('BD')	2. Thus was the thing
3. One man whose sons did not behave according to rule.	3. ---
4. He rose and wrote his property to Jonathan b. Uzziel and rose and wrote them to Shammai.	4. Jonathan b. Uzziel's father prevented him by vow from his property
5. What did Jonathan b. Uzziel do?	5. What did Shammai do?
6. He sold a third	6. He sold part
7. consecrated a third	7. consecrated part
8. and returned a third to his sons.	& and gave him the rest as a gift.
9. Shammai came to him in his staff and bag.	9. ---
10. He said to him, Shammai, if you can take away what I have sold and what I have consecrated, you can take away what I have returned.	10. He [Shammai] said, Whoever will come and complain against this gift, let him retrieve from the hand of the sanctuary, and afterward let him remove from the hand of this one.
11. If not, you cannot take away what I have returned.	11. [As above]
12. He said, Ben Uzziel has confounded me [twice].	12. --

One version completely reverses the account of the other. The first question is, which comes first? It seems to me that the Palestinian version absolutely must precede the Babylonian baraita, and that the latter certainly had to have been shaped in complete dependency upon it. Why so sure? The decisive fact is the intrusion of Shammai into the Babylonian version in no. 9. Who ever mentioned his name? Only in the Palestinian version is Shammai integral to the story. One could, to be sure, divide the baraita into fragments of two independent stories, one in which Jonathan b. Uzziel plays the major, and affirmative role, the other in which Shammai somehow is brought into play. But that theoretical division seems to me unlikely, in the face of the fact that the Palestinian account supplies a complete and unitary story. Both parties there play a part from the outset. No one has to be intruded afterward.

The Babylonian version has translated 'BD' into its conventional superscription, *Ma'aseh b*. It has supplied the reason for the disinheritance. In the Palestinian version we understand at the very outset why Jonathan was included — it was his own father. In the Babylonian, we are as mystified by the fight to Jonathan as by the intrusion of Shammai.

The Babylonian concretizes part to third, obvious but still an improvement. The action of Shammai in the Palestinian version is now copied by Jonathan in the other. Since Shammai is involved in the Palestinian one, the Babylonians have to invent a dramatic encounter to bring in Shammai. Now "whoever will come" is turned into "Shammai, if you." The elements of No. 10 are otherwise not much different. The baraita is somewhat more fluent: if you can do this, you can do that and if you cannot do this, you cannot do that. The Palestinian has thus been improved by the division into affirmative and negative clauses, thus making a binding condition, and the references to hand of purchasers/sanctuary are turned into active verbs. The absence of No. 12 in the Palestinian version is for obvious reasons. So the Babylonian version is certainly later than the Palestinian one.

V. FROM JOSEPHUS TO THE BAVLI

Since Josephus wrote his works in Aramaic, then having them translated into Greek, we may hardly be surprised to find in Rabbinic documents familiarity with materials also known to us in those writings. Since the Rabbinic sages can have read them in Aramaic, we have no reason to begin with to deny that they may have done so. And there is evidence that they adopted stories told by Josephus, since the only way to understand the Rabbinic version of the matter is to invoke details found, otherwise, only in Josephus's narrative, as we shall now see.

To begin with, let us first deal with the relevant passages as they occur in the Rabbinic canon, then turn to Josephus' version of the same matters. There are two important passages, one in the Tosefta, the other in the Bavli. The former serves to establish the fact that exactly the same words occur in both a Rabbinic composition, Tos. Sotah 13:7, and Josephus' narrative. The tatter then shows clear and unmistakable dependence of the Talmudic version of a story upon Josephus' version of the same story.

> Yohanan the High Priest heard from the house of the Holy of Holies, *"The young men who went out to make war against Antioch have conquered"* and they noted that hour, and it tallied that they had conquered at that very hour.

The italicized words are in Aramaic, the rest in Hebrew. The point of the pericope is a miraculous revelation to Yohanan, another indication of the high favor he enjoyed in Rabbinical circles. The kernel of the pericope is the Aramaic passage, in which case the point must be as given, that Yohanan was vouchsafed a heavenly revelation. The Bavli's story of importance in our inquiry is as follows:

A. Abbaye said, "How do I know it [re the silence of a husband in a case in which the wife is charged with committing adultery by one witness only, that the husband must divorce the wife if he remains silent]?"

B. *DTNY'*: The story is told that (M'SH B) Yannai the King went to Kohalit in the wilderness and there conquered sixty towns. When he returned, he rejoiced greatly, and invited all the sages of Israel.

C. He said to them, "Our forefathers would eat salt fish when they were engaged in the building of the Holy House. Let us also eat salt fish as a memorial to our forefathers."

D. So they brought up salt fish on golden tables, and they ate.

E. There was there a certain scoffer, evil-hearted and empty headed, and Eleazar ben Po'irah was his name.

F. Eleazar b. Po'irah said to Yannai the king, 'IO King Yannai, the hearts of the Pharisees are [set] against you."

G. "What shall I do?"

H. "Test (HQM) them by the plate (SYS) that is between your eyes."
I. He tested them by the plate that was between his eyes.
J. There was there a certain sage, and Judah b. Gedidiah was his name. Judah b. Gedidiah said to Yannai the King, "O King Yannai, Let suffice for you the crown of sovereignty [kingship]. Leave the crown of the high priesthood for the seed of Aaron."
K. For people said that his [Yannai's] mother had been taken captive in Modiim. The charge was investigated and not found [sustained]. The sages of Israel departed in anger.
L. Eleazar b. Po'irah then said to Yannai the king, "O King Yannai, That is the law [not here specified as the punishment inflicted on Judah] even for the ordinary folk in Israel. But you are king and high priest — should that be your law too?"
M. "What should I do?"
N. "If you take my advice, YOU will trample them down."
O. "But what will become of the Torah?"
P. "Lo, it is rolled up and lying in the corner. Whoever wants to learn, let him come and learn."
Q. R. Nahman b. Isaac said, "*Forthwith Epicureanism was instilled in him [Yannai] for he should have said, 'That is well and good for the Written Torah, but what will become of the Oral Torah?'*" [In Aramaic.]

R. The evil blossomed through Eleazar b. Po'irah. All the sages of Israel were killed.

S. The world was desolate until Simeon b. Shetah came and restored the Torah to its place.

B. Qid. 66a

A story on a falling out between the Pharisees and Alexander Jannaeus evidently circulated in later times. One form of that tradition placed the origin of the whole difficulty at the feet of Simeon b. Shetah himself, holding that the king believed he had been cheated; therefore Simeon fled for a time but later on returned. A second, and different, set of traditions, of which the above is one exemplum, held that difficulties between Yannai and the Pharisees ("Rabbis") as a group led to the flight of many of them, including Judah b. Tabbai and/or Joshua b. Perahiah to Alexandria. Simeon managed to patch things up — we do not know how — and therefore summoned the refugees to return. But the two traditions, cannot be reconciled or translated into historical language, nor can we profitably speculate on what 'kernel' of historical truth underlay either or both of them. All we do know is that Simeon b. Shetah was believed to have played a role in either the difficulty, or the reconciliation, or bottle

This brings us to Josephus' versions of both items. They occur in the account of John Hyrcanus (135-104), first in War I:54ff. He succeeded his murdered brothers as high priest and led the state for thirty-one years (1:68). He enjoyed the "three highest privileges: the supreme command of the nation, the high priesthood, and the gift of prophecy. He could invariably predict the future." In the pertinent materials in the War, Josephus makes no mention of Pharisees. In

Antiquities XIII, Josephus vastly expands his account. He credits John Hyrcanus with the destruction of the Gerizim temple and the conversion of Idumaea (13:2524). The heavenly message now appears as follows:

> Now about the high priest Hyrcanus an extraordinary story is told, how the Deity communicated with him, for they say that on the very day on which his sons fought with Cyzicenus, Hyrcanus, who was alone in the Temple, burning incense as high priest, heard a voice saying *that his sons had just defeated Antiochus.* And on coming out of the Temple, he revealed this to the entire multitude, and so it actually happened.

The message here preserved in indirect discourse is presented in direct discourse in the Rabbinic materials: "The youths who have made war on Antioch have conquered." But the message is nearly identical, and so is the setting.

Josephus now introduces the story of the Pharisees and Hyrcanus (13:28gff., translated by Louis H. Feldman):

> As for Hyrcanus, the envy of the Jews was aroused against him by his own successes, and those of his sons. Particularly hostile to him were the Pharisees, who are one of the Jewish schools... And so great is their influence with the masses that even when they speak against a high or high priest, they immediately gain credence.
>
> Hyrcanus too was a disciple of theirs, and was greatly loved by them. And once he invited them to a feast and entertained them hospitably, and when he saw that they were

having a very good time, he began by saying that they knew he wished to be righteous and in everything he did tried to please God and them — for the Pharisees profess such beliefs; at the same time he begged them, if they observed him doing anything wrong or straying from the right path to lead him back to it and correct him. But they testified to his being altogether virtuous, and he was delighted with their praise.

However, one of his guests, named Eleazar, who had an evil nature and took pleasure in dissension, said, "Since you have asked to be told the truth, if you wish to be righteous give up the high priesthood and be content with governing the people."

And when Hyrcanus asked him for what reason he should give up the high priesthood, he replied, "Because we have heard from our elders that your mother was a captive in the reign of Antiochus Epiphanes."

But the story was false, and Hyrcanus was furious with the man, while all the Pharisees were very indignant.

Then a certain Jonathan, one of Hyrcanus' close friends, belonging to the school of Sadducees, who hold opinions opposed to those of the Pharisees, said that it had been with general approval of all the Pharisees that Eleazar had made his slanderous statement; and this, he added, would be clear to Hyrcanus if he inquired of them what punishment Eleazar deserved for what he had said.

Hyrcanus did so, and the Pharisees replied: Eleazar deserved stripes and chains; for they did not think it right to sentence a man to death for calumny, and the Pharisees are naturally lenient in the matter of punishments.
Hyrcanus was outraged, and Jonathan in particular inflamed his anger, and so worked upon him that he brought him to join the Sadducean party and desert the Pharisees and to abrogate the regulations which they had established for the people and punish those who observed them.

At this point, Josephus explains who the Pharisees are and alleges that everyone listens to them, while the Sadducees are followed only by the wealthy. Then Josephus returns to the account of War. Hyrcanus lived happily ever after and had the three greatest privileges, as the narrative proceeds to report.

Clearly, the Rabbis' tradition of Alexander Jannaeus at Bavli Qiddushin 66a and Josephus' story of John Hyrcanus in Antiquities exhibit remarkable affinities. On Abbayye's theory that Yannai and Yohanan were one and the same, we have no difficulties whatever, and it is Abbaye who cites the materials in Bavli Qiddushin 66a.

I am impressed by the near-identity of the miracle-story with the Rabbinical one, even more impressed by the antiquity of the language attributed to the heavenly echo, and would be inclined to imagine that to both Josephus and the Rabbis was available a single, brief logion in Aramaic. The parallels certainly are too close to be accidental

The long story about Hyrcanus (=Bavli Qiddushin's Jannaeus) and the Pharisees is another matter. It is long, well developed, and involves riot a single short phrase, but a complex narrative. Josephus has inserted it whole into his larger setting. He does not account for Pharisaic hostility, but takes it for granted; then he makes Hyrcanus a Pharisee, so their hostility is even more incredible. Now comes the famous banquet, with Eleazar (= Judah b. Gedidiah of the Talmud) as the troublemaker, described with much the same adjectives, and his message is identical in substance. Everyone "leaves indignant" in both versions. Then Jonathan (the Talmud's Eleazar b. Po'irah) tells the king to let the Pharisees show their true feelings. They impose the normal punishment. This detail is absent in Bavli Qiddushin 66a. But it is there taken for granted. That is striking indeed. "That is the law even for the most humble... shall that be your law too?" follows the departure of the sages. Let me state with appropriate emphasis:

The version in Bavli Qiddushin 66a, if not garbled or defective, therefore is incomprehensible without the details supplied in Josephus' story.

Now Josephus explains how Hyrcanus left the Pharisees and joined the Sadducees, after which he lived happily. This detail ignores the foregoing narrative. For the Rabbis the break came on the threshold of his death and is left unexplained. Then Simeon b. Shetah comes along and restores the Pharisees to power.

I find it impossible to imagine how the two versions could have been shaped independently of one another. Two facts seem to me decisive. The first is the length and complexity of the narrative, the second, the constant parallels of theme, development, and detail, between the two versions. The two cannot be thought entirely separate traditions, but, on the contrary, may be best accounted for within one of three theories: either Josephus here cites an ancient pre-Rabbinic, Pharisaic story (highly unlikely); or both refer in common to a third, independent source; or the Rabbis cite Josephus. This third seems to me most probable, if in fact Rabbis knew Josephus' writings in the original Aramaic.

The upshot is that the authors of the version now found in the Bavli took over and shaped in their own framework materials of a quite elaborate character.

VI. THE BAVLI AT THE END

For the present purpose the point is simple. The Bavli consistently takes up materials available to us in sources generally assumed to have been brought to closure earlier. It persistently does with these materials pretty much the same thing. That is to add details and to provide a sense of the whole — its purpose, its message — in so doing. If we were given cases of peripatetic parallels without information on the documents from which the several parallel versions were taken, with a high degree of accuracy we could time and again assign to the Bavli the most elaborate version, to prior documents the less fully-articulated one(s). To know precisely that degree of accuracy would require a survey of all cases. All I have established here is a working hypothesis. But it is one that accords with the documentary reading of the canonical compilations, and sufficient evidence has been cited to establish its prima facie plausibility. That is as far as we can go without much more systematic analysis than anyone, in any language, whether English, French, Spanish, German, or Hebrew, has yet conducted.

But my view, based on this evidence, is clear. It is that the Bavli's authors imposed the mark of their own minds upon received materials. They did so in such a way as to revise everything that had gone before. They placed upon the heritage of the past the indelible and distinct, unmistakable stamp of their own minds.

We should not miss the implications, as to the character of the Rabbinic culture, of these facts. The Bavli finds itself represented as the docile bearer of earlier generations' burden, lacking, itself, in critical acumen. That is, most recently, the wrong-headed judgment of Menachem Fish.[5] But even in the framework of the formal analysis conducted here, the opposite is the case. The Bavli's framers — those who took over for use in the Bavli received stories and sayings — did more than preserve verbatim what they got from the past, from documents that had reached closure before they did their work. They imposed their own judgment as to detail and flow of narrative, correcting and revising what they had inherited. And that is the mark of independence of judgment and a thoroughly critical spirit.

The reason is that the Bavli's authorities did not confuse respect with servility. They carefully nurtured critical and creative faculties. Gibbon said (unfairly) of the Byzantine schools, "Not a single composition of history, philosophy, or literature has been saved from oblivion by the intrinsic beauties of style, or sentiment, or original fancy, or even of successful imitation." By contrast, the Bavli is the product not of servility to the past or of dogmatism in the present, but of an exceptionally critical, autonomous rationalism and an utterly independent spirit. The writers gave to pedantry a coot welcome. The authority of the received materials was set aside by the critical judgment of the newest generation. In the fullest sense, the Bavli's authors were not traditionalists. They took traditions of the early generations into their care, respectfully learning them, reverently handing them on. But these they thoroughly digested and made their own. Their minds were filled with the learning of the ancients. But their unrelenting criticism were wholly their own, which is why

---

[5] Menachem Fisch, *Rational Rabbis. Science and Talmudic Culture.* Bloomington, IN, 1997: Indiana University Press. 360 pp.

they added, changed, and rewrote nearly everything they received from, hence shared with, earlier compositions. It follows that the Bavli's changes testify to the intellect of the Bavli's authors.

That, at any rate, is the conclusion that I draw from the facts that have been assembled in these charts. The Bavli emerges with fixed documentary traits and preferences. The same thing that is done to a story deriving from (or represented in) an earlier document in one instance is done in all other instances. What we learn from the corpus of received stories as transmitted by the Bavli concerns the Bavli's fixed tendencies. If that is so, then what the diverse wordings and various versions of sayings and stories show us confirms the documentary hypothesis: Rabbinic compilations exhibit fixed and indicative traits. To be sure, the traits I have identified represent literary, not theological or Halakhic tendencies that recur as the compilation receives materials and reworks them. When it comes to issues of politics or public policy, attitudes and values of a religious character, I cannot show that the Bavli exhibits a fixed trait or perspective in its utilization of received writing. But for the purpose at hand, I do not have to. I have alleged that the several compilations exhibit traits particular and characteristic of one and not another. I have not claimed that the traits are substantive, but have emphasized, in the definition of the particularity of documents, the formal side to things. And that is precisely what the position of the Bavli at the end confirms.

II

THE THRICE-TOLD TALE IN RABBINIC STORIES ABOUT PHARISEES BEFORE 70

Chapter Two

Simeon the Just

We now take up the stories and sayings pertaining to the names in Abot Chapter One. The sayings tend to be worded in a stable text tradition; since tractate Abot is joined to the Mishnah, it follows the Mishnah's pattern of yielding firm versions of its sayings. But stories that move from document to document shift in their wording.

1. *Sayings Attributed to Simeon the Just*

In the first classification is only one saying of apothegmatic character, Abot 1:3 (2):

Abot 1:3(2)	Y. Ta. 4:2	Y.Meg.3:6	Pes. de R. Kahana
1. Simeon the Just was among the remnants of the Great Assembly.	1. TMN TNNYN	1. " " "	1. " " " remnants of the *whole law* (KL HYLKTH)
2. He would say, On three things the world stands, On the Torah, and on the cult, and on deeds of loving kindness.	2. " " "	2. " " "	2. -----
3. ------	3. And all three are in one Scripture, Is. 51	3. " " "	3. -----

Clearly the Abot saying was accurately quoted in the third century, with the addition of an appropriate exegesis, presumably sometime after the Abot-collection was widely available. The version in Pes. de R. Kahana omits the operative moral teaching. The passage probably is garbled. What y. adds is a proof-text.

2. Stories Attributed to Simeon the Just

We have one story told in the name of Simeon the Just about himself. The form is: *Simeon the Just said + story told in the first person*. When other characters appear in the story, their dialogue is supplied by Simeon.

Sifré Num. 22	Tos. Nez. 4:7 (Text: S. Lieberman, *Tosefta Nashim* [N.Y., 1967] p. 138)
1. -----	1. -----
2. Rabbi Simeon the Just said	2. " " " [Omits *Rabbi*]
3. I never (MWLM) ate the guilt-offering of Naziriteship but one	3. " " " (MYMYY)
4. When one came from the south, (MSH B) one who came to me from the south	4. *Story is told concerning*
5. of beautiful eyes, lovely appearance	5. " " "
6. and his locks heaped up into curls	6. " " "

Simeon the Just 51

7. I said (N'M) to him, Quickly must (MHR'YT) one destroy beautiful hair

7. (NM). *My son, Why* [What do you see to destroy this beautiful hair

8. He said (N'M) to me

8. (NM) " " "

9. I was a shepherd in my town

9. " " "

10. And I went to fill (ML') water from the well

10. " " " from the *river*

11. I looked at my shadow

11. " " "

12. and my heart grew haughty (PHZ)

12. my *impulse*

13. It wanted to remove me from the world. (LHBRNY)

13. " " "

14. 1 said (NM) to it, Evil one (RS')

14. " " "

15. Lo, you take pride in what is not yours. It belongs to the dust, worm, and maggot.

15. *You had the right to be jealous* (GRH) *only* of something which is not yours, something *destined to be made* into dust, worm, and maggot.

16. Lo, I shave you [off] for Heaven. I shaved.

16. Lo, it is incumbent on me to shave [Omits: I shaved]

17. Forthwith I kissed him on his head and said (N'M) to him

17. *I bent my head* " " "

18. May such as you increase in Israel, who do the will of the Omnipresent.

18. *My son,* " " "

52 *Peripatetic Parallels*

19. Concerning you is fulfilled	19. " " "
20. Num. 6:2	20. " " "

Y. Ned. 1:1 = Y. Naz. 1:5 [Variations in y. Naz. 1:5 in brackets]	B. Naz. 4b = B. Ned. 9a
1. DTNY	1. TNY'
2. [Omits rabbi]	2. " " "
3. " " "	3. never (MYMY) — guilt-offering of an *unclean Nazir except* for one man
4. came up to me (LH).	4. *came* to me (B')
5. I saw him ruddy ('DMWNY) *with* [Naz: adds DMWT]	5. " " "
6. arranged for him in heaps (TYLY TYLYM) [Naz. omits SDR]	6. *arranged for him in curls*
7. " " " *my son — What did you see* [= why] destroy *this* " " "	7. I said (MR') — *my son* What did you see to destroy *this* beautiful hair?
8. He said (NM) to me, *Rabbi* [Naz: N WM']	8. " " " ['MR]
9. " " "	9. " " " *for my father*
10. " " " to fill a pail (ML'S'WB)	10. " " " [to draw, S'B] with water
11. I *saw* (R'H) *in the midst of the water*	11. " " "

12. my *impulse*	12. my *impulse* " " "
13. to destroy ('BD) " " "	13. to drive me (TWRDNY) " " "
14. " " "	14. " " " ('MR), *Base one* (RYQH)
15. " " " [Omits: It belongs to the]	15. *On what account do you take pride in the world* which is not yours? *For your end will be with* worm and maggot [Omits: *Dust*]
16. It is incumbent on me to *sanctify* you to heaven	16. *By the cult* [Omits: *Lo* (HRNY)]
17. " " " [Naz: I *embraced* and I said ('MR)	17. *I arose and* [in place of *I shaved*]
18. " " "	18. May such *Nazirites* as you [Omits: *who do the will* ...]
19. Concerning you, *Scripture says*	19. Scripture says [Instead of *is fulfilled*]
20. " " "	20. " " "

The Tosefta stands between the fully revised Babylonian baraita and Sifré Num. Important improvements include the addition of *my son* (no. 7), *this* (no. 7), *impulse* in place of heart (no. 12), arid, most striking, the complete revision of no. 15. by which the language is greatly clarified. I have rendered ᶜSH in passive, *to be made*, but it may be translated to *make/produce*. The unclear *shaved my head* of no. 16, which is poor diction, is changed to a clause in Simeon's reply, *I bent my head*. These changes are not fundamental, but superficial and stylistic. The several versions certainly are interdependent. The Palestinian Talmudic versions, which are close to one another, though not identical in all respects, on the whole follow Tosefta, as is to be expected. *Story is told* of Tos. No. 4 is rightly omitted, but the Yer. versions add several words: *ruddy, demut.* The oath it is *incumbent — to sanctify* occurs, only to be changed in the Babylonian baraita to the exclamatory *by the cult.* The reference to *dust, worm and maggot* is omitted in both Palestinian Talmudic versions, perhaps not a lapse of a scribe but a definite literary choice. The most important differences are, in general, between the earliest versions and the latest; the intermediate version, are transitional.

The accounts in Sifré Num. and b. Naz. are closely related, for all differences are minor. No major element in one account is omitted in the other. But the *baraita* consistently supplies details left out of the version of Sifré Num., for instance *unclean* Nazir, explaining what Simeon the Just had against guilt offerings of Nazirs; came *to me, arranged for him* (addition of *sedurot lo*) in curls; *my son* added to the colloquy. The difficult language of Sifré Num., MHR'YT, which I roughly translated, *Quickly must one*, is corrected in favor of a much more lucid *what did you see* [= what made you, why] (i.e. MH R'YT — not much of a change). The diction is then improved with the addition of this beautiful *hair.* The shepherd now works *for my father. Fill* is replaced by *draw*, which settles the matter of the duplicated verbs in the Palestinian versions (no. 10), where both roots occur. *Heart* is dropped in favor of impulse (YSR), possibly more colloquial. The change of TRD) for BR or 'BO' probably is for the same reason. Like no. 7, no. 15 is improved in the baraita by the inclusion of the more complete and lucid statement, phrased in the form of a question, *On what account*, followed by a declarative *For your end...* All that survives of the Sifré version is the stock-reference to *dust worm and maggot*, and the choice of PHZ and G'H. Similarly in no. 16, the *Lo* is replaced by the language of a vow, *By the cult*. In the absence of the oath "by the Temple cult", the force of the vow is diminished; *by the cult* intensifies *lo*. The changes in nos. 17 and 18 conform to the earlier ones: I *arose* and *Nazirites* add, in the former instance, a more colloquial expression, in the latter, a more pointed reference to the *sort* of Nazirites Simeon hopes will multiply. The general *who do the will* is made more specific and precise: *Nazirites*. The Scripture is set into different citation-form. In Sifré Num. the Scripture is *fulfilled* in the Nazirite; in the Palestinian and *baraita*-versions is found the language common in the Babylonian Talmud, "Scripture says *concerning you*..."

It is difficult to deny that the *baraita*-version depends, and improves, upon that in Sifré Num. Valuable details are added to the Sifré's account. The language is clarified and in several points is made to conform to rabbinical diction and word-choice. While some of the differences may represent merely different linguistic conventions (N'M/'MR), Most of them enhance the Sifré version. The *baraita* thus comes later than the version in Sifré Num. This dependence is not merely in the general outline of the story; the differences are not in generalities but in minor details. These cannot have been independent accounts which circulated separately; the authority responsible for the *baraita* seems to have had the Sifré version before him.

The differences between the versions of the *baraita* in b. Ned. and Naz. are negligible. If Sifré were dated later than the other versions, what we have called improvements would have to be regarded as corruptions of superior, earlier versions.

3. Stories about Simeon the Just

Of the four stories told about, or containing references to, Simeon the Just, two historical, and two are of a miraculous, or supernatural, character, a distinction the narrator would not have recognized. The former pertain to Simeon's preparing a heifer-sacrifice and to his encounter with Alexander of Macedonia. The latter are, fir the heavenly-message story, and second, the list of supernatural changes in the life of cult, marking Simeon's death.

a. Heifer

M. Parah 3:5	Y. She g. 4:2	Pes. de R. Kahana
1. Who made them?	1. -----	1. -----
2. Simeon the Just and Yohanan the high priest made two each	2. -----	2. -----
3. -----	3. Ulla objected before Mana, Lo it is taught (TNY):	3. -----[Here: Anony*mous*] Lo it is taught
4. -----	4. Simeon the Just made two [omits: each]	4. Simeon the Just made two *heifers*
5. -----	5. *He did not bring the second out on ramp on which he brought out the first*	5. [Identical to y. Sheq.]

| 6. ----- | 6. *Can you say he was wasteful* [etc.]? | 6. Can you say *that just man* [etc]? |

The Mishnah is referred to in the later versions, but not cited verbatim. The reference Yohanan the High Priest is deliberately omitted. This leaves a lacuna, filled in by the latest Midrashic compilation with the addition of heifers. The other change, for *he* supplying *that just man*, intensifies the ironic force of the question. TNY means that the editor *alludes* to the Mishnah. Clearly the later materials depend upon the earlier, but they have also greatly augmented the Mishnah, by supplying the "fact" that the high priests had wastefully constructed the ramp referred to in M. Parah 3:6, "They would construct a ramp from the Temple Mount to the Mount of Olives." The assumption made by the later masters is that for each sacrifice a new ramp was constructed. But this must then apply to all the priests listed in 3:5, including Simeon the Just. The problem is how to distinguish Simeon the Just, a high priest admired by rabbis, from others on that same list, who are not held in high esteem. The later history of the High priesthood is told in lurid colors by Pharisaic-Rabbinic tradition. No restraints limited expression of Rabbinic hostility against the late priesthood. Hence, if anyone implies all high priests did the same lavish act, Simeon must forthwith be cited to show the act was not disreputable at all.

The inclusion of no. 5 is *not* part of the citation of the Mishnah, though it occurs under the superscription TNY. I do not know whence the *baraita* derives, for Tos. Par. 3:7 follows the Mishnah at the pertinent place. The inference that the ramp could not be used twice was drawn from M. Par. 3:5-6, but we do not know who drew it, why, or when it was important to add to the anti-priestly polemic this particular detail. But at that point the problem of Simeon's inclusion in the list had to be faced.

The *terminus ante quem* is the middle of the third century A.D. Clearly, the detail about the priests' constructing new ramps circulated separately from the Mishnah and was added to the baraita later on. Yet, standing by itself, it is incomprehensible, for a saying *Simeon did not bring the second out* ... would mean nothing outside of the context of "Simeon the Just made two."

The additional detail of the baraita depended upon the Mishnah, having been added later as a commentary on Mishnah 3:6, as I said. We therefore cannot regard no. 5 as an independent tradition.

b. Alexander

B. Yoma 69a	Lev. R. 13:5	Pes. R. Kahana	Pes. Rabbati
1. TNY'	1. -----	1. -----	1. -----
2. Forbidden to mourn on the 25th of Tevet, the day of Mt. Gerizim.	2. ----	2. ----	2. ----
3. Kuteans sought permission to destroy Temple, from Alexander.	3. -----	3. -----	3. -----
4. He gave permission.	4. -----	4. -----	4. -----
5. Simeon the Just wore priestly garments	5. -----	5. -----	5. -----

Simeon the Just 59

6. and arranged processions.	6. -----	6. -----	6. -----
7. When morning star rose, approached Alexander.	7. -----	7. -----	7. -----
8. Who are these? Jews who rebelled against you.	8. -----	8. -----	8. -----
9. At Antipatris sun came out and the processions met.	9. -----	9. -----	9. -----
10. Alexander rose before Simeon, saying if he saw him before battle, he would win.	10. ----- Kuteans asked, Do you rise before a Jew? " " "	10. *A. would say*, Blessed is God of Simeon the Just. Courtiers: Do YOU rise? A.: See Face	10. [As in Pes. de R. Kahana.]
11. Why have you come?	11.-----	11.-----	11. -----
12. You want to destroy the Temple where they pray for you and your kingdom.	12.-----	12.-----	12. -----
13. Gave Kuteans over to Jews, who mutilated	13.-----	13.-----	13. -----

them and
destroyed
Mt. Gerizim.

Clearly, no. 10, which interrupts the narrative of b. Yoma 69a, circulated separately. It was erroneously placed in the Babylonian *baraita*, presumably because it supplied additional information on Alexander's encounter with Simeon the Just. But it did not explain his favor to the Jews, for immediately thereafter Alexander asks them (no. 11) why the Jews have come, and only after they explain their case in terms favorable to the king does he grant their request, and, more than the request, also the right to take vengeance against the Samaritans.

If the materials in no. 10 circulated by themselves, however, then they may antedate the *baraita*, for they fit in too well to suggest later contamination. They presumably were shaped before ca. 250 A.D., but appeared only in the late Midrashic compilations. This is one instance in which the unredacted form of a story *may* have independently circulated early, only to be written down long afterward. On the other hand, it is possible that the *baraita* as we have it was the only redaction of the pericope about Alexander's respect for Simeon, in which case the later Midrashic compilers took only a part of it, without the slightest reference to the context in which it had originally appeared. Lev. R. presupposes the connection by including *Kuteans*. The Pesiqtas improve matters by substituting *courtiers* — leaving no problem as to the identity of the questioners.

c. *Heavenly echo*

Tos. Sot. 13:7 Part A	B. Sot. 33a	Y. Sot. 9:13
1. Simeon the Just heard	1. *Further story is told* (SWB MSH B) *of*	1. The story is told that Simeon the

Simeon the Just 61

	Simeon the Just *that he* heard an echo from the house of the Holy of Holies which was saying	Just heard an echo from the house of the Holy of Holies and said
2. The decree is annulled (BTYLT 'YBYDT)	2. " " "	2. -----
3. which the enemy (SN'H) said (DY'MR)	3. " " "	3. -----
4. to bring (LHYTYH) to the temple	4. " " " to bring (L'YYT'H)	4. -----
5. and QSGLGS has has been slain [*in*	5. " " " GSQLGS	5. GYYS GWLYQS been slain [*in Hebrew*] Hebrew]
6. and his decrees are annulled [*in Hebrew*]	6. " " "	6. and his decrees are annulled [*in Hebrew*]
7. and he heard them in the Aramaic language	7. [= 9]	7. -----
8. -----	8. and they wrote down the hour and it tallied	8. -----
9. -----	9. And *it spoke* in the Aramaic language	9. -----

******

The pericope of Simeon-stories in Tos. Sot. 1 3:7 splits into two separate traditions. The first tradition is represented here. The second occurs in the next synopsis (p. 41). For y. Sot. 9:13, the point of the story is that Simeon heard a heavenly echo. This version therefore excludes the Aramaic translation of the decrees (nos. 2, 3, and 4), for use of Aramaic is no issue. In other respects y. Sot. does not differ from Tos. nos. 5 and 6. The superscription is simply *the story is told concerning*, with no reference to a Tannaite tradent. For the Babylonian Talmud and Tosefta, on the other hand, the point of the story is that the heavenly voice spoke in Aramaic. Therefore nos. 2, 3, and 4 are *in Aramaic*, but these are in substance then summarized in Hebrew in nos. 5 and 6. No. 6 actually translates no. 2!

The relationship of the first element in the three versions is fairly clear. The original was simply Tos. Sot. no 1. This is augmented for editorial purposes *with further* in the Babylonian Talmudic account. Both the Babylonian and Palestinian Talmuds include *story is told* and supply the information on where the voice came from. From that point forward Tos. Sot. and b. Sot. are pretty much identical, except for the improvement of the representation of the verb *to bring*, and the revision of the spelling of the name of the enemy. The addition of no. 8 in b. Sot. is clearly a contamination from the foregoing account, about Yohanan the High Priest (noted above). The passage is quite meaningless here. No. 7 in Tos. is out of place, for the point of the Tos. stories is *not* that the echo spoke in Aramaic. That *is* the point in b. Sot. 33a. It is a probable contamination.

The several traditions therefore serve quite separate purposes. The point is either that Simeon heard as echo, or that angels speak Aramaic, but it cannot be both. The simplest and purest version of the former is y. Sot. Tos. Sot. and b. Sot. have then been contaminated by the inclusion of both tendencies, resulting in the egregious repetition of no. 2 in no. 6. If the point were that angels spoke Aramaic, the pertinent elements ought to have been Tos. Sot. nos. 1-4 and 7, or b. Sot. nos. 1-4 and 9. In neither does no. 8 fit at all.

No. 1 of the Palestinian Talmudic version comes earlier than no. 1 of the Babylonian. But the relationship of the rest of the elements to one another is unclear to me, Certainty without Tos. Sot. we should have concluded that b. Sot. came after the version in the Palestinian Talmud. It would represent a thoroughgoing revision to serve the purpose of the argument for which it is cited in the Babylonian context. Hence the story would have been revised later on in Babylonia. But this supposition is impossible, since the Babylonian version is, except for no. 8, pretty much the same as the one in the Tosefta; indeed, it is almost certainly based upon it. Hence we have to postulate two quite separate versions of the pericope: Tos. + b. Sot., or Tos. + v. Sot. The two may be based upon a common, simple story, of which nos. 5 and 6 in the Palestinian Talmudic version are an accurate reminiscence. If this is so, then y. Sot. is the earliest of the three versions, followed by Tosefta, then the Babylonian based upon the Tosefta — a strange anomaly.

As to the identification of the enemy referred to in no. 5 of all three accounts, we have no idea what name is here rendered into Hebrew characters. I see no profit in attempting to read Gaius Caligula into any of the consonantal representations before us.

d. *Miracles*

Tos. Sot. 13:7b	Y. Yoma 6:3	B. Yoma 39a-b
1.-----	1. All the days that Simeon the Just was	1. TNW RBNN: *In the forty years that Simeon*

	alive, it [the goat] would not reach half-way down the mountain before it was turned into bits. When it would flee to the wilderness, and the Saracens would eat it.	*the Just served* -- [omits goat-miracle]
2.-----	2. All the days that Simeon the Just was alive, the lot of the Name would come up in the right [hand]. When Simeon the Just died, sometimes it would come up in the right, sometimes in the left.	2. " " " [Omits Ali-alive]
2*.-----	[2*. See 7*]	2*. The red strap would turn white. Henceforward, sometimes it would turn white, sometimes it would not turn white. [See y. Yoma 7* below]
3. All the time that Simeon the Just was alive	3. *days* " " "	3. [Omits *all-alive*]
4. The Western lamp was continual (TDYR)	4. would *burn* (DLQ)	4. *burn* [= y. Yoma]

Simeon the Just 65

5. When he died	5. " " "	5. *Henceforward*
6. they went and it had gone out	6. -----	6. -----
7. Afterward, sometimes it went out, sometimes it burned	7. " " "	7. " " "
7*.-----	7*. All the days that Simeon the Just was Alive, the red strap would turn white. When Simeon the Just died, sometimes it would turn white, sometimes it would turn red.	[7*. = 2* above]
8. And the fire of the wood-offering was continual	8. All the days etc., the *fire* of the wood-offering *would flame up*	8. [Omits *all-alive* fire of wood-offering was *strong, and the priests did not have to bring wood to the fire except for the two logs to carry out the commandment of the wood.*
9. Once they had arranged it in the morning, it was strong (HYTH MTGBRT)	9. Once they *had placed two logs* in the morning " " "	9. -----

10. and they would of sometimes in the offerings and supplementary offerings and their drink-offerings	10. -----	10. -----
11. and they only added to it two logs of the evening offering	11. -----	11. -----
12. Lev. 6:5	12. they added nothing all day long [omits Lev. 6:5]	12. -----
13. When Simeon the Just died	13. " " "	13. ----
14. the strength (KH) of the fire-offering diminished (TSS)	14. " " "	14. Henceforward, sometimes it was strong and sometimes it was not strong
15. and they did not refrain from adding wood all day long	15. " " "	15. " " "
16. And there was a blessing on the two loves of bread and the show-bread.	16. blessing *sent* upon " " "	16. blessing *was sent* on the omer and " " "
17. The two loaves of bread were divided at the Gathering (SRT) and the show-bread at the festival (RGL) for all the watches.	17. -----	17. -----

Simeon the Just

18. Some ate and were sated, and some ate and left over	18. *Each one would get an olive's bulk and* " " "	18. *Each priest to whom as much as an olive's came* — *some ate*" " "
19. and only as much as an olive's bulk came to each one.	19. [See above; order is reversed]	19. [See above, order is reversed.]
20. When Simeon the Just died the blessing departed	20. " " "	20. A *curse* was sent on the *omer* etc.
21. -----	21. -----	21. [Predicted own death]

*****

B. Yoma 39b	B. Men. 109b	Y. Yoma 5:2
1. TNW RBNN	1. DTNY'	1. -----
2. In that year in which Simeon the Just died	2. " " "	2. *Forty years Simeon the Just served Israel in the high priesthood.* In the last year, he said to them, In this year I am going to die.
3. he said to them that in this year he would die	3. " " "	3. [As above]
4. They said to him, Whence do you know?	4. " " "	4. " " "

68 Peripatetic Parallels

5. He said to them, Every Day of Atonement an old man would meet me, dressed in white and cloaked in white.	5. " " "	5. He said to them, Ever
6. He would enter with me and leave with me.	6. " " "	6. " " "
7. Today an old man met me dressed in black and cloaked in black. He went in with me but he did not leave with me.	7. " " "	7. *This year* he entered with me but did not leave with me. [Omits *black clothes*]
8. After the festival he fell ill for seven days and he died.	8. " " "	8. -----
9. His brethren the priests held back from blessing with the [Ineffable] name.	9. " " "	9. -----
10. -----	10. When he was, dying he said to them, My son Onias etc. [The rest of the story appears only here.]	10. -----
[11.-----]	[11. ----]	[11. Colloquy of

Simeon the Just 69

R. Abbahu: Man was the Holy One.]

The changes in the supernatural setting of the cult and the prediction by Simeon that he would die are as follows:

Tos. Sot. 13:7b Y. Yoma 6:9 B. Yoma 39a-b Men. 109b Y. Yoma 5:2

1. Western lamp	1. Goat	1. Lot	1. Predicted death	1. Prayed too long
2. Fire of wood-offering	2. Lot	2. Red strap	2. Ineffable Name	2. Predicted death
3-Blessing of loaves	3. Western lamp	3. Western lamp		
	4. Red strap	4. Fire of wood-offering		
	5. Fire of wood-offering	5. Blessing of loaves		
	6. Blessing of loaves	6. Predicted death		
	7. Ineffable Name			

If we could reconstruct a single, unitary source that underlay the several pericopae, it logically would look something like this:

1. Prayed too long
2. Predicted death and died

Day of Atonement 3. Priests stop saying Ineffable Name
4. *After he died: Goat*
5. Lot
6. Red Strap

7. Western lamp
Daily Cult 8. Fire of wood-offering
9. Blessing of loaves

Nos. 1-6 all pertain to the Day of Atonement. Nos. 7-9 stand by themselves as a comparable, but separate list of supernatural changes. Strikingly, Tos. Sot. does preserve nos. 7-9 as a separate pericope. Similarly, b. Yoma 39a-b, nos. 6-7, probably circulated separately, as seen in the identical version in b. Men. 109b. There the pericope serves to introduce the long singleton about the succession to Simeon. Palestinian Talmud Yoma 5:2 similarly supplies the Yom Kippur pericope, but without the miracles in connection with the cult of that day. That leaves the lists in y. Yoma 6:3 and b. Yoma 39a-b, in which the Yom Kippur miracles are presented together with those of Tos. Sot.; but b. Yoma keeps the Yom Kippur materials separate from the other miracles, while y. Yoma inserts no. 3, Western lamp, into the midst of the others. We may therefore take it for granted that Tos. Sot. does constitute a single, separate pericope. The stories about the prediction of Simeon's death probably circulated separately as well, therefore serving diverse editorial purposes later on. To these were attached the detail about the Ineffable Name or the prayer that went on too long; neither was integral to the prediction-story, but both found a satisfactory place. The miracles connected with the Day of Atonement service likewise may have circulated by themselves, but in the form before us they have already been contaminated by the list of Tos. Sot.

As to the relationships among the several components of the pericopae, we find that the Babylonian *baraita* imposed its own conventional language, as would be expected. Normally, this meant choosing words common in Babylonian rabbinical Hebrew and rendering vague details more precise and pointed, e.g. *all the days* of y. Yoma becomes *in the forty years*. But the substance of the several miracles varies very little between the Palestinian and Babylonian versions. The important differences are between both and Tosefta. Thus Tos. Sot. 13:7b, nos. 6, 9, 1 0, II, and 17 have no close equivalent, or no equivalent at all, in either Talmudic version. The Babylonian version, to be sure, transforms the participle of y. Yoma 6:3 no. 16 into a verb, adds omer (no. 20), and makes a few other, minor alterations. But in the main Tos. presents a striking contrast to the two Talmuds' versions, and these by and large closely resemble one another.

The *baraita* in b. Yoma 39b is unchanged in b. Men. 109b. I imagine the editor of b. Men. 109b took it from existing materials to serve as an introduction to the story of real interest to him, about the Temple of Onias. Without the foregoing materials (nos. 1-9) the story told by R. Meir could have stood by itself. The death-story in b. Yoma 39b and y. Yoma 5:2 presents some contrasts. The Palestinian Talmudic version makes explicit the ears but that detail had already occurred in b. Yoma 39a-b. Perhaps the editor of the baraita saw no reason to repeat the information. Since the y. Yoma pericope stands by itself, it was natural to include the more concrete detail. Hence we cannot in this instance suppose the Palestinian version to have been more detailed or concrete than the Babylonian one. The indirect discourse of the Babylonian baraita becomes direct discourse (or vice versa) in no 2. The detail about the old man dressed in white is omitted in no. 7 of the Palestinian version. It seems to me a striking omission, and the likelihood is that the editor of the

Babylonian baraita supplied it to complete the symmetry of the story. He likewise invented nos. 8 and 9; no. 8 is absolutely necessary to complete the tale -- that is, Simeon actually did die. No. 9 is not essential. In any event, the Babylonian baraita probably comes after the Palestinian version of the same story and likely depends upon it. The augmentations are not derived from a separate oral or written tradition circulating by itself, but all were provoked by literary and artistic considerations. None presents a detail of independent, historical interest.

What can we say of the entire collection of sayings and stories? What seems to me clear is that the variations from document to document affect details, but the main components are firm, start to finish. It is difficult to find in these exercises grounds for the Goldberg-Schaefer-Becker school's judgment that the Rabbinic text-tradition is too flimsy and diverse to sustain the construction of a cogent version of a given document. For the cases before us, each document receives a fundamentally stable and fixed account of matters and hands on an improved but essentially unimpaired version. There is a pronounced tendency for documents redacted earlier to have a simpler version of things, and those later, a more complex and fully spelled out version. That once more sustains the documentary hypothesis by showing fixed relationships characteristic of documents in a line of transmission, each doing to whatever materials it receives pretty much the same thing. What we saw in the case of the Bavli recurs for Yerushalmi and so on backward.

Chapter Three

Antigonos of Sokho.
Yosé b. Yoezer and Yosé b. Yohanan

A. YOSÉ B. YOEZER AND YOSÉ B. YOHANAN

I. Reproach against Grapeclusters

Tos. B.Q. 8:13	Y. Sot. 9: 10	B. Tem. 15b-16a
		1.*And Rab Judah said *in the name* of Samuel, All the Grapeclusters ” ” ” from *the days of Moses until Yosé b. Yoezer died would learn Torah like Moses our rabbi. Thenceforward, they did not learn Torah like Moses our rabbi.*
1. All the grapeclusters that arose from Israel from when Moses died until until Yosé b. Yoezer of Seredah and Yosef b. Yohanan of Jerusalem	1. TNY: *Pairs* (ZWGWT) ” ” ”	1. TNY: All the Grapeclusters that arose for Israel from *the days* of Moses until Yose b Yoezer *died*
2. it is *not* possible to place reproach against them.	2. It *is* possible	2. *There was not in them* any reproach

3. And until arose Judah b. Baba	3. " " " [omits: *and*]	3. ——
4. It *is* possible to place against them reproach	4. It is *not* possible	4. *Thenceforward, there was in them reproach*

The Tos. has been much garbled in transmission to the Babylonian *baraita*, no less so to the Palestinian version. As to the latter, we observe that the sense of the tradition has been reversed. The baraita begins with the teaching in Samuel's name about study of Torah, followed by TNY as in 1.* above. It seems to represent at best a paraphrase of Tos. Yosé b. Yohanan has been dropped in both parts of the Babylonian Talmudic version; Judah b. Baba (no. 3) is likewise omitted here, but is referred to in the immediately following Talmudic discussion. This proves that the *baraita* originally contained no reference to him, for if it had, the subsequent discussion, aimed at showing Judah *is* referred to, would have been superfluous. The Babylonian *baraita* thus has drawn the sting from the Judah b. Baba-tradition, by leaving the impression that while the end of the Grapeclusters concluded old-time virtue, no particular sage later on can be credited with reverting to that former glory. Without the praise of Judah b. Baba as the restorer of ancient merit, the *baraita* has been deprived of its former contemporary relevance. It stands merely as an untendentious supplement to the grapecluster-Mishnah.

    I imagine the *baraita* was shaped after the version in Tos. B.Q., indeed after Judah, the language of whose citation of Samuel suggests that the original formulation of Tos. B.Q. was unknown. Had it been known to Judah (Samuel), he would have directly referred to it and would not have offered

Antigonos of Sokho. Yosé b. Yoezer and Yosé b. Yohanan 75

his own formulation, involving study of Torah, of the change in the history of the grapecluster.

Alternatively, Samuel Judah did know Tos. B.Q., but, because of its political aspect (Judah b. Baba), preferred to formulate it in other, quite original, but neutral terms. But the *baraita* in any event accomplished the same end. It may, to be sure, have been formulated after the Judah b. Baba-version and circulated independently thereafter. The emission of Yosé/Yosef b. Yohanan later on could not have been consequential. He was merely a name on a list. No one had ties to him or direct access to traditions originally deriving from him.

2. *Uncleanness of Land of Peoples and Glassware*

B. Shab. 14b	Y. Shab. 1:4	Y. Pes. 1:6	Y. Ket. 8:11
1. DTNY	1. Did not R.	1. Did not R. Zeira b. Abuna in R. Jeremiah's name say	1. Did not " " " Zeira P. Abuna " " "
2. Yosé + Yosé	2. Yosef + Yosef	2. Yosé + Yosé	2. Yosé + Yosé
3. decreed uncleanness	3. " " "	3. " " "	3. " " "
4. on the land of the peoples	4. " " "	4. " " "	4. " " "
5. and on glassware	5. " " "	5. " " "	5. " " "
5.*———	5.* R. Yonah *Judah b. Tabbai*	5.*" " "said,	5.*R. Yosé said, Judah b. Tabbi R. Yonah said,

76 *Peripatetic Parallels*

			Judah b. Tabbi and Simeon b. Shetah decreed...
6. Simeon b. Shetah ordained (TQN)	6. *And* Simeon b. Shetah *decreed*	6. [= y. Shab.]	6. [As above]
7. marriage-settlement for a wife	7. ——	7. ——	7. ——
8. and decreed uncleanness on metal utensils	8. " " "	8. " " "	8. " " "
9. Shammai and Hillel decreed	9. *Hillel and Shammai* " " "	9. *Hillel and Shammai* " " "	9. *Hillel and Shammai* " " "
10. uncleanness on the hands	10. " " "	10. cleanness " " "	10. cleanness " " "

What the Babylonian Talmud knows as a *baraita* allegedly formulated by Tannaim is available to the Palestinian Talmud only in the names of fourth-century Palestinian Amoraim from Babylonia (Jeremiah, Zeira). That is not surprising, as we saw in Chapter One. Apart from the marriage-contract (no. 7), the materials are nearly identical in all important matters. Variations are in such minor details as the names Yosé/Yosef. The Palestinian versions are virtually identical with one another. b. Shab.'s S + H is the better order; and *uncleanness* (no. 10) must be more accurate than *cleanness*, which makes no sense. But the inclusion of no. 7 is irrelevant to decrees on purity laws—indeed, the language TQN is substituted, obviously unsatisfactorily, for GZR, otherwise used throughout. Alternatively, the *baraita* before us has been contaminated by materials from other sources.

B. YOSÉ B. YOEZER ALONE

1. Cleanness of Fluids in Temple Slaughter-house

Sifra 8:5	M. Ed. 8:4	B. Pes. 16a	B. Ned. 19a	B. A.Z. 37a
1. Rabbi Eliezer says	1. ——	1. WHTNY: Eleazar	1. [As b. Pes.]	1. DTNN
2. Uncleanness (TWMH) etc.	2. ——	2. " " "	2. " " "	2. ——
3. You should know that it is so	3. ——	3. [Omits: that]	3. [As b. Pes.]	3. ——
4. for behold, Yosé b. Seredah testified concerning	4. [Omits: for behold; Adds: b. Yoezer]	4. " " "	4. [As b. Pes.]	4. " " "
4.* ——	4.*on ayil QMSDKY	4.*DKN	4.* [As b. Pes.]	4.* " " DKN
5. BYMTHBHY	5. and on fluid of the slaughter-house (MSQH BYT MTBHY)	5. MSQYN	5. [As b. Pes.]	5. MSQH
6. that[they are] pure (DKYNN)	6. that they are pure (DYNWN DKYN)	6. " " " DKN	6. " " "	6. DKN

7. ——	7. And that one who touches a corpse is impure (WDYQRB BMYT MSTB)	7. ——	7. ——	7. [As in Mishnah] LMYT MSB
8. ——	8. And they called him Yosé the lenient (WQRW LH YWSY SRY)	8. ——	8. ——	8. [As in Mishnah] LYH YWSP

The citation of the Mishnah in b. A.Z. 37a is accurate and reveals only minor variations, none of which changes the meaning. The *baraita*-versions of b. Pes. and b. Ned are identical. Both differ markedly from the Mishnah in omitting nos. 7 and 8. But the real comparison is between Mishnah and Sifra. Sifra is shorter, leaving out all but the question of fluids (nos. 5-6). The rulings however pertain to uncleanness. I suppose the Mishnah preserves the earliest formulation of the saying, that is, the full list in Aramaic. Then Sifra presents merely part of it, for R. Eliezer's purposes. To be sure, the brief citation (nos. 5-6) could have been an independent tradition, circulating quite separately from the list of three Yosé-rulings supplied by M. Ed. In any event the entire list in M. Ed. now forms a unified pericope. Two of the three rulings are lenient and are so characterized at the end (no. 8).

The variations from document to document show not independent text traditions but intertwined ones; the differences concern a shared narrative and sayings common to the several documents. The peripatetic parallels attest to a firm tradition, varied by documents in some measure within their established patterns of dealing with received stories and sayings.

Chapter Four

Joshua b. Perahiah and Nittai the Arbelite. Judah b. Tabbai and Simeon b. Shetah

A. Judah b. Tabbai and Simeon b. Shetah

1. Man Illegally Put to Death and Anomaly of Law against Circumstantial Evidence

Mekhilta Kaspa III 31-41	Tos. Sanh. 6:6 = Mid. Tan.Tos. Sanh. 8:3 ed. Hoffmann, p. 112	
1. Once (KBR) S. Killed (HRG) a false witness	1. Judah said -----	1. -----
2. Judah b. Tabbai said to him	2. -----	2. -----
3. May I [not] see consolation if you have riot shed innocent blood [= Tos. 7*]	3. May I " " *if I have not slain a perjurer to uproot from the Boethusians who saythe accused must be put to death* [before the perjurer is slain] (Mid. Tan. = *Sadducees*)	3. -----
4. and the Torah said	4. -----	4. -----
5. Slay at the testimony of witnesses, slay at	5. -----	5. -----

the testimony of
perjurers

6. Just as the witnesses are two	6. -----	6. -----
7. so the perjurers are two	7. -----	7. -----
7.*-----	7.* Simeon said, to him May I [etc.] if you have not shed innocent blood	7.* -----
7**-----	7** = Mekhilta 6, 7	7**-----
8. and once (WKBR)	8. -----	8. Simeon said, May I [etc.] if I did not see one running after his fellow with a sword in his hand. He entered before him into a ruin, and ran after him.
9. Judah b. Tabbai entered a ruin.	9. -----	9. I entered *after him*.
10. and found there a slain man still writhing (MPRPR)	10. -----	10. and found him slain
11. and the sword dripping blood (MNTP DM)	11.-----	11. and the sword in the hand of the murderer

12. from the hand of the slayer	12. -----	12. [see above]
13. Judah b. Tabbai said to him, May [evil] come upon me	13. -----	13. *I said to him, Wicked one*
14. if not you or I have slain him	14. -----	14. " " "
15. But what should I do	15. -----	15. " " " *for your case is not given into my hand*
16. for lo, the Torah said, At the testimony of two witnesses (Deut. 19:15)	16. -----	16. " " "
17. But he who knows and the Master of thoughts (HYWD WBL HMHSBWT)	17. -----	17. [Omits: *master of*]
18. he will exact punishment of that man	18. -----	18. " " "
19. He had hardly come out when a serpent bit him and he died.	19.-----	19. He did not move from there
20.-----	20. At that moment Judah took on himself not to teach law except	20. -----

>according to Simeon.
>[Mid. Tan. copies b. Mak.
>5b, no. 20.]

The Tosefta has split the single but composite pericope of Mekhilta Kaspa into its two components; the first, about killing a perjurer, is separated from the story about circumstantial evidence. In both instances Judah is replaced as the hero by Simeon. Further, the Tosefta's Simeon now tells Judah he has shed innocent blood; the Mekhilta's Judah says the same to Simeon. The Tosefta's Judah explains his action: to inflict exemplary punishment. Of this Mekhilta knows nothing. Tos. no. 3 seems to depend on Mekhilta no. 1. The Tosefta's version of the unpunishable murder is similar to the Mekhilta's and in most respect depends upon it, e.g. in the correction of *master of* (no. 17), which is redundant, and in strengthening the conclusion (no. 19) by killing the man in the very presence of the rabbi. Likewise no. 13 is intensified by the expletive *wicked*. The whole account is now given in the first person, as the narrative of Simeon himself. Both Toseftan versions are developments of the Mekhilta's composite pericope. But the developments are not merely of detail, which would permit us to impute dependency. Rather, the names of the masters are consistently reversed, and this suggests deliberate doctoring, not merely the augmentation of one detail or another. The further versions all depend in general upon the Toseftan one, as we shall now see. Mekhilta stands mostly apart from the later developments of the pericope. For the next stage in the comparison, we shall give y. Sanh. 4:9, to which the other versions will be compared.

Joshua b. Perahiah and Nittai the Arbelite... 85

y. Sanh. 4:9 = Mid. Tan. ed. Hoffmann, p. 101	y. San/ 6:3	b. Mak. 5b
1. Simeon said, May I see consolation	1. -----	1. ----
2. If I did not see one pursuing another	2. -----	2. -----
3. He entered [Mid.	3. -----	3. -----
4. I entered after him	4. -----	4. -----
5. and found him slain	5. -----	5. -----
6. and this one going	6. -----	6. -----
7. and the sword was dripping blood	7. -----	7. -----
8. I said to him	8. -----	8. -----
9. May I see consolation	9. -----	9. ----
10. that this one slew	10. -----	10. -----
11. but what shall I do	11. -----	11. -----
12. for your blood is not	12. -----	12. -----
13. but the one who knows	13. -----	13. -----
14. He did not even leave	14. -----	14. -----
15. before a serpent bit him and he died.	15. -----	15.-----
16. -----	16. Judah b. Tabbai said, May I see consolation If I did not slay a	16. TNY ,, ,, ,, ,, ,, ,,

		False witness. For they would say, Until he is slain [the false witness is not punished], as it is said (Ex. 21:23), *Soul for soul*	to remove from the *heart of the Sadducees* who would *say* " " "
17. -----		17. Simeon b Shetah said to him, May I see consolation	17." " "
18. -----		18. if it is not regarded to you as if you shed innocent blood.	18 .*if you did not shed* " " " for the sages said, *no punishment until the accused perjurers are both found guilty* [+ *flagellation* and *fines*, in same formula]
19. -----		19. At that time he took upon himself not to teach except from the mouth of Simeon b. Shetah	19." " " except *in the presence*
20. -----		20. -----	20. *And all the rest of Judah's life he prostrated himself on the grave of that witness,*

and his voice was heard, and people thought it was the voice of the slain man. He said, It is my voice. You ill know it tomorrow when he dies.

*****

B. Sanh.	B. Shebuot 34a	B. Hag. 16b
1. TNY " " "	1. " " "	1. -----
2. " " " another into a ruin	2. " " " "[as b. Sanh.]	2. -----
3. *I ran after him*	3. " " "	3. -----
4. -----	4. -----	4. -----
5. *I saw him with a* sword *in his hand*	5. I *found him* " " "	5. -----
6. -----	6. -----	6. -----
7. and *his blood was* dripping and *the slain man was writhing*	7. " " " [as b. Sanh.]	7. -----
8. " " "	8. " " "	8. -----
9. -----	9. -----	9. -----

10. *Wicked! Who killed this man? You or me*	10. " " "	10. -----
11. " " "	11. " " "	11. -----
12. " " " for lo, the	12. " " "	12. -----
13. " " " from that man who slew his fellow	13. The *Omnipresent* will " " "from *you* [omits who-fellow]	13. -----
14. *They said* he did not *move* from there before a snake *came*	14. "*they* did not move before a snake bit him [omits *came and*] and bit him and he died	14. -----
15. [As above]	15. [As above]	15. -----
16. -----	16. -----	16. TNW RBNN
17. -----	17. -----	17. [As b Mak. 5b]
18. -----	18. -----	18. [As b Mak. 5b]
19. -----	19. -----	19. [As b. Mak. 5b]
20. -----	20. -----	20. [As b. Mak. 5b]

The *baraita* about Judah's exemplary but illegal punishment of the false witness, b. Mak. 5b = b. Hag. 16b, is an improvement on the equivalent version in y. Sanh. 6:3. There *they would say* is unclear. The Babylonian version supplies the identity of *those* who held the false opinion, namely the *Sadducees*. This further depends upon Tos. Sanh. 6:6, but *Boethusians* is dropped in favor of *Sadducees*. The exact quotation of the Boethusians/Sadducees varies somewhat. Y. Sanh. Supplies a proof-text for their opinion, which is absent in Tos. Sanh. And later dropped in b. Mak. = b. Hag. The most striking change occurs in no. 18, where the language *if it is not regarded to you as if you shed* is changed to the more direct *you shed*. This is a simplification and an improvement. Tos. Knows nothing of Judah's pledge not to teach instruction/law except according to Simeon, which occurs in more dramatic detail — *in the presence of* — in the Babylonian *baraita*. The Palestinian is intermediate; it does not specify what it was that Judah would not teach. The *baraita*, in summary, is unquestionably later than, and an improvement upon, y. Sanh., being smoother, dropping irrelevant details (e.g. the proof-text), but supplying important "omissions", e.g. what Judah would not teach, and adding *flagellation* and *fines*. In one respect, namely no. 16, *to remove* etc., the *baraita* obviously must depend upon Tos. But in all other important aspects, it is a development of y. Sanh. 6:3 — thus eclectic or a composite, a puzzling result.

The Mekhilta Version provides the briefest and least satisfactory story, omits the dramatic details of Judah's (Simeon's) report of what he had done, and of Judah's vow not to teach except following Simeon's opinions. No. 20 of the *baraita* is certainly a dramatic and colorful addition to the whole, known only in the latest version.

The story about the murderer whom the law cannot punish is linked to the foregoing in Mekhilta Kaspa, but everywhere else stands separately. In Mekhilta Kaspa we again find the simplest and least embellished form. The changes from y. Sanh. 4:9 to b. Sanh. 37b = b. Shebuot 34a are not considerable. The scene is somewhat clarified and sharpened. *He entered... I entered* of y. Sanh. Becomes the dramatic confrontation of b. Sanh.: *I ran after him and saw him a moment after he did the deed*. Then the details (no. 7) are greatly augmented, but again are drawn mainly from Mekhilta Kaspa, further from the anonymous accounts, not summarized here, which invariably include the gory details. *What shall I do* of y. Sanh. 4:9 is greatly expanded by reference to the proof-text, but here this is artfully introduced in the context of the exchange between the sage and the murderer. Then, in no 14 of b. Sanh., the narrator takes over for the unclear *he did not leave,* so we are now told who has provided the details of the denouement.

As we observed above, the two stories are distinct and circulated by themselves. Only the Judah b. Tabbai-version was kept together. The Simeon-ones were allowed to develop separately. The *beraitot* in both cases provide additional information, but we have not reason to suppose they contain material drawn from other, independent traditions. In each instance, on the basis of the earlier versions we can readily account for the alterations. Only no. 20 is entirely independent of the foregoing, but it is certainly a dramatic embellishment, nothing more; it is the sort of addition that editors of *beraitot* loved to make.

Now, assuming the Mekhilta is the earliest version of the pericopae, we note that the later accounts are in general dependent upon, or at least related to, it in all important details except for the identification of the hero. The whole can be said to be a living tradition, in that details found later on normally derive from earlier accounts and can be readily traced from one version to the next. But what lies before Mekhilta Kaspa? I find it difficult to imagine that the literary relationships we have observed do not signify the dependence, upon the Mekhilta, of the accounts in which Simeon is the hero. The Mekhilta of R. Ishmael-version is what Meir would have supplied; all the others in general follow opinion of Judah b. Ilai, making Simeon *Nasi.* All elements of the Simeon-materials thus are revisions of the foregoing, including the important fact that Simeon is the hero, Judah the judge who erred. In that case, the correct tradition must be the one which places Judah b. Tabbai superior to Simeon b. Shetah. The others testify to the ability of Judah b. Ilai and those who shared his view not only to develop the older tradition, but also completely to revise its historical and biographical facts. The relative importance of Simeon and Judah seems to have constituted an important issue for the late second century Tannaitic schools.

2. Nasi -- Head of Court

Tos. Hag. 2:8	Y. Hag. 2:2a	Y. Sanh. 6:6a
1. There were five pairs.	1. -----	1. -----
2. Three of the first pairs who said not to lay on hands	2. -----	2. -----
3. and two of the last who said to lay on hands	3. -----	3. -----
4. were *Nasis*,	4. -----	4. -----
5. and the second were heads of court, according to R. Meir	5. -----	5. ----
6. R. Judah says, Simeon b. Shetah was *Nasi*, Judah b. Tabbai head of the court	6. [As in 6*]	6. [As in 6*]
6.*-----	6.* We have learned (NN TNYNN): Judah b. Tabbai was *Nasi*, Simeon b. Shetah was head of the court.	6.*Some Tannaim teach (YT TNYY TNY) Judah b. Tabbai was *Nasi* and

92 Peripatetic Parallels

		Simeon b. Shetah was *Nasi*.
7. -----	7. Some teach it in reverse. [The story of Judah in Alexandria and Simeon in Ashqelon follows.]	7. -----

The Tos. version thus has not been reproduced, merely cited, in the Palestinian Amoraic discussion. But y. Hag. rephrases the whole in explicit form: Judah was *Nasi* Simeon was head of the court. In y. Sanh. two separate attributions to Tannaim simply assign the position of *Nasi* to each of the authorities. In any event the language of Tos. has been abandoned, while Tannaitic authority is claimed for its content.

3. Judah b. Tabbai in Alexandria

Y. Hag. 2:2b	Y. Sanh. 6:6b
1. The men of Jerusalem wanted to appoint Judah b. T. as *Nasi* in Jerusalem. He fled to Alexandria.	1. -----
2. The men of Jerusalem would write	2. " " "
3. From Jerusalem the great, to Alexandria the small	3. " " "
4. How long will my betrothed dwell with you, and I set etc.	4. How long will my *husband* in your *midst* " " " *in my house*

5. He departed, coming in a boat. He said, you remember etc.	5. [Omits the affair with the student.]

The version in y. Sanh. omits the introductory materials and knows nothing of the incident with the student at all. The augmentations in no. 4 suggest a somewhat later version, and my guess is that y. Sanh. depends upon, but abbreviates, y. Hag. The same pattern of summary and abbreviation of y. Hag. by y. Sanh. recurs in the Simeon-story.

4. The Decree on the Uncleanness of Metal Utensils

B. Shab. 14b	Y. Shab. 1:4	Y. Pes. 1:6	Y. Ket. 8:11
1. DTNY Abuna in the	1. R. Zeira b. R. Abuna name of R. Jeremiah	1. [As y. Shab.]	1. [As y. Pes.]
2. Yosé b. Yoezer	2. " " " and Yosé b. Yohanan decreed uncleanness on the land of the peoples and glassware.	2. " " "	2. " " "
3. Simeon b. Shetah ordained (TQN) the marriage contract for the woman	3. *R. Yonah said, Judah b. Tabbai. R. Yosé said, Judah b. Tabbai and* Simeon b. Shetah decreed uncleanness on metalware [Omits	3. *R. Judah* said, Judah b. T. and Simeon b. S. [As. y. Shab.]	3. *R. Yosé* said Judah b. T. *R. Yonah* said, Judah b. T. and Simeon b. S. decreed uncleanness on metal-

94 Peripatetic Parallels

	marriage-contract]		ware [Omits marriage-contract]
4. and decreed (GZR) uncleanness on metalware	4. [See no. 3]	4. [See no. 3]	4. [See no. 3]
5. Shammai and Hillel decreed uncleanness on the hands	5. " " *concerning the cleanness* of the hands	5. [As y. Shab.]	5. [As y. Shab.]

Since y. Ket- 8:1 t contains the list of Simeon's decrees, we shall add the synopsis of that list here:

Tos. Ket. 12:1	B. Ket. 82b	Y. Ket. 8:11
1. At first... Simeon b. S. ordained that her marriage-contract should be with her husband, and he should write to her, All the property which I have is liable and pledged for this, your marriage-contract	1. Rab Judah.... Simeon b. S. ordained all his property is liable for her marriage-contract. TNY NMY HKY: ...until Simeon b. S. ordained that he should write should write to her, All *my* property is liable for *her* marriage-contract	1. Simeon b. Shetah decreed three things
2. -----	2. -----	2. That a man may do business with his wife's marriage-contract

3. -----	3. -----	3. That children should go to school
4. -----	4. -----	4. and he ordained (TQN) uncleanness on glassware

All the references to the marriage-contract pertain to details. None holds Simeon b. Shetah invented the marriage-contract. The reference in b. Shab. no. 4 appears in y. Ket. 8:11 no. 4, now an ordinance. The version in b. Shab. no. 4 is unrelated to more detailed accounts of the matter. The marriage-contract materials are not closely related. Tos. Ket. has certainly produced b. Ket., but y. Ket. (like b. Shab. no. 3) stands pretty much by itself. Perhaps the intent of the ordinance is what is specified.

As to the decree on the uncleanness of metal utensils, all the traditions are identical in language, except y. Ket. No. 4, which, like b. Shab. No. 4, omits reference to Judah b. Tabbai. Since the lists of b. Shab. 14b and y. Ket. 8:11 have in common the omission of Judah b. Tabbai and a reference to the marriage-contract (but *not* the same reference, there may be some correspondence between them. But a list of Simeon's decrees ought not to have omitted the founding of the school-system, and TQN of y. Ket. Changes to GZR in b. Shab. Hence the lists are not closely related. Moreover, the intent of y. Ket. 8:11 is to list Simeon's decrees; one might argue Judah b. Tabbai is not deliberately omitted, mere bypassed for stylistic purposes. But the same cannot be said for B. Shab. 14b, which either is defective or represents a purposeful revision of the tradition referred to by the Palestinian Amoraim. I presume the latter were influenced by the juxtaposition of Judah and Simeon in M. Hag. 2:2 and M. Abot (see Chapter Fourteen), but I do not understand why the framer of the Babylonian *baraita* was not similarly impressed with those lists, if he knew them.

B. SIMEON B. SHETAH ALONE

1. *Heavy rains*

Sifra	B. Ta. 23a	Lev. R.
1. M^cSH	1. So we find	1. " " "
2. In the days of Simeon b. S., in the days of SLMSW the queen	2. [Omits: *Salome the Queen*]	2. " (SLMSY) [Adds:]
3. that the rains would descend from Sabbath night to Sabbath night	3. " " " *on eves of Wednesdays and Sabbaths*	3. " " "
4. until the wheat was made like kidneys	4. " " "	4. " " "
5. the barley like olive	5. " " "	5. " " "
6. and the lentils like gold *denars*	6. " " "	6. " " "
7. and the sages bound up (SRR) some of them	7. " " " *as an example* (DWGM)	7. " " "
8. and left them for coming generations	8. " " " [Omits: *and left them; coming*]	8. " " "
9. to make known how much sin causes,	9. " " "	9. *All this why* " " "

| 10. to fulfill that which is said Jer. 5:25 | 10. *As it is said* " " " | 10. " " " |

The differences between Lev. R. and Sifra are negligible. Only *all this why* betrays the mark of a later hand. The phrase could have been omitted without loss of meaning. It serves to underline the purposive sense of the infinitive, *to make known*. The Babylonian Talmudic version follows the usual Amoraic form, *as it is said,* in place of the Tannaitic Midrashic *to fulfill*. Salome is now omitted, certainly an improvement, dropping a redundant detail; her name could have meant little to people out of touch with the stories of King Yannai and Simeon. *Wednesdays* is added because of the legal context. *As an example* likewise clarifies the sages' intent, thought it does not augment the meaning. The version in b. Ta. Is certainly a development of that in Sifra. Lev. R. is a more exact copy. This is a common phenomenon. Where traditions appearing in early collections recur in very late ones, they are normally copies, showing little evidence of either growth of a living tradition, or response to vivid discussions of the subject-matter of the pericope. Both phenomena by contrast are apparent in b. Ta. Sometimes, to be sure, late compilations supply all sorts of new elements, but these rarely appear to be integral to the earlier version or part of an internal process of augmentation of words or phrases. Rather, they tend to be manufactured or whole cloth.

2. Hung Eighty Women in Ashqelon

Sifré Deut. 221	M. Sanh. 6:4	Y. Sanh. 6:3
1. The man is hung, but not the woman. R. Eliezer says, Even a Woman is to be hung.	1. *The woman is hung facing backward, the man facing the people, so* R. Eliezer. *The sages say,* The man is hung, but not the woman.	1. -----
2. R. Eliezer said to them, Did not Simeon b. S. hang women in Ashqelon?	2. " " "	2. -----
3. They said to him, He hung eighty women, and one does not judge two on the same day	3. " " "	3. -----
4. But hour required to teach other by that means	4. -----	4. -----
5. -----	5. -----	5. Simeon's hands were heated. A conspiracy of scoffers came and said, Come, let us take counsel and testify against his son and kill him. They testified against him and his case was settled that he be killed. As

he was going
forth to be killed,
they said to him,
"My lord, we
are liars." His
father wanted to
bring him back.
He said to him,
"Father, if you
want salvation to
come at your
hand, make me
like a threshold."

*****

Y. Hag. 2:2c   Y. Sanh. 6:6c

1. There were two pious men who   1. " " "
   shared their food and studies.

2. One died and was not properly   2. " " "
   mourned.

3. When a villager, a tax-collector   3. " " "
   died, the whole town took time
   off to mourn him.

4. The pious man began to be   5. " " " *to cry*
   troubled and said etc.

5. Do not disgrace the sons of your   5. " " " [minor variations, one sin
   Lord, for this one did one sin.   *and went in it,* one good deed and
   And the other one did one good   *went in it*]
   Deed and it went well for him

6. [Specifies the sin; then second dream: pious man saw fellow in heaven, tax-collector suffering, Because she fasted etc.]	6. [Specifies sin; *omits*: sin of Miriam.] and Miriam etc. Why is this so?
7. How long thus?	7. " " "
8. Until Simeon takes it from her ear	8. " " "
9. Why? Because he said, If I am made *Nasi* I shall kill witches, and lo, he had been made *Nasi* and has not killed witches. There are eighty in a cave in Ashqelon. Go and tell him.	9. What is his *lapse*? *He vowed* and said " " "
10. I am afraid, for he is *Nasi* and will not believe me. If he believes you, well and good, and if not, this is your sign [*re* eye].	10. " " "
11. Simeon believed him.	11. " " "
12. Took eighty young men etc.	12. [From here to end, the account is abbreviated and simplified.]
13. This is what we learned, The story is told of Simeon b. Shetah that he hung women in Ashqelon. They said he hung eighty women; while one does not judge two on the same day, the hour required it.	13. This is what we learned, Eighty women did Simeon b. S. hang in Ashqelon and one does not judge two in one day, but the hour required it.

The tradition on the hanging of (eighty) women (witches) in Ashqelon comes in two forms. The earliest is a reference merely to hanging women. Nothing more is told. This tradition is virtually ignored in y. Hag. and y. Sanh., which produce the elaborate account about the witches and how they were outwitted by Simeon's superior knowledge of magic and of the libido of witches. A still further detail records the vengeance of the people of Ashqelon. It seems to me Sifré must be regarded as earliest, and the Palestinian Amoraic versions as quite separate, but much later assemblies of traditions. According to the former, Simeon did put to death a large number of women, but we do not know why. The elaborate accounts of y. Sanh. and y. Hag. supply the reason and much more. Of the two, y. Hag. is the more detailed, while y. Sanh. seems to be an abbreviation and a summary. But neither is likely to date before Amoraic times. The Babylonian Talmud contains no equivalent materials, and we may perhaps assign the magical accounts to third- or fourth-century Palestinian schools.

3. Rebuked Honi

M. Ta. 3:8	Y. M.Q. 3:1	Y. Ta. 3:1 0
1. ...Simeon b. S. sent to him	1. [All omitted to here.] " " " *He said to him*	1. [Mishnah ends with Prov. 23:25. Then] If a decree were decreed as in the days of Elijah, would you not be found bringing the public to profanation of the name [etc. as in y. M.Q. no. 2.1
2. Were you not Honi	2. You ought to be excommunicated. For if a decree were decreed as in the	2. [as y. -M.Q.]

102 *Peripatetic Parallels*

	days of Elijah, would you not be found bringing the public to profanation of the name, for all who bring the public to profanation of the name require excommunication.	
3. I should decree excommunication upon you	3. -----	3. -----
4. But what should I do to you	4. -----	4. -----
5. For you come petulantly (HTY) before the Omnipresent	5. -----	5. -----
6. and he does your will for you	6. -----	6. -----
7. like a son who comes petulantly against his father	7. -----	7. -----
8. and he does his will	8. -----	8. -----
9. and concerning you Scripture says Prov. 23:25	9. -----	9. -----

*****

<u>B. Ber. 19a</u>

1. DTNN [Omits story until *Simeon sent to him*] " " " *You require to be excommunicated*

<u>B. Ta. 2 3a</u>

1. [Foregoing story much developed. Then as in M. Ta.] " " "

2. " " "	2. For if the years were like the years of Elijah, for the keys of rain were in the hand of Elijah, would not the name of heaven be found profaned by your hand.
3. " " "	3. [As above]
4. " " "	4. " " "
5. " " "	5. " " "
6. " " "	6. " " "
7. " " "	7. " " "
8. " " "	8. " " " [Adds:] *and he says to him, Father, take me to wash me in warm water, pour cold water over me, give me nuts, almonds, and pomegranates and he gives him*
9. " " "	9. " " "

The Palestinian Amoraic versions introduce the theme of Elijah, but drop the rest of the colloquy of Simeon. The Babylonian *baraita* (b. Ber. 19a) borrows a single phrase, *You require*. The extended version in b. Ta. 3a not only adopts the whole of the Palestinian version, but then inserts the remainder of the Mishnah passage, and finally supplies a complete conversation between the son and the father — a full repertoire, leaving out not a single detail of the earlier versions.

4. *Simeon, Yannai, and the Nazirites*

Y. Ber. 7:2	Y. Naz. 5:3	B. Ber. 48a	Gen. R.
1. TNY	1. " " "	1. -----	1. -----
2. Three hundred Nazirites came up in the days of Rabbi Simeon b. S.	2. " " " Omits Rabbi]	2. -----	2. " " "
2.*One hundred fifty he found grounds for absolution (MS PTH), and one hundred fifty he did not find grounds for absolution	2.*" " " *they* found	2.*-----	2.* " " "
3. He came to Yannai the King	3. " " "	3 - -----	3. " " " went up (SLQ)
4. He said to him, There are here three hundred Nazirites requiring nine hundred sacrifices	4. " " "	4. -----	4. " " "
5. So (L) you give half from yours, and I half from mine	5. [Omits L]	5. -----	5. [As Y. Naz.]

6. He sent him four hundred fifty	6. " " "	6. -----	6. *Yannai gave half*
7. An evil report went forth and said to him	7. " " "	7. -----	7. " " "
8. He gave nothing of his own.	8. " " "	8. -----	8. " " "
9. Yannai the King heard and was angry. Simeon b. S. was frightened and fled.	9. " " "	9. -----	9. [Omits: *Yannai-angry*]
10. After some days important men came up from the Kingdom of Persia to Yannai the King.	10. " " "	10. ----- [Begins:] *Yannai the King and the Queen were eating together. Since he had killed the rabbis, there was no one to bless for them, He said to his wife. Who will give us a man to bless for us? She said to him Give me your oath that if I bring you a man you will not torment him. He*	10. " " "

106 *Peripatetic Parallels*

		gave his oath and she brought him Simeon b. S. her Brother.	
11. When they were seated eating they said to him, We remember that there is here a certain old man and he said before us words of wisdom.	11. " " "	11. -----	11. at the *table of Yannai the King* " " "
12. Let him teach	12. " " "	12. -----	12. -----
13. They said to for us a matter (WBD).	13. " " "	13. -----	13. -----
14. He sent and	14. " " "	14. [As above]	14. " " "
15. He came and he sat between the king and the queen.	15. " " "	15. He seated him between him and her	15. " " "
16. He said to him, Why did you deceive me?	16. " " "	16. -----	16. He said to him, What is this
17. He said to him, I did not deceive you.	17. " " "	17. -----	17. [Follows 19]

18. You from your money and I from my Torah	18. " " "	18. -----	18. [Follows 19]
19. As it is	19. " " "	19. -----	19. [Quotes Ben Sira.]
			19* [Now come 17 and 18]
			19.**Why did you not tell me? If I told you, you would not have done it.
20. He said to him, And why did you flee?	20. " " "	20. -----	20. " " "
21. He said to, him I heard that my lord was angry against me, and I wanted to fulfill this Scripture, Is. 26:20	21. " " " [Omits wanted to]	21. -----	21. " " "
22. And he read concerning him Qoh. 7:12b	22. " " "	22. -----	22. -----
23. He said to him, And why did you sit between king and queen.	23. " " "	23. *You see how much honor I pay you?*	23. -----

24. He said to him, In the Books of Ben Sira it is written [etc.]	24. Book of *Bar Sira* " " "	24. *It is not you that honors me, but the Torah honors me, as it is written Prov. 4:8*	24. -----
24* -----	24* -----	24* *He said to her, Do you see he does not accept authority.*	24* -----
25. He said to him, Give him the cup so he will bless	25. " " "	25. " " "	25. *Mixed cup, said to him, bless*
26. He took the cup and said	26. " " "	26. *He said to him, How shall I bless? Blessed is he whose* [gift] *Yannai and his companions have eaten?*	26. " " "
27. Let us bless the food which Yannai and his companions have eaten	27. " " "	27. [As above]	27. *I never heard this from you before*
28. He said to him, To such an extent are you in your stubbornness?	28. " " "	28. [See 24*]	28. -----
29. He said to him, What should 1 say, For the food which we have not eaten?	29. " " "	29. [As above, no. 26]	29. " " "

30. He said, Give him to eat. He ate.	30. " " "	30. *He drank it* [the cup] they brought him *another cup and he blessed.*	30. " " "
31. and said, Let us bless the food which we have eaten	31. " " "	31. -----	31. " " "

Gen. R. does not greatly differ from the Palestinian versions. The order of some of the elements changes, and there are a few minor changes in word-choice, not here indicated. But for the rest, we may regard Gen. R. as a fairly accurate representation of the Palestinian Talmud's accounts. There also are some differences in grammar and spelling between the two Palestinian versions. They have not been signified.

The real comparison is between the three Palestinian versions and the Babylonian one. The latter shows how material would be reshaped by an editor for the purposes of legal discussion. The version in b. Ber. omits all reference to elements extraneous to the inquiry of that discussion. It therefore drops the Nazirites and thus loses the explanation provided by that incident for Simeon's absence. The more generalized *since he had killed the rabbis* make up the difference. The Babylonian tradition further omits all conversations related to earlier incident with the Nazirites. The honor paid to Simeon is now credited to the king, rather than having Simeon take the place of honor on his own. This certainly improves matters and permits an even better sermon to make much the same Point. Proverbs replaces Ben Sira, which is consistent with the Babylonian Rabbinic denigration of Ben Sira. Finally the story of the blessing is repeated, in the established for n, except here, Simeon *drinks* the first cup, and they have to provide a second. But the explanation of his action is the same; so the argument has been converted into a dramatic gesture.

    Once more, we observe close relationships between the documents' several versions of a given story or saying, respectively. The variations concern details, minor ones at that.

Chapter Five

Shemaiah and Abtalion

1. Splitting the Sea

Mekh. of R. Ishmael	Mekh. of R. Simeon b. Yohai
1. Shemaiah says,	1. " " "
2. Worthy is the faith that Abraham their father believed in me	2. [omits HY] the [faith], *their father*
3. that I shall open for them (LHM)	3. I am opening for them (LHN) the sea
4. as it is said, Gen. 15:6	4. [Omits *as it is said*]
5. Abtalion says,	5. " " "
6. Worthy is the faith that they that believed in me	6. [Same changes as above, no. 2] Israel in Egypt believed
7. that I should open for them the sea	7. [Same changes as above, no. 3]
8. as it is said, Ex. 4:31	8. " " "

The Mekhilta of R. Simeon b. Yohai exhibits fixed stylistic differences from the Mekhilta of R. Ishmael. No. 6 represents a considerable clarification. The point of Abtalion is that their faith, not merely that of the fathers, is being rewarded. Hence Mekhilta of R. Simeon b. Yohai stresses this by supplying *Israel in Egypt* in place of the less precise *they*. The versions are otherwise very close and the differences merely stylistic. The Ishmael-version is older.

2. *Weavers quote Shemaiah and Abtalion*

M. ED. 1:3-4	Tosefta Ed. 1:3	b. Shab. 15a
1. Hillel says, A *hin* of drawn-water spoils the *miqveh*	1. " " " [Adds:] *a full hin* of *twelve log* " " "	1. " " "
2. But (LS) a man is obligated to say in the language of his master	2. ------	2. *for* a man " " "
3. Shammai says, Nine *qabs*	3. *a full hin of thirty-six log* " " "	3. " " "
4. And the sages say, Not according to the words of this one, and not according to the words of this one.	4. " " " *but three logs of drawn water spoil the miqveh* [= M. Ed. No. 6]	4. " " "
5. But until (LDS) two weavers came from the Dung Gate which is in	5. *The story is told* (MSHB) *that* " " "	5. " " "

	Jerusalem and gave testimony in the name of (MSWM) Shemaiah and Abtalion		
6.	Three *logs* of drawn water spoil the *miqveh*	6. " " "	6. " " "
7.	and the sages confirmed their words	7. " " "	7. " " "

The measurements thus are as follows:

M. Ed.	Tosefta Ed.
Hillel: One *hin* [= three *qabs*]	one *hin* = twelve *logs*
Shammai: [Three *hin*] = nine *qabs*	one *hin* = thirty-six *logs*
Sages: Three *logs* [= 1/4 *hin* = 3/4 *qab*]	three *logs*

Mishnah-Tosefta preserve the same relationships:

$$3-9-3/4 = 12-36-3$$

	M. Ed. 1:3-4	Tosefta Ed. 1:4	b. Shab. 15a
8.	And why do they mention the words of Shammai and	8. *And why are the names of their places and their occupations*	8. " " " Hillel to no purpose (LBTLH)

	Hillel to no purpose (LBTLH)		*mentioned? Do you have a more lowly occupation than weaving, or a more despised place in Jerusalem than the Dung Gate?*	
9.	To teach coming generations that a man should not insist on his opinion.	9.	*But just as the fathers of the world*	9. " " "
10.	for lo, the fathers of the world did not insist on their opinion.	10.	did not insist on their opinion *in a place where oral tradition* (SMWH) *is available, how much the more so that a man should not insist on his opinion in available.*	10. " " "

In b. Shab. 15a the Mishnah is accurately cited, with only a small but essential improvement. There the strange L becomes S, *for*. Tosefta preserves the story about the weavers as a separate unit. The sages have already given "their" opinion — the opinion which in the Mishnah as in the story of the weavers (MSHB) derives from Shemaiah and Abtalion. Tosefta Eduyyot thus has the sages' opinion circulate separately from the pericope involving Hillel and Shammai. I have already remarked on the exculpation of Hillel and Shammai. For the Mishnah what requires explanations the citation of the two masters, Hillel and Shammai, when in fact their opinions do not constitute law.

For Tosefta the problem is different. No one is bothered about mentioning Hillel's and Shammai's opinion when it is not law. It is taken for granted that this may happen. The Tosefta story emphasizes the modest origins of the opinion attributed to Shemaiah and Abtalion — it came from weavers from the poorest district. The sermon is in form much the same. But the "fathers of the world" now are *not* Hillel and Shammai, but Shemaiah and Abtalion! And the operative element is the availability of an oral tradition (SM cH). The irony is that Hillel achieved the office of *Nasi* only because he had such an oral tradition from Shemaiah and Abtalion, yet here ignores it. The irony is underlined in Tosefta no. 10. All this is revised by Judah the Patriarch, in his Mishnah, which naturally makes Hillel and Shammai the fathers of the world, and *their* forbearance the point of the sermon.

Here we may attribute to Judah the Patriarch a clear-cut preference for the Mishnaic version of the materials. Hillel, his alleged ancestor, is at the center of things. Judah makes Hillel the example of modesty and humility. The story of the weavers occurs — presumably there was no other version of Shemaiah and Abtalion's opinions — but it is subordinated. We may therefore take it for granted that the story circulated separately in the form in which it occurs in the Tosefta. Only afterwards was it revised to serve the purposes of the editor of Mishnah Eduyyot. MSHB is dropped. And so are the significant lessons to be learned from the Dung Gate.

3. Gave Bitter Water to Suspected Adulteress

M. Ed. 5:6 = Sifré Num. 7	b. Ber. 19a	y. Sot. 2:5
1. [Aqabiah and sages dispute whether to administer bitter waters to convert or freed female slave. Aqabiah says one does not do so. The sages say one does.]	1. TNY: He would say, One does not cause to drink (MSQYN) the female convert nor the freed slave girl, and the sages say, You do.	1. R. Aqiba said, I shall explain: From one man, the wife does not drink and repeat; from two men, the wife drinks and repeats. And the sages say, Whether from one or two men, the wife drinks and repeats.
2. They said to him, The story is told (MSH B) concerning Khorkemit, a freed slave girl, who was at Jerusalem.	2. " " "	2. *Khorkemit will prove it, for she drank and repeated and* [did it still a] *third* [time]. (Drops *ma'aseh b*).
3. And Shemaiah and Abtalion administered the waters to her.	3. " " "	3. ———
4. He said to them, They administered the waters to her as an example (DWGM HSQWH).	4. *and* he said " " "	4. ———

As we see, y. Sot. Has Aqiba's opposition citing *not* the Mishnah before us, but rather a quite different reminiscence of, or allusion to, it. The story no longer concerns whether a convert or a freed slave-girl is made to drink the waters. She is not a freed slave-girl at all. Now she is just an ordinary wife, in the situation explained above. We therefore cannot suppose the Mishnah is accurately quoted by the sages opposed to Aqiba. A different, slightly related version is used for settling a separate issue. The kernel of both traditions must be an association of Shemaiah and Abtalion with the administration of the bitter waters to Khorkemit — who was either a freed slave-girl, or a wife in an especially complicated situation, but not both. Once more, the variations from document to document prove trivial.

Chapter Six

Yohanan the High Priest

1. Did Away with Confession

M.M.S. 5:15 M. Sot. 9:10	B. Sot. 48a	Tos. Sot. 13:10	Y.M.S. 5:5	Y. Sot. 9:11 (" " "=as in y.M.S.5:5)
1. Yohanan the High Priest did away with (BR) the Confession of the Tithe	1. TNY Also he annulled (BTL) " " "	1. ------	1. R. Yohanan said	1." " "
2. Also the annulled (BTL) the Wakers and the Knockers	2. ------	2. ------	2. ------	2. ------
3. And until his days the hammer was striking in Jerusalem	3. ------	3. ------	3. ------	3. ------
4. And in his days a man did not have to ask about *demai*	4. And he *decreed concerning demai*	4. He *annulled (BTL) demai*	4. ------	4. ------

5. ------	5. for he sent through the whole boundary of Israel and saw they separated only *terumah gedolah*.	5. " " "	5. *Yohanan the High Priest sent and searched in all the cities of Israel and found* " " "	5. " " "
6. -----	6. As to First Tithe and Second Tithe, some were tithing, and some were not tithing	6. " " "	6. " " "	6. " " "
7. -----	7. He said to them, My children, Come and I shall say to you.	7. -----	7. -----	7. ------
8. -----	8. Just as in *terumah gedolah* mortal sin inheres, so in Heave-offering of tithe	8. " " "	8. He said to them, *Since First Tithe* [is] *in death and Second Tithe is in the sin of tebel*	8. " " "

Yohanan the High Priest

9. -----	9. He arose and ordained (TCN) for them: He who purchases fruits from an *am haares* separates from the Heave-offering of tithes and gives it to the priest	9. [= y. M.S. 5:5]	9. Let a man designate *Heave-offering* and Heave-offering of Tithe and give it to the priest	9. " " "
10. -----	10. Second Tithe—he goes up and eats it in Jerusalem	10. [y. M.S. 5:5]	10. and Second Tithe *—he profanes it with coins*	10. " " "
11. -----	11. First Tithe and poor man's Tithe—he who takes away from his fellow must bring the proof	11. " " "	11. and the rest –poor man's Tithe " " " *and let him confess*	11. " " "

12. -----	12. What are knockers? Rab Judah-Samuel [as above]	12. -----	12. ------	12. ------
13. -----	13. BMTNYT' TN'	13. -----	13. -----	13. ------
14. -----	14. They would smite it with hammers as they do beforehand	14. [y. M.S. 5:5]	14. *Yoḥanan the High Priest said to them*	14. " " "
15. -----	15. He said to them, Until when are you going to feed corpses (NBYLWT) to the altar	15. " " " TRPWT	15. How long are you going to feed " " "	15. " " "
16. -----	16. NBYLWT?	16. ------	16. -------	16. -----
17. -----	17. they slaughter them, but TRPWT lest the membrane of	17. ------	17. altar [Omits *on ground*]	

18. -----	18. He arose and ordained (TQN) for them	18. ------	18." " " and made	18." " "
19. -----	19. rings on the ground	19. ------	19. rings [Omit on ground]	19." " "
20. -----	20. ------	20. ------	20. for he set up pairs	20. ------

We see that both the Babylonian and Palestinian *gemarot* preserve substantial expansions of the tradition. The two Palestinian versions differ very little, except in the striking failure of y. Sot. 9:11 to correct NBYLWT to TRPWT, the secondary, therefore necessarily later version. Tos. Sot. 13:10 does make the necessary correction, perhaps a scribal "improvement." The earlier form of the Amoraic material must be the Palestinian version attributed to Yohanan, with the baraita's coming later. The Palestinian form omits the colloquy introducing Yohanan the High Priest's message, *My children, come and I shall teach you*. The Babylonian further improves the diction of his message, *just as... so...* and corrects *sin of tebel* (whatever that might mean) to *in... tebel, mortal sin...* which makes sense. The Babylonian prefers to have the man eat his tithe in Jerusalem, while the saying of Yohanan is congruent to Palestinian realities of his day. No one could then go up to Jerusalem. The Babylonian improves on this, by rightly, *but* anachronistically, setting the whole thing back into Temple times. The Palestinians have him confess he has paid his dues, but this is manifestly dishonest, and the Babylonian drops that detail. The interruption of Judah-Samuel obviously will be absent in the Palestinian version.

Then the Babylonian further improves on the brief colloquy, by supplying the detail of what they would do (b. Sot. 48a, no. 14), thus augmenting the Palestinian version's simple *he said to them.* The Babylonian further explains the legal dilemma, no. 17 lest *the membrane*, further developing the Palestinian version's no. 17. The concluding detail, no. 19, is augmented by *on the ground* in Babylonia.

There can be no reasonable doubt that the Babylonia *baraita* not only comes later than Yohanan's version, but in fact depends, and improves, upon it in numerous details. But we have no grounds to suppose that Yohanan possessed some sort of "very ancient" tradition, or, if he did, that he transmitted it in the language in which it would have been formulated centuries earlier. On the contrary, in effect he did much as did Samuel, but instead of phrasing the whole in his own language, he told a story in standard Mishnaic narrative style. This then became the basis for the still later Babylonian *baraita.* The variations of the story from one document to another are minor and do not suggest that we have a set of distinct stories. Rather, they underscore the continuity in the unfolding of a single story, as it moves from document to document over time.

2. *Heard Heavenly Echo*

Tos. Sot. 13:5	B. Sot. 33a	Y. Sot. 9:13
1. Yohanan the High Priest heard from the house of the holy of holies	1. WHTNY: " " "	1. M^{c}SH S " " "
2. ------	2. ------	2. Young men went forth to do battle at Antioch

3. [See above, 1]	3. " " "	3. *And* Yohanan *the high priest* heard *an echo coming forth from the* house of the holy of holies
4. " " " [= y. Sot.]	4. " " "	4. *The youths who made war in Antioch have conquered* [in Aramaic]
5. And they tallied (KWN) that hour and they tallied that they conquered at that hour	5. -----	5. and they wrote down that time and set in it the hour
6. [See above, 5]	6. -----	6. and they tallied it that it was in that very hour

In no. 3, y. Sot. adds BT OWL, strikingly absent from Tos. Sot. no. 1. The Babylonian version is furthest from the other two, which are quite close to one another, as we saw in connection with Simeon. The Babylonia *baraita* has dropped nos. 5 and 6, since the issue is whether or not the angels speak Aramaic, and those details therefore are of no consequence here. Otherwise, the differences among the three versions are not substantial. The Palestinian version no. 5 removes some of the verbal repetitions of Tos. Sot. and is certainty dependent upon it. The Babylonian *baraita* copies Tos. Sot. so far as it is relevant. But its omissions took deliberate and indicate dependence on the Tosefta version, not an independent formulation or the transmission of a separate tradition.

3. Ended as a Sadducee

B. Ber. 29a	B. Yoma 9a	Pesiqta deRab Kahana.
1. TNN	1. ------	1. *They said concerning*
2. Do not believe in yourself, etc.	2. ------	2. -------
3. For lo, Yohanan the High Priest served in the high priesthood for eighty years	3. ....and the eighty that Yohanan the High priest served	3. Yohanan the high priest *that* " " "
4. and at the end became (Lit: was made) a Sadducee	4. ------	4. " " "

The *baraita* of b. Ber. 29a is referred to, but not closely quoted, in b. Yoma 9a. What is more interesting is the form of the citation in Pes. R. Kahana. There the compiler has imposed a quite different form from TNN. Now it is *they said concerning* with the additional *that* necessary for the new form. Otherwise it is identical to the *baraita* and presumably represents a citation of it. The editor of a Midrashic compilation was prepared to impose his own redactional forms on antecedent materials, even those attributed to Tannaim.

Chapter Seven

Menahem. Shammai

A. MENAHEM

The only explicit reference to Menahem is in M. Hag. 2:2: "Hillel and Menahem did not differ, but Menahem went forth and Shammai entered in." This enigmatic saying is discussed in Amoraic pericopae, as follows:

[Menahem went forth and Shammai entered.] Where did he go?

Abbaye said, "He went forth to evil culture."

Raba said, "He went forth to the king's service."

It has also been taught (TNY' NMY HKY): Menahem went forth to the king's service, and eighty pairs of disciples dressed in silk (SYRYQWM) went forth with him.

B. Hag. 16b

Where did he go forth?
Some say, "He went forth from measure to measure (MYDH)."
And some say, "He went against his face (KNGD PNYW), he and eighty pair of disciples of the sages, dressed in golden silk [following Jastrow, read SYRQY instead of TYRQY] that brightened their faces like the saucer attached to a pot."

For they said to them, "Write on the horn of an ox that you do not have a portion in the God of Israel."

Y. Hag. 2:2

128 *Peripatetic Parallels*

The Babylonian pericope is unrelated to other materials in the same context. Raba's saying is expanded in the *baraita*, or perhaps he cited the tradition contained in the *baraita*. I assume the *eighty pair of disciples* is a counterpart to Hillel's, in a baraita also from Pumbedita; perhaps it is a stock-phrase.

The Palestinian pericope, isolated from its setting, is enigmatic. The meaning of "from measure to measure" has been variously explained; I do not know what it means. *He went against his face* generally is interpreted to mean, he went out unwillingly, but here again, I do not know the philological basis for that explanation. The passages compare as follows:

B. Hag.	Y. Hag.
1. Where did he go?	1. " " "
2. Abbaye said	2. *Some* say
3. He went forth	3. *from measure to measure* he went forth
4. Raba said	4. *Some* say
5. He went forth to the service of the king	5. He went forth *against his face*
6. TNY' NMY HKY	6. ------
7. Menahem went forth to the service of the king	7. ------
8. And there went forth with him eighty pairs of disciples	8. He and eighty pair [sing.] of disciples *of the sages*
	9. dressed in silk (LBWSYN SYRYQWN)

10. ------	9. dressed (MLBWSYN) [in] silks of (TYRQY = SYRQY) gold
	10. For they said to them, etc.

The Babylonia *baraita* has improved the Palestinian Amoraic tradition in a number of respects. First, the enigmatic language, *from measure to* measure and *against his face*, has been dropped in favor of commonplace and immediately comprehensible expressions. Second, the *baraita* changes pair to pairs clarifies SYRYQY and drops the redundant gold. All of no. 10 is dropped in the Babylonian version. My guess therefore is that the Babylonian version depends upon the Palestinian one. It seems to me unlikely that the two traditions developed independent of one another, and in this instance the shorter and clearer probably improves upon the longer and less lucid. But I do not understand why the substantial detail of no. 10 should have failed to serve the editor of the Babylonian *baraita*. We have no reason to attribute any tradition concerning Menahem to a period before the circulation of M. Hag., for both Palestinian and Babylonian pericopae begin with the language of the Mishnah, "Where did he go," although the *baraita* has hidden that question in the declarative statement of no. 7. The Mishnah, in its present form, must have been known to all parties responsible for the foregoing pericopae. On this basis we must regard all the traditions as efforts to provide glosses for the Mishnah, not as independent traditions deriving from the period before it.

B. Shammai

1. Rules about the Sabbath

Sifré Deut. 203	Tos. Erub. 3:7	B. Shab. 19a
1. *When you besiege a city*	1. ------	1. TNW RBNN
2. Tells that one offers peace two or three days before making war against it…	2. ------	2. ------
3. One does not start a siege against a city less than three days before the Sabbath happens to be, the Sabbath does not interrupt the war.	3. A camp that goes forth to optional war does not besiege a *gentile* city less than three days before the Sabbath, and if they *began, even on the Sabbath they* do not interrupt	3. One does not besiege *cities of aliens* (NKRYM) less than three days before the Sabbath and if they began, they do not interrupt [Omits: *even on the Sabbath*].
4. This is one of three things that Shammai the Elder expounded	4. -----	4. ------
5. One does not weigh anchor (PLG) to the Great Sea less than three days	5. ------	5. ------

6. Of what things are spoken?	6. ------	6. -----
7. On a long journey, but on a near journey, one weighs anchor.	7. ------	7. -----
8. ------	8. Thus (KK) did Shammai the Elder expound, *Until it fails*—And even on the Sabbath	8. And so (KN) did Shammai *say* " " " [Omits *and*]

Sifré contains numerous elements lacking in the two Talmuds, but has no knowledge of Shammai's exegesis of Deut. 20:20. Tos. Erub. refers to an optional war, while to make a required war one presumably may lay siege at any time. Sifré Dent. is unclear on this point. The detail on the siege is the same; Once the siege has started, it must not be lifted despite the Sabbath. The *baraita* in b. Shab. follows Sifré in omitting reference to the optional war, but otherwise is identical to the Tos. version, except in leaving out what must have been thought redundant, *even on the Sabbath*. In this instance it is difficult to argue that the baraita is necessarily later than, and dependent upon, the Tosefta's version. It bears at least one important affinity to Sifré. On the other hand, the exegesis of Shammai is copied, with only a minor omission. I therefore imagine the framer of the *baraita* depended upon Tos., but has improved on it by generalizing *a camp that goes forth* into one does not *besiege*—presumably more satisfactory for a legal context. Hence in the balance the *baraita* must be judged dependent upon, and later than, Tos. The appearance of no. 8 in both is the decisive factor, but the rest of the language is sufficiently close, except for the detail at the outset, no. 3, so that this conclusion is highly probable.

2. *Would Not Feed with One Hand*

B. Yoma 77b	B. Hul. 107b
1. They said concerning Shammai the Elder	1. " " "
2. That he did not want to give to eat with his one hand	2. " " "
3. and they decreed on him	3. " " "
4. to give to eat with two hands	4. " " "

The two passages in fact are identical. The only differences are in the context in which they are cited. The essential materials exhibit no changes whatever.

3. *The synopsis of the story about Shammai and Jonathan b. Uzziel has already been given above, Chapter One.*

The parallel-versions of stories about and sayings of Shammai yield no consequential variations that I notice. We have a firm textual tradition running from document to document.

Chapter Eight

Hillel

1. Would Fold Together

Mekhilta de R. Simeon b. Yohai 131.12	Tos. Pisha 2:22	Y. Hal. 1:11	B. Pesahim 115a	B. Zebahim 79a
1. Ex. 12:8	1. ------	1. ------	1. TNY They said of Hillel	1. = b. Pesahim
2. It is a misvah	2. ------	2. ------	2. ------	2. ------
3. Hillel the Elder could fold them together and eat them	3. " " "	3. [Omits: together ... and eat them]	3. that " " " them at once (BBT 'HT) and eat them.	3. = b. Pesahim
4. ------	4. ------	4. ------	4. As it is said Num. 9:11	4. MSWM = b Pesahim

The two Babylonian versions are identical, except that b. Zebahim 79a adds *because* (MSWM), a minor change. The version of Mekhilta deR. Simeon is briefest. Tos. Pisha adds *the three of them*, apparently to clarify what we are talking about. The omission of the Scriptural citation (Ex. 12:8/Num. 9:11) may have necessitated the more explicit statement. y. Hal. 1:1 drops *would eat them*—perhaps because it was obvious. The

Babylonian versions have entirely lost, or dropped, the exegetical framework of Ex. 12:8, so Hillel's action is no longer an "illustration" or a narrative pertinent to that Scripture. Another Scripture, Num. 9:11, is cited now as *justification* for Hillel's behavior, rather than as an independent exegesis. The Babylonian baraita-form comes last of all; the composite version of Mekhilta is the clearest version, since it preserves the relationship between the exegesis and the Hillel-story, lost in both Tos. and Palestinian versions. It is interesting to see how the exegetical framework is later dropped, then changed and restored, and the story circulates as an independent biographical account.

2. *For Three Things Did Hillel Come Up Received Law.*

Sifra Shemini 9:5	Sifra Tazria 9:16	Tos. Neg. 1:16	Y. Pes. 6:1
1. Lev. 11:24	1. Lev. 13:37	1. ------	1. -------
2. Hillel says, Even if he is in the midst of the water	2. Hillel says, LSNTQ NTQBTWK NTQ	2. -----	2. -----
3. ------	3. ------	3. -----	3. Lev. 13:37
4. ------	4. Priest declares him clean	4. " " "	4. = Sifra 9:16
5. -------	5. If priests say of clean unclean, and *vice versa*, perhaps he is clean?	5. " " "	5. = Sifra 9:16

6. ------	6. Scripture says, *He is clean* and *priest makes him clean*.	6. " " "	6. = Sifra 9:16
7. -----	7. On account of this matter Hillel came up from Babylonia	7. And this is *one of the things* on account of which Hillel came up from Babylonia	7. = Sifra 9:16
8. -----	8. -----	8. -----	8. [Contrast and harmonization of Deut. 16:2, Ex. 12:5; Deut. 16.8, Ex. 12:15]
		9. -----	
		9. -----	9. And he expounded and agreed and went up and received law

Sifra Shemini has nothing to do with the other materials. Sifra Tazri'a and Tos. Neg. nos. 4-7 are identical, except that in no. 7, Tos. makes *the thing* into *one of the things*, without listing others. The revision may reflect knowledge of a tradition about other "reasons" for Hillel's migration, part of the tendency that Hillel came up and restored the Torah to Palestine. Or, alternatively, the subscription is a stock-phrase. y. Pesahim makes one of the things into *three* things, copies

136 *Peripatetic Parallels*

Sifra Tazri'a word for word, and then adds, for the other two things, the conventional harmonizing exegeses (no. 8). At the end comes a new subscription (no. 9). This phrase makes no sense at all outside of the context of the Bené Bathyra stories, to which the pericope is loosely attached in y. Pesahim So y. Pesahim no. 9 is a redactional device, external to the pericope and linking it to the antecedent materials in context. Clearly the tradition on the *thing/things/three things* on account of which Hillel came up has been garbled. Some such list must have existed, perhaps centered on purity laws and/or Passover rules for the Temple. But in the versions that have reached us, we him clean. cannot find equivalents to the purity law materials (nos. 4-6), and the others were probably process to give some semblance of order to the Palestinian version and to tie it to the of clean unclean, foregoing materials in y. Pesahim about Hillel's rise to power.

3. Redeem Property at End of Year

Sifra Behar 4:8	M. Arakh. 9:4	B. Git. 74b
1. [Lev. 25:30 alluded to:] LSMYTWT	1. When the day of the completion of the twelve months comes and it is not redeemed, it was permanently sold to him. It is all the same for one who buys and one to whom it is given as a gift, as it is said LSMYTWT.	1. ------

2. To include one who gives a gift	2. [as above]	2. -------
3. At first he would hide on the day of the twelve months [completion] so it would be permanently sold (HLWTH) to him.	3. " " "	3. TNN HTM " " "
4. Hillel the Elder ordained	4. " " "	4. " " "
5. that he should assign his coins in the temple fund (LYSKH) and he would break down the door and enter.	5. " " "	5. " " "
6. Whenever he wants, that one will come and take his coins	6. " " "	6. " " " [HLZ of Sifra becomes HLH; adds: *and* whenever]

The minor change in no. 6 of b. Git., supplying *and*, clarifies the subject of the verb *wants*. Setting *whenever* apart from *enter*, we now are clear that it is the *purchaser* who can choose the time, not the *redeemer* of the property. But this was not unclear in the earlier versions, which had supplied *that one* (HLZ, HLH) to clarify the same issue. Once the Sifra version was fixed, it was cited with practically no modification. The only important changes are in no. 1; the Mishnah superscription conforms to the normal Mishnaic conventions, but the Hillel story is unaffected.

138 Peripatetic Parallels

Sifré Deut. 113	Midrash Tannaim p. 80	M. Shebiit 10:3-4 (cited b. Git. 36a)	M. Git. 4:3
1. Deut. 15:3	1. " " "	1. *Prosbul is not released. This is one of the things that Hillel the Elder ordained.*	1. ------
2. But not he who gives his mortgages to the court.	2. " " "	2. ------	2. ------
3. From here they said	3. " " " [Omits: *they said*]	3. ------	3. ------
4. Hillel ordained the prosbul	4. " " "	4. ------	4. " " "
5. On account of the order of the world.	5. ------	5. ------	5. " " "
6. That [for] he saw the people that they held back from one another.	6. ------	6. [Omits *that*] *When* " " "	6. ------

7. And they transgressed against what is written in the Torah.	7. -----	7. and *were transgressing* + *Deut. 15:9*	7. -----
8. He arose and ordained the *prozbul.*	8. -----	8. " " " [Omits: *arose and*]	8. -----
9. And this is the formula of the *prosbul*	9. -----	9. " " "	9. -----
10. I give to you, so-and-so, the judges that are in such-and-such a place, every debt which I have that I may collect it whenever I want, and the judges seal below, or the witnesses.	10. -----	10. " " "	10. ------
11. ------	11. *And thus expounded Hillel:* Deut. 15:3—but not he who gives his	11. ------	11. -----

mortgages to the court.

As we observed above, Sifré Deut. 113 combines two versions of the reason and basis for Hillel's ordinance, an exegesis of Deut. 15:3 and the order of the world. Midrash Tannaim preserves the former, nos. 1-4, with practically no variations. M. Shebiit preserves the latter, but now supplies Deut. 15:9 as a proof-text; the proof-text has already provided the outline of the historical "event" which Hillel had observed. M. Shebiit 10:3-4 knows nothing of the exegesis of Deut. 15:3; the *gemara* in y. Shebiit 10:2 raises the question of how Hillel could have ordained a law in contravention of the Torah. M. Git. 4:3 is a brief summary of nos. 4-5. Midrash Tannaim explicitly attributes *to* Hillel the anonymous exegesis cited in nos. 1-2.

4. *Forbade Interest in Kind*

M. Baba Mesia 5:9	Tos. Baba Mesia 6:20	B. Shab.148b
1. Man should not say to fellow, Lend me a *kor* of wheat, and I shall give you at the harvest, but he says to him, Lend me until my son will come, or until I find the key.	1. A man says to his fellow, Lend me a *keg of wine until my son comes, or until I open the cistern. If he had a jar in the middle of the cistern and the cistern was opened and it fell and broke, even thought he is liable, it is permitted*	1. ------

2. And Hillel prohibits	2. " " "	2. ------
3. And so would Hillel say:	3. ------	3. DTNN " " "
4. A woman may not lend a loaf to her neighbor until she determines its value in money, lest wheat increase in price and they be found coming into the hands of usury.	4. ------	4. " " "

The Toseftan version preserves Hillel's prohibition (no. 2) but *riot* the case to which no. 2 refers in the Mishnah, and drops nos. 3-4 entirely. b. Shab. 148b simply preserves part of the Mishnah, without significant variation.

5. *Scatter/Gather*

Tos. Ber. 6:24	Y. Ber. 9:5	B. Ber. 63a
1. Hillel the Elder says	1. " " "	1. TNY': Hillel the Elder says
2. When (BSCT) they are gathering (KNS), scatter (PZR)	2. " " " (adds *d* to KNS), scatter (BDR)	2. BS'T HMKNYSYN PZR (as Tos. Ber.)
3. When they are scattering, gather	3. " " " (BDR)	3. BS'T HMPZRYN (As Tos. Ber.) " " "

4. When you see that the Torah is beloved on all Israel and all are rejoicing in it, you be scattering in it, as it is said, Prov. 11:24	4. *And so Hillel would say, If* you *have seen* " " " (BDR) [Omits Prov. 11:24]	4. *If you have seen a generation* upon whom the Torah is not beloved, scatter, as it is said, Prov. 11:24
5. When you see that the Torah is forgotten from Israel, and not everyone is paying attention to it, you be gathering it in, as it is said Prov. 119:126	5. *And if not, gather*	5. *And If you have seen a generation* upon whom *the Torah is not beloved*, gather, as it is said Prov. 11:24

The Babylonian *baraita* is based upon the Tos. version, and in some ways improves it. First, the duplicated verbs of Tos. Ber. no. 5 are made into a single, strong image; then the conclusion is imperative, rather than participial, so that the reversed condition of no. 4, which in Y. Ber. is simply a brief allusion, is neatly spelled out in concise language. No. 4 adds *generation*. The possibility of the Torah's being forgotten is not raised in the Babylonian *baraita*. The Tosefta may contain an echo of the Hiyya-saying that when the Torah was forgotten in Israel, Ezra, Hillel, and Hiyya restored it, *but* here the message is that, if it is forgotten, one should not get involved. The transformation of the verbal participles of Tos. Ber. to substantive participles in b. Ber. may not be of consequence. The Palestinian version presents an abbreviated version of Tos. I assume all three versions are interdependent. Since the interdependence is not merely thematic but verbal, b. Ber. 63a is almost certainly a careful revision of Tos. Ber.; but Y. Ber. is more of a rough precis. As usual, the Babylonian *baraita* exhibits considerable stylistic improvements over earlier versions.

6. Pesah Overrides Sabbath — Rise to Power

Tos. Pisha 4:13	Y. Pesahim 6:1	Y. Shab. 19:1	B. Pesahim 66a-b
1. One time	1. *This law was hidden from the Elders of Bathyra.* " " "	1. ------	1. TNW RBNN. [As y. Pesahim]
2. the fourteenth coincided with the	2. *" " " and they did not know whether the pesah overrides the Sabbath or not.*	2. ------	2. " " " [As y. Pesahim]
3. They asked Hillel the Elder	3. *They said, There is here a certain Babylonian and his name is Hillel the Babylonian, who served Shemaiah and Abtalion, knows whether pesah overrides the Sabbath or not. Perhaps there will be profit from him. They sent and called him. They said to him, Have you ever heard when*	3. ------	3. [As y. Pesahim With glosses, e.g. *two great men of the generation,* S + A etc. Drops *perhaps-him.*]

	the fourteenth coincides with the Sabbath whether it overrides the Sabbath or not?		
4. *Pesah*—what is it that it should override the Sabbath?	4. [As above]	4. ------	4. [As y. Pesahim]
5. He said to them,	5. " " "	5. ------	5. [As y. Pesahim]
6. Do we have one *pesah* in the year that overrides the Sabbath?	6. " " "	6. ------	6. [As y. Pesahim]
7. Many more than three hundred *pesahs* do we have in the year and they override the Sabbath	7. Do not *many* " " " Some teach, 100, 200, 300, etc.	7. -------	7. More than *two hundred*.
8. All the courtyard collected against him.	8. They said, We have already said, if there is with you profit.	8. ------	8. They said *to him*, How do you know [Here follows *heqqesh* and *qal vehomer*] Forthwith they seated him at the

Hillel 145

head and appointed him *Nasi* over them. He was expounding all day long in the laws of the *pesah*. [*After* no. 27, follow y. Pesahim Arguments against his proofs, in the form *A master said*.]

9. He said to them, *Tamid* is a community sacrifice and *pesah* is a community sacrifice.	9. He began expounding to them from *heqqesh, qal vehomer,* and *gezerah shavah.* " " "	9. -----	[9. As summarized above]
10. Just as the *Tamid* is a community sacrifice and overrides the Sabbath	10. " " "	10. ------	[10. As summarized above]
11. So the *pesah* is a community sacrifice and overrides the Sabbath	11. " " "	11. -----	[11. As summarized above]

12. Another thing	12. From *qal vehomer* [See Tos. *Pisha* No. 17]	12. -----	
13. Concerning *Tamid*, *In its season*, is said	13. *From gezerah shavah* " " "	13. -----	[13. As summarized above.]
14. and concerning *pesah*, *In its season* is said	14. " " "	14. -----	[14. As summarized above.]
15. Just as *Tamid*, concerning which *In its season* is said, overrides the Sabbath	15. " " "	15. -----	[15. As summarized above.]
16. So *pesah*, concerning which *In its season* is said, overrides the Sabbath	16. " " "	16. -----	[16. As summarized above.]
17. And furthermore, *qal vehomer*	17. [See above, No 12]	17. -----	[17. As summarized above.]
18. *Tamid*, that one is not liable for cutting off, overrides the Sabbath, *pesah*,	18. " " " *They said to him, We have already said, If there is* [not] *profit from the Babylonian.*	18. -----	[18. As summarized above.]

that one is liable for cutting off, is it not logical that it should override the Sabbath?	[Here y. Pes. Supplies arguments against the proofs, in direct address, e.g. *Heqqesh, that you said, has a reply* etc.]		
19. And furthermore I have received from my masters that *pesah* overrides the Sabbath	19. *Even though he was sitting and expounding for them all day, they did accept [proof] from him kuntil he said to them, May [evil] come on me, Thus have I heard from Shemaiah and Abtalion.*	19. -----	[19. As summarized above.]
20. And not the first *Pesah* but the second *pesah* and not the community but the individual *pesah*.	20. -----	20. ------	20. -----
20'. -----	20'. *When they heard thus from him, they arose and appointed him nasi over them. He began*	20'. -----	20'. -----

	to criticize them [for not having studied with S + A, and therefore he forgot his law.]		
21. They said to him, What will be for the people who have not brought knives and *pesahs* to the sanctuary?	21. " " "	21. *They asked Hillel the Elder* " " "	21. -------
22. He said to them, Let them alone. The holy spirit is upon them. If they are not prophets, they are sons of prophets.	22. *I heard this law and forgot but* " " "	22. [As y. Pesahim]	22. [As y. Pesahim]
23. What did Israel do in that hour?	23. -----	23. ------	23. *The next day*
24. Whoever had as his *pesah* a lamb hid it in its wool, a goat, tied it be-	24. " " "	24. *Forthwith* " " "	24. " " "

tween its
horns.

25. And they brought knives and *pesahs* to the sanctuary and slew their *pesahs*.	25. " " " [Omits *and* —*pesahs*.]	25. " " "	25. " " "
26. On that very day they appointed Hillel *Nasi* and he would teach to them concerning the laws of *pesah*.	26. [See 20 above.]	26. -----	26. -----
27. ------	27. When he saw the deed, he remembered the law. He said, Thus have I heard from Shemaiah and Abtalion.	27. " " "	27. " " "

Y. Shab. Has taken nos. 21-2 and 24-7 and introduced the whole with *they asked*. Y. Pesahim is a considerable expansion of Tos. Pisha, which knows nothing of the Bené Bathyra, has heard not a word about Hillel's studies with Shemaiah and Abtalion, and does not have Hillel forget the law, but rather introduces the little story about the people as prophets (or good deceivers) by supposing the Hillel had given a law today, but what can the people do to keep it tomorrow? The arguments in the three versions are pretty much the same: *qal vehomer*, *heqqesh*, and *gezerah shavah*.

The important developments come between Tosefta and Palestinian Talmud. The Babylonian version in general follows the Palestinian, with various glosses indicating that it depends upon it; it occasionally improves the order. In dropping the refutations of Hillel and allowing Hillel to take office upon the conclusion of his successful arguments, the Babylonian version provides a more continuous narrative; but then Hillel's own proofs, and *not* his citation of his masters, are made the cause of his elevation to power. The order is Tosefta, Palestinian Talmud, Babylonian Talmud.

7. Come to My House

Tos. Sukkah 4:3	B. Sukkah 53a	Y. Sukkah 5:4
1. Hillel the Elder says	1. TNY' *They said concerning Hillel the Elder: When he was rejoicing at the Rejoicing of the Place of Drawing, he said, If I am here, all are here* [alternatively: *The Whole is here*] *and I am not here, who is here? He used to say thus*	1. [In Aramaic] *Hillel the Elder, when he saw them acting with pride, he would say to them, If we are here who is here, and does he need our praise? And is it not written* Deut. 7:10. *When he saw them acting properly he would say, If we are not here, who is here, for* [in Hebrew] *even though there are before him many praises, beloved is the praise of Israel before him more than all. What is the reason?*

Hillel

		II Sam. 23:2, Ps. 22:3
2. To the place which my heart loves, there my feet lead me.	2. " " "	2. -----
3. If you will come to my house, I shall come to your house.	3. If you will come to my house, I shall come to your house	3. -----
4. If you will not come to my house, I shall not come to your house	4. " " "	4. -----
5. As it is said Ex. 20:24	5. " " "	5. ------
6. -----	6. *Also he saw a skull that floated on the face of the water. He said to it,* [in Aramaic] *Because you drowned they drowned you, and those that drowned you will be drowned.*	6. -----

Tos. Sukkah is the simplest version, but is not tied to the celebration of the Festival. y. Sukkah, by contrast, invents a "historical" event: When Hillel saw the people misbehaving, he rebuked them, saying their presence means nothing. But when he saw them behaving properly, he praised them, saying their presence means everything. In b. Sukkah this is turned from first person plural, and historical, into first person singular, and gnomic. The Scriptures are dropped, and the whole has, or is given, a theological-mystical echo. Indeed, without reference to y. Sukkah we should have imagined the original saying to be a mystical sentiment said by Hillel (in behalf of God). b. Sukkah also preserves the saying attached to Ex. 20:24, and adds a still further saying. Thus b. Sukkah has taken Tos. Sukkah and introduced it with a double introductory formula (TNY', 'MRW 'LYW); it has the same apophthegm as y. Sukkah; but, left in the singular, the saying has no historical or narrative function. Then b. Sukkah tacks on another Hillel-saying. y. Sukkah is entirely unrelated to Tos. Sukkah, and b. Sukkah stands between the two. But I am not sure that b. Sukkah no. 1 necessarily comes before y. Sukkah no. 1. The relations between the two versions are clear, but the implications of those relations are not obvious to me.

8. *Expounded Ketubah*

Tos. Ketubot 4:9	Y. Yebamot 15:3	Y. Ketubah. 4:8	B. Baba Mesia 104a
1. Hillel the Elder expounded language of Common folk (HDYWT).	1. ------	1. " " "	1. *would expound DTNY'*
2. When the sons of Alexandria would betrothe women	2. *They would write in Alexandria, for one of them would*	2. [= y. Yebamot.]	2. *The men of Alexandria would betroth their wives and when they entered*

Hillel 153

			the canopy, others come and seize them from them.
3. One come and seized her from the market	3. and his *fellow* " " "	3. [= y. Yebamot.]	3. [See No. 2 above.]
4. And the deed came before the sages.	4. and *when* " " "	4. [= y. Yebamot]	4. -----
5. They sought to make their sons *mamzerim*	5. " " " to make *them* " " "	5. [= y. Yebamot]	5. *And the sages* sought to make their sons *mamzerim.*
6. Hillel the Elder said to them	6. " " "	6. [= y. Yebamot]	6. " " "
7. Bring out to me the *Ketubah* of your mothers	7. " " " [Drops *to me*]	7. [= y. Yebamot]	7. [= y. Yebamot]
8. They brought to him	8. " " " *the marriage-contract of their mothers*	8. [= y. Yebamot]	8. [=y. Yebamot]
9. And written in	9. *they found* written in them	9. [= y. Yebamot]	9. and *he found* that it was written in them.

10. When you enter my house, you will be my wife according to the law of Moses and Israel	10. " " " and the Jews	10. [= y. Yebamot.]	10. When you enter *the canopy be my wife* [drops *according-Israel*].
11. -----	11. -----	11. -----	11. *And they did not make their sons mamzerim*

The Babylonian *baraita* improves upon the former versions in every last detail. First, it has provided a new superscription, so the generalized reference to Hillel's practice is followed by an *example* given the status of a Tannaitic tradition, DTNY'. Then the story is carefully narrated. The problem is not violence in the market, but under the marriage-canopy. The whole is made a singular event, so we are no longer dealing with a generalized situation, but with a one-time happening, as the storyteller has already indicated. In the earlier versions there is confusion on just this point, with a mixture of singular and plural nouns (*mothers*). Now the problem of no. 5 is not to declare the litigants, but rather their children, *mamzerim*. This further clarifies the situation, for in the Palestinian versions we are not sure which generation we are dealing with. The actual Situation is corrected in no. 10 to conform to the narrative conditions specified earlier. Then no. 11 tells us the outcome of the case, which is omitted in all the earlier versions. Most important, therefore, the story is now made a single event, rather than the description of a generally prevailing situation to which a single court-case is awkwardly attached. But in this respect the improvement is not complete.

The two Palestinian versions are identical. y. Ketubot is presumably copied by y. Yebamot, or vice versa. But y. Yebamot no. 2 is garbled, unlike Tos. no. 2. b. Baba Mesia could well be based on Tos. Ketubot, without the intervening Palestinian versions, for no. 2 of b. Baba Mesia omits reference to what the Alexandrians would write, and follows Tos. Ketubot in this respect; the story of Tos. Ketubot is much elaborated in b. Baba Mesia, to be sure. Tos. no. 5, *their sons*, is preserved in b. Baba Mesia as we observed.

10. *Worthy of the Holy Spirit*

Tos. Sotah 13:3	Y. Sotah 9:13	B. Sanhedrin 11a	B. Sotah 48b
1. M'SH S	1. " " "	1. ------	1. [TNW RBNN: When last prophets died, holy spirit ceased, but would use the echo, for]
2. The sages entered the house of Guryo in Jericho	2. " " " " GDY'	2. Once they were reclining in the upper room of " "	2. [= b. Sanhedrin]
3. And they heard an echo saying	3. An echo *went forth and said*	3. An echo *placed on them from heaven*	3. [= b. Sanhedrin]
4. There is here a man who is worthy (R'WY) of the holy spirit	4. There is *among you* " " "	4. " " " that the *Shekhinah should rest on him*	4. [= b. Sanhedrin]

5. But his gene- | 5. " " " (KDYY) | 5. " " " | 5. R'WY
ration is not righteous (ZK'Y) for it (LKK)

6. And they placed their eyes on Hillel the Elder | 6. " " " | 6. " " " | 6. " " "

7. And when he died they said about him | 7. " " " | 7. " " " | 7. " " " (They *lamented* him)

8. Woe for the meek man, woe for the pious man, disciple of Ezra. | 8. " " " | 8. " " " | 8. " " "

9. Again they were sitting in Yabneh and heard an echo saying, There is here a man [etc. as no. 4-5] | 9. " " " [With same changes as above] | 9. " " " [Same changes as above] | 9. [= b. Sanhedrin]

10. and they set their eyes on Samuel the Small | 10. " " " | 10. " " " | 10. " " "

11. And when he died ...disciple of Hillel | 11. [With intervening gloss on why he is called the Small] " " " | 11. " " " | 11. " " "

Hillel 157

*****

Y. Abodah Zarah 3:1	Y. Horayot 3:5
1. R. Jacob b. 'Idi in the name of R. Joshua b. Levi " " "	1. [= y. Abodah Zarah]
2. upper room of GDYY' Yabneh and a heavenly echo came forth and said to them, There are among you two worthy of the holy spirit and Samuel the Small is one of them, and they set their eyes on R. Leazar, and they were rejoicing that their opinion had agreed with the opinion of the holy spirit.	2. [= y. Abodah Zarah]
3. [= y. Sotah]	3. [= y. Abodah Zarah]
4. There are among you *two* who are worthy of the holy spirit, and Hillel the Elder is one of them. And they set their eyes on Samuel the Small.	4. [= y. Abodah Zarah]
5. ------	5. ------
6. ------	6. ------
7. ------	7. ------
8. ------	8. ------
9. Again the elders entered the upper chamber in	9. [= y. Abodah Zarah + *Eliezer b. Hyrcanus*]

The Babylonian versions supply what may be Babylonian idioms, e.g. the holy spirit is replaced with *Shekhinah*. Otherwise, the changes are of no consequence, except for the placing of the story into a *baraita*. The interesting versions are y. Abodah Zarah = Y. Horayot Here we see a new state of affairs. The story is told by Joshua b. Levi. It derives from Eleazar's or Eliezer's school; or the Samuel the Small-version has been revised so as to make room for Eliezer. Hillel is taken for granted. Samuel the Small is moved to Jericho. But at the same time the *upper chamber* is moved to Yabneh, replacing the better known *vineyard*, probably because the story is an exact counterpart. Certainly y. Abodah Zarah = y. Horayot depend upon the Tos. Sotah-y. Sotah versions and are not independent, but still separate forms of the story. If so, this is an instance in which the Babylonian baraita evidently antedates a Palestinian Amoraic version of a story appearing in both places.

B. Sanhedrin adds *upper room*; the echo comes specifically *from heaven*; "they" become the *sages*; and the *holy spirit* is dropped entirely. The Babylonian baraita depends upon the Palestinian-Toseftan version. The reformulation by Joshua b. Levi is anomalous.

A pattern has established itself and forms its own testimony. The later documents take up a received story and embellish it. The large gaps run between the Tosefta and the two Talmuds. The amplifications and extensions do not suggest that we deal with autonomous stories or sayings. Rather, they point to an unfolding tradition, a story taken up from one document to another without enormous variations. Peripatetic parallels from document to document do not greatly differ but exhibit a cogent core — narratives and wording alike — in common.

Chapter Nine

Shammai and Hillel

1. Retroactive Uncleanness of Menstruant

M. Eduyyot 1:1	M. Nid. 1:1	B. Shab. 15a
1. Shammai says, All the women sufficient for them [is] their period (S'TN)	1. " " "	1. " " "
2. And Hillel says, From examination to examination (PQYDH).	2. " " "	2. " " "
3. And sages say, Not according to the words of this, and not according to the words of this.	3. " " "	3. " " "
4. But from time (T) to time [twenty-four hours] diminishes (MM^{C}T) by means of examination to examination [and vice versa]	4. " " "	4. (MM^{C}TT)

The Mishnaic tradition is cited in nearly identical form throughout. That is nearly always the case. We may now propose the rule that the variations in the wording of Mishnah-passages are less in volume and range than those of Tosefta-passages, all the more so Talmud- and Midrash-passages.

2. Liability of Loaf for Hallah

M. Eduyyot 1:2	Tos. Eduyyot 1:11	B. Shabbat 15a
1. Shammai says, From *qab* for *hallah*	1. ...*They said, Let us begin from Hillel and Shammai.* Shammai says, From *qab hallah* [Omits: *For*].	1. Shammai says, From *qab, hallah*
2. And Hillel says, From two *qabs*	2. " " "	2. " " "
3. And sages say, Not according to the words of this and not according to the words of this, but a *qab* and a half (HYYBYM) are liable for *hallah*.	3. " " " [HYYB singular].	3. [= Tos. Ed.]
4. ———	4. As it is said Num. 15:20	4. ———

Except for the narrative superscription and exegetical subscription, b. Shabbat 15a follows Tos. Eduyyot 1:1 rather than M. Eduyyot 1:2 wherever Tos. and M. Eduyyot differ. But the differences are not important. The Mishnah has dropped the Tosefta's exegetical traditions, as is normally the case. Otherwise the materials are pretty much identical in the several versions.

3. Source of Disputes is Inadequate Study with Shammai-Hillel

Tos. Hagigah 2:9 = Tos. Sanhedrin 7:1 (Yosé-logion)	Tos. Sotah 14:9 (MSRBW –form only)	Y. Hagigah 2:2 = Y. Sanhedrin 1:4	B. Sot.47b = B. Sanhedrin 88b (MSRBW-form) (Yosé-logion)
1. When multiplied the disciples of Shammai and Hillel that had not served efficiently.	1. " " "	1. *At first there was no dispute in Israel except on laying on of hands only, And Shammai and Hillel arose and made them four.* When multiplied the disciples *of the House* of Hillel *and* they did not serve their masters sufficiently	1. " " "
2. They caused to multiply (MRBW) disputes in Israel	2. " " " Multiplied (RBW) [qal]	2. *and the* dispute " " "	2. [= Tos. So.].

3. and they were made two Torahs	3. " " "	3. *And they were divided into two parties, these declare unclean and these declare clean. And it is not destined again to return to its former place until the son of David will come.*	3. And *the* Torah was made *like* two Torahs

Y. Hagigah depends upon, but greatly augments, Tos. Hagigah The two Babylonian versions reject the possibility that the Torah was really divided, therefore add *like* two Torahs (even though they were really one). The preference for *qal* RBW rather than Tos. Hagigah's HRBW does not seem meaningful. So Tos. Hagigah, Tos. Sotah, and the two Babylonian versions differ from one another in no important ways, except for one. Tos. Hagigah and b. Sanhedrin insert the lemma into Yosé's long saying on the administration of justice, though it interrupts the rhythm and order of that logion, while Tos. Sotah and b. Sotah preserve the saying as an independent lemma in MSRBW-form. Clearly, the saying stood separately and was introduced into the Yosé-logion later on, which suggests the explanation for the division of the two Houses comes before the middle of the second century. However, there is always the possibility that the lemma has been inserted into the Yosé-materials by a later hand. This was done consistently, however, in both instances of the Yosé-saying, which can be explained by later scribal correction. Hence form-critical considerations are hardly decisive in proposing a credible date for the logion.

In this instance, the Babylonian version is independent of the Palestinian one, and depends, rather, on the Tosefta's—a rare phenomenon in materials we have considered.

4. Lay on Hands: Hillel vs. Shammai's Students

Tos. Hagigah 2=11	Y. Hagigah 2:3 – y. Besah 2:4	B. Besah 20a-b
1. M'SH B	1. " " "	1. TNW RBNN+
2. Hillel the Elder who laid hands on the whole-offering (LH)	2. who *brought his whole-offering to the courtyard and* laid hands on it.	2. who *brought his whole-offering to the* courtyard *to* lay hands on it on the festival.
3. and the disciples of Shammai collected against him.	3. " " " House of Shammai	3. " " " House of Shammai *the Elder, They said to him, What is the nature of this beast*
4. He said to them, Come and see that she is female	4. *He began to feel* (KSKS) *its tail.* He said to them, See " " " *and peace-offerings*	4. He said to them, It is female, *and I brought it* for peace-offerings. *He felt its tail for them.*
5. and I need to make her sacrifices of peace-offerings.	5. ——— [Above]	5. ——— [Above]
6. He put them off with words and they went away.	6. " " "	6. and they went away [Omits *he—words.*]

7. Forthwith the hand of the House of Shammai grew strong, and they sought to establish law according to them.	7. *After some days* " " " according to *their words*	7. *That day* " " "
8. There was there Baba ben Buta, who was of the disciples of the House of Shammai and knew that law is according to the words of the House of Hillel in every place	8. " " " (Omits *in every place*). *One time he entered the courtyard and found it desolate. He said, May the houses of those who have desolated the house of our God be made desolate. What did he do?*	8. " " " [Omit *in every place*.]
9. He went and brought all the Qedar-sheep and set them up in the courtyard, and said	9. He *sent* and brought *three thousand goats from* " " " *and inspected them from their faults* " " "	9. " " " *that were in Jerusalem*
10. Whoever needs to bring whole-offerings, let him lay on hands.	10.-11. *Hear me my brothers, House of Israel,* Whoever *wants* let him bring whole-offerings *and lay on hands,* peace-offerings and lay on hands.	10. Whoever wants *to lay on hands, let him come and lay on hands*
11. They came and took the beast and offered whole-offerings	[11. As above]	11. ———

Shammai and Hillel

12. On that very day the law was established to the words of the House of Hillel and no one objected to the matter.	12. " " " and no one *said anything*	12. That day *the hand of the House of Hillel was stronger* and they established the law like them and *there was no man* there who objected to the matter *in any way* (KLWM)

The progression from the earliest version, Tos. Hag., to the latest, b. Besah 20a-b, is in general smooth and routine, except for the substantial intrusion of speeches in nos. 8 and 10 of y. Hag., unavailable to b. Besah. That is surprising, for the accounts in other respects are mutually independent, and the versions in both Talmuds clearly depend upon Tos. Hagigah Therefore b. Besah probably did not have access to Baba's dramatic speeches. I cannot in any other way account for the omission. This also explains why b. Besah no. 9 does not know how *many goats* were involved, and why the dramatic, second speech, y. Hagigah no. 10, is omitted. So we have an example of what happens when the two Talmuds' versions depend upon the same anterior source, but *not* upon one another. The differences show that the Palestinians were quite as capable as the Babylonians of creating their own speeches and conversations, and that literary artifice was no monopoly of the Babylonian schools, despite the consistent stylistic excellence of Babylonian *baraitas*.

Comparing Tos. Hagigah with the two Talmuds' versions, we find that both later accounts make Hillel's opposition the House of Shammai adding House of to *disciples of*. Both add the dramatic detail that Hillel lifted the sheep's tail to show its sex. However, in y. Hag., he simply supplies the information without being questioned, even hinting at it through his gesture, while in b. Besah a dramatic colloquy as usual is introduced: the disciples *ask* before he says anything, then he *says* what it is, and then proves it by showing them the sexual parts. Both versions drop no. 5, having included the detail in no. 4. b. Besah leaves out the first element of no. 6. 1 cannot say why. All versions preserve, with minor variations, nos. 7 and 8. As noted, y. Hagigah has greatly expanded nos. 8-9. All b. Besah adds to Qedar sheep is *that were in Jerusalem*, a normal expansion to add color. Tos. Hagigah is similar to b. Besah But why b. Besah then omits the story of what the people actually did I cannot understand. There should be a clause, as in Tos. Hag., saying that the people really did accept Baba's invitation and did conform to Hillel's law. Otherwise no. 12 is unfounded. Hence I imagine the parallel clause has been lost. The conclusion, no. 12, is everywhere the same, though b. Besah has rendered it into the Babylonian baraita-idiom and drawn on no. 7 to supply a counterpart, *the hand of Shammai* was not stronger; *now* it is the hand of *Hillel*.

5. *Uncleanness of Vintaging Grapes for the Vat*

B. Shabbat 15a	B. Shabbat 17a	B. A.Z. 39b	B. Hul. 36b
1. He who gathers grapes for the vintage	1. " " "	1. " " "	1. " " "
2. Shammai says, Ready [to receive uncleanness]	2. " " "	2. " " "	2. " " "
3. And Hillel says, Not ready	3. " " "	3. " " "	3. " " "

4. Except for that instance, for there Hillel silenced Shammai (STYQLYH HLL LSMPY)	4. ———	4. *And Hillel* (WDY) *agreed with Shammai*	4. " " "
5. ———	5. Hillel said to Shammai, Why do they gather grapes in cleanness and they do not cut olives in cleanness?	5. ———	5. ———
6. Hillel said to Shammai, Why do they gather grapes in cleanness and they do	6. He said to him, If you press me, I shall decree uncleanness even on cutting olives.	6. ———	6. ———
7. ———	7. A sword was implanted in the school house. They said, He who enters will enter, but he who goes will not go out. That day, Hillel was submissive and sat before Shammai like one of the	7. ———	7. ———

> disciples, and it was hard for Israel like the day on which the calf was made.

Nos. 5-7 of b. Shabbat 17a stand entirely alone. No. 4 in the other three versions surely alludes to b. Shabbat 17a, nos. 5-7, but b. Shah. 15a = b. Hul. 36b has Hillel silencing Shammai, contrary to the extended version of b. Shah. [7a, while b. A.Z. 39b has Hillel agreeing with Shammai! Both certainly are invented on the basis of the subscriptions, *Shammai and* Hillel decreed, presumably unanimously. Perhaps b. Shabbat 17a, nos. 5-7, represents a story told to account for that "unanimous" decree. In their present forms we cannot identify one version as earlier than another. All that seems certain is that the primary pericope consisted of nos. 1-3, and then was variously embellished to explain how the decree was attributed to both men when they had disagreed about it to begin with.

It is hardly necessary to take note of the obvious fact that a firm text-tradition runs from document to document, exhibiting only cosmetic changes.

Chapter Ten

Gamaliel

1. Ate in Sukkah

M. Suk. 2:5 is accurately cited in b. Yoma 79a, with the following gloss: "Not because the law is so, but because they wished to be stringent with themselves," pertinent to the Mishnah; this comes between Gamaliel-Yohanan and the following clause, about Sadoq.

2. Approved Admon's Decisions

M. Ket.13:5	M. Tos. Ket. 12:4	Y. Ket.13:5	B. Ket.109a
1. He who agrees on a sum of money with his [future] son-in-law, and he fled—let her sit until her head turns white. Now that father has agreed for me, what can I do? Either marry or free [me].	1. R. Yosé b. R. Judah said, Admon and the sages did not differ where the father agreed with her, that she should say, Father agreed for me, what can I do, etc. In what did they disagree? Where she herself agreed. Admon says, She can say, I thought that father would give to me, now that father does not	1. [= Tos. Ket.]	1. [= Tos. Ket.]

	give to me, what can I do, marry or free.		
2. Admon says, She can say, If I had agreed on my own, I should sit until my head turns white. Now that father has agreed for me, what can I do? Either marry or free [me].	2. ------	2. ------	2. -----
3. Rabban Gamaliel said, I see the worlds of Admon.	3. " " " *says*	3. " " "	3. " " "

The logion of Gamaliel persists in both versions, M. and Tos. Clearly, the tradition was that he agreed with Admon, but there was disagreement on just what was the opinion of Admon. This means that Gamaliel's opinion in the matter never registered, but was merely a fixed logion pertaining to his opinion of whatever Admon might say. Therefore in all four exempla no. 3 is a stock-phrase tacked on at the end for formal, not substantive, reasons.

3. Banned Targum of Job

Tos. Shab. 13:2	Y. Shab. 16:1	B. Shab. 115a
1. R. Yosé said,	1. ------	1. R. Yosé
2. M^cSH S	2. " " " B	2. " " " B
3. R. Halafta went to R. Gamaliel to Tiberias	3. -------	3. *Abba* Halafta" " "
4. and he found him that he was sitting by the table of Yohanan b. Nazif	4. -------	4. " " "
5. and in his hand was the Book of Job *Targum* and he was reading in it.	5. ------	5. " " "
6. R. Halafta said to him, I remember Rabban Gamaliel the Elder, the father of your father, that he was sitting	6. --Rabban Gamaliel [Omits: *the Elder*] who was standing on the Temple mount	6. He said to him, I remember [Omits *the Elder*] that he " " "
7. on (^cL GB) the step on the Temple Mount	7. ------	7. " " "
8. and they brought before him the Book of Job *Targum*	8. " " " *to him* the Book Job *written* [in] *Targum*	8. " " " *and he was reading it*

9. He said to his sons [sic] | 9. " " " the *builder* | 9. " " " [= y. Shab.]

10. Hide it (GNZ) under the rubble (NDBK) | 10. " " " | 10. *Plaster* it (SQˤ) " " "

The Toseftan version has been taken over by the Babylonian *baraita* with only a few changes. R. Halafta becomes Abba. Gamaliel is standing, rather than sitting (in conformity to b. Meg. 21a); and the concept of *genizah* is changed, for reasons I cannot tell. But b. Shab. Has dropped the whole situation in which the story is told. We are not informed that it is R. Yosé, Halafta's son, who reports the story as a criticism of Gamaliel *BeRabbi* in Tiberias. The story stands as an independent narrative. We are not told which Gamaliel is involved (though the same presumptions apply as elsewhere). *His sons* become the *builder* (Lieberman's preferred reading), so the detail about hiding the Targum under the rubble becomes comprehensible. *Written* is supplied as well. I see no grounds to doubt that y. Shab. Is dependent on Tos. Shab., for where the version of y. Shab. Does use materials of Tos. Shab. (nos. 2,6,8,9, and 10), it has done so practically verbatim. Then why is the setting of the story so radically revised? Why no specification that it is Gamaliel *the Elder*? I cannot say, but it is clear that Tos. Shab. Has combined two stories, one contained in nos. 1, 3, 4, 5, with the story of Gamaliel the Elder. The combination is smooth and straightforward, and we do not have to doubt that a single tradent is responsible for the whole pericope of Tos. Shab. The parts not appearing in y. Shab. Seem to me to have been dropped, not absent to begin with. b. Shab. is somewhat influenced by y. Shab. in no. 6, specifically, but I doubt that b. Shab. has copied that single element from y. Shab.; perhaps the same reasons that caused the tradent of y. Shab. to make

Gamaliel stand up and to drop *the Elder* motivated the Babylonian tradent, but I cannot imagine what those reasons might have been.

4. *Letters* re *Leap Year*

Tos. Sanh. 2:6	Y. M.S. 5:4	Y. Sanh. 1:2	B. Sanh. 11b
1. M^cSH B	1. Rabbi Yuda said " " "	1. TNY Rabbi Yudan said " " "	1. DTNY' " " "
2. Rabban Gamaliel and the Elders who were sitting on (^cL GB) steps on the Temple Mount	2. " " " of the WLM on the Temple Mount	2. " " " *step*	2. [Omits *and the Elders*] " " " *step*
3. and Yohanan the certain scribe (SWPR HLH) before them	3. " " " (HLZ) *was sitting* before " " "	3. [= y.M.S.]	3. " " " (HLZ) *was standing* before him and three cut sheets were lying
4. He said to him, Write	4. They said to him, *Go and write*	4. *Rabban Gamaliel* said to him, *Write*	4. *He* said to him *Take one letter and* write
5. To our brothers, Men of Upper Galilee, and to men of Lower (THT'H) Galilee	5. Our brothers ('HYNW) " " "	5. " " "	5. " " "

6. May your peace increase	6. " " "	6. " " "	6. " " "
7. I inform you (MHWDN')	7. " " "	7. " "	7. We inform you (MHWDYN).
8. That the time of burning has come, to bring out (L'PWQY)	8. " " " *Bring out* (TPQWN) " " "	8. " " "	8. " " " to *separate* tithe from the olive vats (L'PRWSY)
9. And to our brothers Men of the Upper Sough and men of the Lower South And to our brothers Men of the Upper South and men of the Lower South	9. " " "	9. " " " [Reverses order: *South, then Galilee*]	9. And take one letter and Write " " " [Omits: *Lower South*]
10. May your peace increase May your peace increase	10. -----	10. " " "	10. " " "
11. We inform you that the time of burning has come, to bring out tithes from the sheaves of wheat.	11. " " "	11. " " " [As above, nos. 7-8]	11. " " " [As above, nos. 7-8]

12. And to our brothers, Men of the Exile of Babylonia and men of the Exile of Medea and the rest of all the Exiles of Israel	12. " " " and Men of the Exile of Greece and the rest " " "	12. [= y. M.S.] " " "	12. *Take one letter and write* " " " [Omits *Greece*]
13. May your peace increase	13. " " "	13. " " "	13. " " " *forever*
14. We inform you that the pigeons are tender and the lambs weak, and the time of spring has not come.	14. " " "	14. " " "	14. " " "
15. And it is well in my view of my colleagues	15. " " "	15. the *matter* is good " " "	15. [= y. Sanh. 1:2]
16. and I have added to this year thirty days.	16. " " "	16. *to* add " " "	16. " " "

The texts to the letters are virtually identical; the changes are minor, involving a shift from infinitives to finite verbs, adding words here and there. The narrative superscriptions show important changes. B. Sanh. Drops *and the Elders*, which completely misses the point of citing the story: Gamaliel was willing to consult his colleague, while later patriarchs were not; the antecedent reference to *colleagues* in no. 15 is lost. The setting of no. 2, however, is standard: the Temple mount. But the *steps* become *step* and are moved here and there. Then b. Sanh. Supplies some instructions to Yohanan, absent in the earlier accounts. This addition is certainly an improvement of, and based upon, the foregoing versions. It is striking that while the normal changes made in earlier Palestinian versions by the editors of late *beraitot* do occur, these changes have scarcely touched the substance of the letter.

The upshot remains the same as before. What we see before us are not diverse versions of a single story or saying, in unrestricted circulation. Rather what we have is a single story or saying, worked and reworked by successive documents. It is the close relationship between the several versions as portrayed by the respective documents that calls into question the competing theory. That is, if there were completely free-standing "parallels," the range of variation ought to be much broader than it is. The data before us point to the opposite: a document with its stories, continued and utilized by successor documents and their authors and compilers. The model is the Mishnah, cited, taken over, and recast by the Tosefta; then the Mishnah with the Tosefta, cited, taken over, and recast by the authors of compositions and the compilers of composites working on what emerged as the Yerushalmi and the Bavli, respectively. In other words, as I have long argued, just as the Mishnah is its own best commentary, so too, what we are seeing here, is that the canon is its own best historian.

Chapter Eleven

Simeon ben Gamaliel

1. Lowered cost of Sacrifice

The only important difference between Sifra Tazria 3-7 and M. Ker. 1:7 is in the question of whether the rest of the offerings must be brought later on. M. Ker. (B) says *no*, Sifra lacks the negative, following M. Ker. (A).

2. Non-Believer and Erub

M. Erub. 6:2	B. Erub. 68b
1. Rabban Gamaliel said,	1. " " "
2. M^{c}SH B	2. " " "
3. One Sadducee who was living with us in an alley in Jerusalem	3. " " "
4. And father said to us	4. " " "
5. Make haste and bring out all the vessels to the alley	5. " " "
6. before he brings out and prohibits [it] for you	6. " " "
7. R. Judah says in another language:	7. ------
8. Make haste and do all your needs in the alley before he brings out and prohibits [it] for you.	8. [No. 10 below]

9. -----

9. *And the story is told concerning one Sadducee who was living with Rabban Gamaliel said to his sons, My sons, Make haste and take out what you are taking out, and bring in what you are bringing in , before this abomination brings out and prohibits [it] for you, for low, he has annulled his right for you, the words of R. Meir.*

10. [No. 8, above]

10. R. Judah says in a different language: Make haste and do your needs in the alley *before it gets dark* and he prohibits [it] for you.

The Mishnah has preserved the version of Meir in the story of Gamaliel (nos. 1-6), then supplied Judah's version in his own name. This is an excellent illustration of Judah the Patriarch's preference for Meir's traditions. It also illustrates that the Tannaitic authorities were quite well prepared to transmit legal materials in the form, of fabricated stories, and, without the Babylonian *baraita*, in this case we should not have known that

M. Erub. no. 1-6 was in fact a Saying of Meir. We should have supposed it was a logion of Gamaliel 11 himself. Hence we cannot conclude that words directly attributed to an early authority in a legal matter or a story pertaining to law must necessarily have been said by him. The contrary presumption is that the logion is framed to put into his mouth a saying in conformity with law later on accepted as authoritative.

3. Juggled

Tos. Suk. 4:4	Y. Suk. 5:4	B. Suk. 53a
1. MᶜSH B	1. ’MR ᶜWLYW ᶜL	1. TNY’ MRWᶜLYWᶜL
2. Rabban Simeon b. Gamaliel who would dance with eight torches of fire	2. *Rabbi* " " " torches *of gold*	2. " " " *when he would rejoice at the Rejoicing of the Place of the Drawing* would dance with eight torches of fire *and throw one and take one*
3. and one of them did not touch the ground	3. " " " tough *another*	3. [= y. Suk.]
4. and when he would prostrate himself (MSTHWH), he would place his finger in the earth of the floor	4. " " " (KWRᶜ) *he would push his thumb into the earth*	4. " " " he *places his thumbs* in the earth *and bows* (SWHH) and kisses the floor and straightens up
5. bow (SWHH) and kiss and forthwith straighten up (ZWQP)	5. and bow (KWRᶜ) and forthwith *would* straighten up (NZQP)	5. [As above]
6. -----	6. -----	6. *And no one (else) can do so, and this is Qiddah*

The Babylonian Talmud has reworked and improved earlier materials. First, it has supplied the usual double-subscription by adding TNY'. Of greater importance, it has added the occasion of the juggling, perhaps implicit in the context of both Tos. Suk. and y. Suk., but not spelled out in either place. Now the juggling is an example of how he would rejoice (lest anyone think that Simeon was like the Magi, who would juggle for thaumaturgical purposes). No. 3 of b. Suk. follows y. Suk.; no. 4 of b. Suk. makes it *both* thumbs, instead of one; b. Suk. further improves on the duplicated *earth/floor* of Tos. Suk. no. 4 — the thumb goes into the earth, and he kisses the floor, then straightens up. b. Suk. further explains that no one else can do such a trick, and a gloss at the end adds that this is the biblical *Qiddah*. The torches of *gold* of y. Suk. no. 2 must be a mistake. b. Suk. thus is a combination of important details of y. Suk. (as in no. 3) and the version of Tos. Suk., nos. 4-5, where the word-choices of Tos. Suk. are selected in preference to y. Suk. b. Suk. borrows and develops details in *both* earlier versions, rather than standing in a single line after the Palestinian Talmudic one. That b. Suk. depends upon the language of *both* seems to me beyond reasonable doubt. This is not a common phenomenon.

The upshot is familiar. A stable text tradition is adorned in details, but the stories and sayings move from document to document in an essentially cogent version, start to finish. We do not find evidence of a wildly changing set of free-standing stories and sayings but the very opposite.

Chapter Twelve

Yohanan ben Zakkai

1. The Rite of the Red Cow

Sifré Num.	Common to Both	Tos. Parah
	1. His disciples asked	
2. In what garments is the red-heifer done		2. The red heifer—in what is it done
	3. He said, in golden...	
4. They said to him, Have you not taught us, our rabbi, in white garments		4. You have taught us in white garments
5. -----		5. He said to them, Well spoken, and
6a. What my own eyes saw and my own hands served I have forgotten, how much the more so		6a. A deed which my own hands did and my own eyes saw, but I have forgotten, but when my ears hear, how much the more so
6b. that which I have taught		6b. ----
7a. ----		7a. Not that he did not know

7b. And all this why? In order to stimulate the disciples	7b. but that he wanted to stimulate the disciples
8. And some say it was Hillel	8. And some say it was Hillel the Elder when they asked.
9. ----	9. Not that he did not know but that he wanted to stimulate the disciples
10. ----	10. For R. Joshua said…
11. But he could not say, What my own hands served	11. -----

The versions are close, but by no means identical. The variations of no. 2 are minor and insignificant. Those in no. 4 are of somewhat more interest, for the Tosefta version is briefer and less polite. The real differences begin at no. 5. Tos. 5 is clearly an embellishment of the story. Tos. 6 *a deed which* is added; Sifré 6b is additional; there is no equivalent in the Tos. version, which leaves the *gal vehomer* to dangle.

A further clear addition is Tos. 7a, *Not that he did* not know which replaces *all this why* with an explication of the problem. 8a is identical in both versions, but Tos. 9 is copied from Tos. 7a, and the intrusion, then exclusion, of Hillel is never actually accounted for. I should regard Tos. 7a-b as a garbling of Sifré 8, 11, which is a coherent statement. Tos. 9 is absent in the Sifré.

In sum, the Tos. version is not only longer than the Sifré one, but also at several points both augmented and more verbose; Joshua's saying is brought gratuitously. I should therefore regard the Tos. version as a later development of the Sifré. Here again we see that what appears in a later document depends upon, and augments, a version in an earlier compilation. The Sifré story not only appears in the earlier document, but it gives indication of being the earlier *version*.

2. One-hundred-twenty Years

Sifré Deut. #357	Mid. Tan. to Deut. 34:7	B. R.H. 31b =	B. Sanh. 41b	Gen. R. 100:24 100:24
1. Deut. 34:7	----	----	----	(Begins #7-#13)
2. These are they: Moses, Hillel, Yohanan, 'Aqiba		----	----	[Then:]
3. Moses: *was* Egypt, 40 Midian, 40 Sustained	*worked* *served*	---- ----	---- ----	lived in palace of Pharaoh, 40 Midian *served*
4. Hillel: Migrated at 40 Midian, 40 Sustained 40	*served*	----	----	*served sages served*
5. Yohanan *busied* Business, 40 Disciples, 40 Sustained, 40	*worked*	All the years (*see b. R.H. 31b*) of Yohanan were one-hundred-twenty Business, 40 Studied, 40 Taught, 40		*worked* *learned served*

6. Aqiba
  Studied, 40
  Sustained 40
	studied
	served sages
	served Israel
			worked as a boor, 40
			studied
			served

7. Six pairs lived same number of years		----	----
8. Rebecca/Kohath		----	----
9. Levi/Amram		----	----
10. Joseph/Joshua		----	----
11. Samuel/ Solomon		----	----
12. Moses/Hillel		----	----
13. Yohanan/Aqiba		----	----

The *one-hundred-twenty-years* pericope thus comes in two versions. In the first, represented by Sifré, Mid. Tan., and Genesis Rabbah, Yohanan is listed among four, then six pairs who lived one-hundred-twenty years. We may further subdivide these versions into two separate units, the "four," then the "six," or in reverse order in the latest version. Sifré and Mid. Tan. are practically identical; the only variations are in the choice of *worked* for *was*, *served* for *sustained*, in the latter version.

Further, Mid. Tan. corrects the omission in the earlier version of the first forty years of Aqiba's life. The tradition on Aqiba's early ignorance was well-known and widely attested. It would destroy the symmetry of the passage to make no reference to one-third of Aqiba's life, and hence the improvement, which at the same time perfects the saying and cleans up Aqiba's early years.

Gen. R. not only reverses the order—which is an editorial change—but elaborates the Egyptian period of Moses, changing the general "in Egypt" to the specific "in the Palace of Pharaoh." Likewise Aqiba's early years are properly characterized as years of ignorance. But for the rest, the account is close to the early versions.

The two *baraitot*, which are identical, are quite another matter. The *baraitot* are as follows:

> Has it not been taught, Rabban Yohanan ben Zakkai lived for one-hundred-twenty years. Forty years he was in business, forty years he studied, and forty years he taught.
> B. R. H. 31 b

> Has it not been taught, Rabban Yohanan ben Zakkai lived for one-hundred-twenty years. Forty years he was in business, forty years he studied, and forty years he taught.
> b. Sanh. 41 b

They ignore all others in the one-hundred-twenty set and concentrate on Yohanan alone. But otherwise the *baraita-version* exhibits striking similarities to the earlier formulations. The forty-year divisions are repeated. Business (*pragmata*) is preserved. The disciplehood/sustaining Israel of Sifré Deut. becomes studied/taught, a play on LMD. The *baraita* cannot be divorced from the earlier documents' version. Rather, it revises the tradition to concentrate on Yohanan alone; of the four/six, Yohanan is singled out. The exegetical framework is dropped as well.

The significant comparison, therefore, is to be made between the version in the earliest document, Sifré Deut., and that in the Babylonian *baraita*. Are the two versions independent but of equal antiquity? Or has the baraita formulation been *extracted* from the former and been slightly rephrased? My guess is that the latter has taken place. What was formerly a complete list is now a story about Yohanan alone. The reference to one-hundred-twenty years is the key. Without the exegesis of Deut. 34;&, as well as the list of all those therein included, the reference to Yohanan's exception life-span is meaningless; he could be one of hundreds. The tripartite division of his life-span likewise is pointless outside of the earlier convention. The *baraita* standing outside of the exegetical framework and the four/six pattern is enigmatic; within that framework, it makes real sense: These were the four/six who both lived a very long time and whose years were equivalently divided.

3. Disputes with Gentiles

The enumeration of the Levites (Num. 4:46) is the common theme in the following:

B. Bekh. 5a	Y. Sanh. 1:4	Num. R. 4:9
Qintroqis asked Yohanan	Antoninus Hegemon asked Yohanan	Agentus the Hegemon asked Yohanan
When Levites are enumerated in detail, you find 22,300. But when counted as a group, 22,000. where did the 300 go?	In general they lack, in particular they are too many.	Moses your teacher was either a thief or poor at arithmetic. Why?
Three hundred were first-born and a first-born cannot redeem a first-born (Num. 3:44)	The three hundred extras were the first born of the priesthood, and holy cannot redeem holy.	Because there were 22,273, and God commanded: Levites redeem the first-born. Now there were still 300 Levites left over when counted in de-

----	----	-tail, for we find 273 gave five *sheqels* each.
----	----	Further, when he sums up the number, he deducts the 300 of the original number. So he left them out so that
----	----	those 273 first-born might each give 5 *sheqels* to his brother Aaron.
----	----	or bad at arithmetic.
----	----	Yohanan: he was no thief and was good at arithmetic. But you read but cannot expound Scripture.
----	----	Moses thought, The 22,000 Levites will redeem the 22,000 first-born, and the 300 Levites will remain, and of the first-born, so when he summed up the number he omitted them because they were first-born.

Num R. has obviously provided a careful spelling out of the reasons for the dispute, in the form of supplied dialogue. The Palestinian version is too brief to have been comprehended without additional explanation. Whether this depended on the Babylonian story or not I cannot say. Perhaps some sort of brief reference was meant to call to mind a well-known, more complete account. But in its current form, without Scriptural references, even without an antecedent for *they lack* and *they are too many*, the Palestinian version is garbled. The assertion that Moses was either poor at arithmetic or a thief, of Num. R. 4:9 is borrowed from y. Sanh. 1:4, which concerned *not* the enumeration of the Levites, but the collection of the *sheqel* for use in the sanctuary and the final accounting for the use of the money. The passage continues, after some intervening material, in both b. Bekh. 5a and y. Sanh. 1:4, as follows:

B. Bekh. 5a	Y. Sanh. 1:4
And again he was asked	Antonius the Hegemon asked Yohanan
With reference to collection, you count *kikkar* and 11 *maneh*.	Moses was either a thief or not good at arithmetic, Ex. 38:27. If a centarius ...he stole one sixth/one half.
But when Moses gave the money, you find only 100 *kikkar*. Was Moses a thief or bad at arithmetic? He gave half, took half, and did not return a complete half. Yohanan: Moses was reliable and good at arithmetic. The sacred *maneh* was double the common one.	Yohanan: Moses was a faithful treasurer and good at arithmetic.

The *again he was asked* becomes a separate story in y. Sanh., and while the point of both stories is roughly the same, namely that Temple measurements were different from ordinary ones, there is no close relationship between the two accounts. Clearly some sort of common tradition underlies both versions; it had to do with the gentile's ignorance of Scripture and of the Temple's measurements, on the one hand, and of the redemption rules, on the other. But beyond that, I see little in common in the literary accounts.

4. Analogical Exegesis (Kemin Homer)

The *homer* exegeses occur both with that designation and without. The list in Tos. B.Q. 7:2-5 counts five in all, but as we shall note, there are additional exegeses in the *homer-style*, both so designated and otherwise. We shall first compare the versions of the five in Tos. B.Q. 7:3-7:

Tos. B.Q. 7:3. Why was Israel exiled to Babylonia?

-- no parallels.

Tos. B.Q. 7:4: First tablets, second tablets

-- no parallels.

Tos. B.Q. 7:5	Sifra VaYiqra	Y. Hor. 3:2	B. Hor. 10b Teno Rabbanan
----	----	----	
Lev. 4:22	(see Tos. B.Q. 7:5)	(see Tos. B.Q. 7:5)	(see Tos. B.Q. 7:5)
Happy is the generation whose prince brings a sin-	(see Tos. B.Q. 7:5)	(see Tos. B.Q. 7:5)	(see Tos. B.Q. 7:5)

offering for his
unwitting sin.

----	----	----	If the prince brings, do you have to ask about an ordinary person?
----	----	----	If for an unwitting sin, do you have to ask an intentional sin?

What is striking, first of all, is that no version of the saying on Lev. 4:22 ever designates the exegesis as analogical, except for the superscription of Tos. B.Q. The Babylonian *baraita* expounds Yohanan's meaning, extending his message. It obviously is a later elaboration, and once again illustrates the tendency of the Babylonian *baraitot* to augment and improve upon earlier materials.

Tos. B.Q. 7:5-6	Mekhilta Neziqin	Y. Qid. 1:2	B. Qid. 22b
And it says Ex. 21:6	Yohanan interprets it *kemin homer*.	His disciples asked Yohanan	Yohanan *would* interpret this Scripture *kemin*
Why ear pierced more than all other limbs?		Why is this slave to be pierced in his ear more than all limbs?	Why is the ear differentiated from all the limbs of the body?

Since it heard from Mt. Sinai Lev. 25:55	The ear heard Ex. 20:13		He said to them, The ear heard Ex. 20:2	The Holy One, blessed be he said, the ear which heard my voiced on Mt.
Yet it broke from itself the yoke of heaven and accepted the rule of mortals	Yet went and stole.		Yet broke the yoke of the kingdom of heaven and accepted the yoke of mortals	Sinai when I said Lev. 25:55 and not slaves to slaves.
-----	-----		The ear heard Lev. 25:55 yet went and acquired for itself another master.	Yet it went and acquired for itself a master
Therefore Scripture says, Let the ear come and be pierced, for it did not keep what heard.	Therefore it alone of all limits will be pierced. ----		Therefore let the ear come and be pierced. Because it did not keep what it heard.	Let it be pierced. ----
Another matter: It did not wish to be subjugated to its creator, let it come and be subjugated to his daughters.	----		-----	----

The version of Pesiqta Rabbati 21 is closest to y. Qid. We see that the simplest version is the Mekhilta, in which Ex. 20:13 is cited. The assumption is that by stealing and being unable to pay recompense, the man was sold into slavery. This version stands apart. Even though it is briefer than Tos. B.Q., we cannot suppose that the latter was built upon it, for the whole exegetical framework in Tos. B.Q. is different.

The comparisons are to be made, rather, between Tos. B.Q. and the two Talmudic versions. We note that the

Palestinian version inserts Ex. 20:2 before Lev. 25:55, and omits the "other matter," which seems adequately spelled out in reference to Lev. 25:55 and to require no further repetition. The version in b. Qid. is closer to Tos. B.Q. and I assume it is copied from it, with the inclusion of the *kemin homer* designation. Lev. 25:55 is further expounded, an improvement on, *therefore Scripture says*. In place of *Scripture*, the verse is introduced by reference to *God*, a voice, *Mt. Sinai*, and so forth; that is, it is made more vivid. The interrelationship between Tos. B.Q and b. Qid. thus is close, but the differences all point toward the latter's being a later development of the former. The account in y. Qid. does not depend upon the Babylonian one, and is a secondary development of the Tos. B.Q. one, also considerably improved.

Tos. B.Q. 7:6	Mekhilta de R.Ishmael
And it says Deut. 27:5 Why was iron prohibited more than all metals?	This is what Yohanan says: (*see Tos. B.Q. 7:6*)
Because the sword may be made from it.	(*see Tos. B.Q. 7:6*)
The sword is a sign of punishment and the altar of atonement.	(*see Tos. B.Q. 7:6*)
Remove something which is a sign of punishment from something which is a sign of atonement.	(*see Tos. B.Q. 7:6*)
And it is a *qal vehomer*:	(*see Tos. B.Q. 7:6*)

Stones which do not see, hear, speak—	(see Tos. B.Q. 7:6)		
Because they bring atonement between Israel and their father in heaven.	(see Tos. B.Q. 7:6)		
Scripture says Deut. 27:5.	(see Tos. B.Q. 7:6)		
Sons of Torah who are atonement for the world	(see Tos. B.Q. 7:6)		
How much the more so that any of all the demons should not touch them.	(see Tos. B.Q. 7:6)		

Tos. B.Q. 7:7	Mekhilta Bahodesh	Sifra Qedoshim
Behold it says Deut. 27:6	Yohanan says, Behold It says Deut. 27:6	(see Mekhilta Bahodesh)
Stones which bring peace between Israel and their father in heaven, the Omnipresent says, should be perfect before me	Stones which bring peace. *It is a qal vehomer:*	(see Mekhilta Bahodesh) (see Mekhilta Bahodesh) (see Mekhilta Bahodesh)
Sons of Torah, who perfect the world	Stones do not see, hear speak.	(see Mekhilta Bahodesh) *Scripture*
How much the more so should they be perfect before the Omnipresent.	Because they bring peace between Israel and their father in heaven, the Holy One said Deut. 27:5	(see Mekhilta Bahodesh) [Man/man *omitted*]

How much the more so the *one who brings peace* between man and man, husband and wife, nation and nation, family and family, government and government.	*family*/family, city/city, state/state, nation/nation.
be protected so no harm should come to him.	How much the more so should punishment not overtake him.

We see that the *stones which bring peace* and the prohibition of iron appear both together and also separately in Tos. B.Q. 7:6-7. The first version contains the prohibition of iron, and adds to it the *stones*, the second treats *stones* alone. The *qal-vehomer* appears only in connection with *stones*. Differences between Mekhilta's and the Sifra's accounts are striking, and it is not difficult to assign priority. Revisions of the exegesis were intended to change condemnation of war and swords and praise of peacemakers into praise of study of Torah and disciples of Torah.

5. Because You Did Not Serve

The sermon on the occasion of seeing a starving child exists in a number of formulations, appearing in the earliest to the latest documents. We shall compare the versions by the sequence of documents.

Mekhilta Bahodesh	Sifré Deut.	Y. Ket. 5:11	Tos. Ket. 5:9-10
They were not satisfied to count.	----	[Marta daughter of Boethus had large dowry...]	[The daughter of Naqdimon had a large dowry]
Ezek. 40:1 Hag. 1:15 And thus it says, *if you know not* (Song 1:18) And It also says, *Because you did not serve* (Deut. 28.47-8)	---- ---- ---- ----	Eleazar b. Zadoq said he saw her gathering barley under hooves of horses in Acre, and I cited concerning her Deut. 28:56 and Song 1:8]	Eleazar b. Zadoq says he saw her gathering barley under the hooves of horses in Acre. And I *cited* concerning her Song 1:8]
Yohanan going to Emmaus saw girl picking barley-corn from horse dung. To disciple: What is girl?	*Story is told* that Yohanan was riding an ass and students walking after him, and he saw girl picking barley-corn from the feet of Arab cattle		
She is Jewish The horse belongs to an Arab.	When she saw Yohanan she wrapped herself in her hair and stood before him, asking for food.		

Yohanan to disciples: Now I know meaning of *Song 1:8*			
	She: Naqdimon b. Gurion, don't you remember my *ketubah*?		
You are unwilling to be subject to God, are now subject to Arabs.			
	He remembers *ketubah* also that her family went on carpets to Temple.	-----	-----
You were unwilling to— pay head-tax (Ex. 38:26) now pay fifteen sheqels			
—repair roads for pilgrims now do so for enemy	And all my life I sought meaning of *Song 1:8* Read not…	-----	-----
Thus it says, *Because you did not serve* (Deut. 28:47-8)	For when Israel do the will of the Omnipresent, no one can rule them, but when they do not, the lowest nation rules them, even the cattle of the lowest nation.		

B. Ket. 66b

Teno Rabbanan: Story is told that Yohanan was riding on ass and *going out of Jerusalem* and his students were walking after him. He saw a girl picking barley-corn from between feet of Arab cattle.

When she saw him, she wrapped self in hair, stood before him, and said, Rabbi, feed me.

He asks, Whose daughter are you?

She: Naqdimon b. Gurion.

Yohanan: What happened to your father's wealth?

Girl: Cites proverb.

She: don't you remember my marriage contract?

Yohanan: I remember I signed it.

Yohanan wept and said, Happy are you O Israel, when you do God's will on one can rule you, but when you do not, even meanest people rule you, even their cattle.

ARNa chap. 17

Yohanan saw girl in marketplace, picking barley from feet of Arab cattle.

Who are you?

No answer.

Covered self wit hair, sat before him, I am daughter of Naqdimon b. Gurion.

Yohanan: What happened to wealth of father, father in law.

Girl: Cites proverb.

Yohanan: Now I understand Song 1:8.

Israel has been surrendered to meanest of peoples, even to cattle-dung.

Girl: Reminds him about marriage-contract.

Yohanan: By the Temple service, I signed her marriage-contract and also that her family went on carpets to Temple.

I have cited the Palestinian Talmud and the Tos. Ket. stories merely to indicate how the same Scriptures are used in several different ways. The Toseftan story may be the earlier of the two, for in the Palestinian Talmudic account, we see a proliferation of Scriptures; on the other hand, the daughter in the Tosefta is Naqdimon's, in the Palestinian Talmud, Boethus's. The stories are related, but the latter is not simply an amplified version of the former.

The four accounts in which Yohanan appears are certainly interrelated, though the exact relationships are by no means clear. Mekhilta is a play on Deut. 28:47-8 and Song 1:8, while in Sifré Deut., Deut. 28:47-8 does not appear at all. In Mekhilta the girl is unnamed; Yohanan has never met her; the pathos of her fall from prosperity is ignored. The meaning of Song 1:8 is elucidated by Deut. 28:47-8. But the girl's plight plays no intrinsic role. And the disciples play an active part. In Sifré Deut., by contrast, the girl is the central figure, asking for food, then identifying herself, reminding Yohanan about her *ketubah*; and he further remembers the luxurious way her family lived. then comes Song 1:8, now the point of it all. Finally comes the closing homily, "When Israel do ...

Perhaps Sifré Deut. is a development of Mekhilta Bahodesh, in which the detail about the girl becomes greatly embellished, indeed is made the point of the encounter. Then *You were unwilling* ceases to be an exegesis and becomes an outright homily, independent of a Scripture. But some details of Mekhilta are dropped, first, the conversation with the disciples, second, the location of the trip. When the girl becomes central, the disciples pass out of the picture, serve as a silent audience.

The Babylonia *baraita* clearly depends upon Sifré Deut. Now the location of the trip is once again supplied. The encounter with the girl if further amplified by the question, *What happened to your father's money*? This is inserted before the marriage-contract, so the girl now introduces the topic not in order to identify herself, but as a separate colloquy. Strikingly, all Scriptural exegeses are omitted, but the homily of Sifré Deut. is further expanded by *Happy are you, O Israel.* Otherwise it is identical.

As usual, ARNA is highly literary. The disciples are absent, having no role to play. The marketplace is now the setting. The conversation is dramatic, eloquent. The girl then identifies herself; Yohanan asks about her father's money; she replies citing a well-known proverb. Yohanan now introduces Song 1:8 and the homily immediately follows, in somewhat abbreviated form. Finally, the details of the marriage-contract and the luxurious way of living of her family are tacked on.

In effect, the version of the Mekhilta stands by itself; Sifré Deut. forms the basis for both the Babylonian *baraita* and the ARNa. The components common to all versions are as follows:

1. Starving girl picks barley-corn from dung of Arabian horses/cattle.
2. Yohanan sees, asks who she is.
3. He cites Song 1:8 in reference to the girl.

Unique to Mekhilta Bahodesh is the further exegesis of Deut. 28:47-8; but the homilies appearing in all other accounts in fact are based upon the plain sense of that very Scripture: "If you do well, you will be blessed, but if not, you will be cursed." The additional elements common to Sifré Deut., b. Ket. *baraita*, and ARNa, are as follows:

4. The girl identifies herself as Naqdimon's daughter.
5. Do you not remember you witnessed my marriage-contract?

6. Indeed I do, and what happened to your father's wealth? I remember also how your family went to the Temple on carpets.
7. [Song 1:8 appears in Sifré and ARNa.]
8. When you do God's will, no one can rule you, but when you do riot, you are given into the hands of mean people and their cattle.

We may further conjecture that the association of the unnamed girl of Mekhilta with the daughter of Naqdimon in Sifré and afterward derives originally from the fact that an exegesis of Song 1:8 is common to both Yohanan and Eleazar b. Zadoq, leading to the further assumption that the "you" of "if you do not know" is, in fact, Naqdimon's daughter. Henceforward, the citation of Song 1:8 will remind everyone to whom Yohanan was talking, and further details naturally will be supplied from other stories about her. The association of Yohanan with her father is drawn quite routinely in the escape stories, but these are very late, certainly much later than the materials before us, and I imagine that the escape-stories have been shaped by *Because you did not serve materials*, rather than vice versa.

The b. Ket. 66b and ARNa Ch. 17 versions of the encounter with Naqdimon's daughter probably are developments of Sifré Deut., which is likely to be related to, but separate from, Mekhilta Bahodesh. Thus stories appearing in documents of approximately the same age do not appear to improve on one another, but do exhibit complex relationships with one another. Stories appearing in later documents as usual seem to be developments of stories appearing in earlier documents. In general, marks signifying a later version normally, though not invariably, include augmentation and other kinds of development. In the historical stories this invariably is the distinguishing trait of the later versions.

I hardly need repeat the conclusion reached in the foregoing units of this part of the study. The variations in stories as they flow from document to document are less weighty than the essential uniformities.

III

THREE THEORIES OF THE PERIPATETIC SAYING

Chapter Thirteen

"He Often Used to Say"

Among the three familiar interpretations of the fact that a story appears in more than one document and that a saying occurs a number of times, the oldest is also the silliest. If a given saying occurs in numerous passages, then the person to whom the saying is ascribed is alleged to have said that saying a lot. Since the "he often used to say"-explanation circulates in both simple and sophisticated versions, we have to take a moment to "refute" it. Not only in Israeli, European, and American *Yeshivot* and universities will people yet find such a refutation provocative. But since the theory is just silly, the refutation will prove equally trivial.

The simplest proof that the present explanation cannot serve derives from the fact that two or more stories of an event that cannot have been repeated do circulate in the Talmudic corpus. Since several versions of the same story in the present case by definition report only a one-time event, one which simply cannot have been repeated, it must follow that the explanation at hand has now to leave the stage of rational discourse, though believers, of course, will always believe whatever they find convenient. For the purposes of argument I can think of two never-to-be-repeated events, one, the destruction of the Second Temple, the other, the death of a rabbi. As we saw above, Chapter One, Eliezer b. Hyrcanus dies twice in Talmudic writings. How explain the two versions? No fundamentalist maintains that the Temple was destroyed twice. None to my knowledge (here I am less certain of what is to be found in the dim reaches of the Yeshiva-periodicals) can claim that a rabbi died, was resurrected, then died a second time, allowing for two events, to which two quite different stories of the same rabbits death may then be made to refer. Since, on the face of it, the theory at hand cannot explain important facts, the theory has to wend its way off the stage of reasoned discourse. A new theory will have to take shape to account for the same facts — all of them, all the time.

The case at hand involves Yohanan ben Zakkai's escape from Jerusalem during the Roman siege. I think even the most primitive Orthodox and Israeli scholars will concur that Yohanan surely did not escape from Jerusalem one way, crawl back into the city, then make an escape another way — the one time dealing with one group of people, the next with another, the one time seeing Vespasian and having one conversation with him, the next time seeing Vespasian but having a different conversation with him. So it would appear to me sufficient to point to the following case. We shall leave in ruins the first of the three theories on the meaning of diverse versions of a given event.

To the texts at hand: we have two fundamentally different accounts of Yohanan's escape, each in two versions, those in ARNa and ARNb, and in b. Git. 56b and Lam R. It is obvious that all are very late stories. None can possibly date from before ca. A.D. 200. In Tannaitic traditions, attributed to authorities before A.D. 200, we find not the slightest reference to an escape. Indeed, we should not know how Yohanan reached Yabneh, if we had to rely on the Tannaitic Midrashim, Mishnah-Tosefta, and even the *beraitot* in the Babylonian Talmud. Nor does the Palestinian Talmud contain a reference to an escape. if we knew the date of The Fathers According to Rabbi Nathan (= ARN), we should probably have a clear idea about the literary beginnings of the escape legend, though the several components of the ARNa account are probably older and now have been reshaped. We may only imagine that at some point after 200, it became important to tell escape-stories; no single account was ever widely accepted. I can propose no conjecture on when, where, or why it became important to make up such a story, or to whom it would have been useful. Perhaps opposition to Julian's attempt, in 360, to rebuild the Temple provoked it, but my guess is that components of the escape-legends are older than that.

The Babylonian version is clearly a composite, while ARN is, as usual, more literary, smoother, but also formed from earlier materials. We shall first compare the two ARN versions, then the second pair, and finally contrast one account with the other.

ARNa	ARNb Ch. 6, Schechter, p. 10a
I. Vespasian asks sign of submission.	1. *see* ARNa
Yohanan counsels Jews to give it, save the Temple, the refuse.	*see* ARNa
Vespasian's me heard of Yohanan's loyalty.	*see* ARNa
II. Yohanan tells Joshua and Eliezer to help him escape.	II. *see* ARNa
Make a coffin. Eliezer and Joshua carried coffin. Gatekeepers object, but are told it is a corpse.	*see* ARNa Gatekeepers object, want to stab corpse. Disciples reply, You will be said to have stabbed Yohanan's corpse.
III. Coffin carried to Vespasian, Yohanan rises from coffin before emperor.	III. Yohanan gets out of coffin, goes and asks after welfare of Vespasian as one asks about a king, saying *Ridumani Imperion*.

Are you Rabban Yohanan? What can I give you?	Are you Ben Zakkai?
Yabneh, so I may teach, establish prayer-house, do commandments.	Yohanan predicts coming rise to power, citing Is. 10:34.
Go	
IV. Yohanan tells Vespasian you are about to be made emperor, on basis of Is. 10:34.	IV. [*After* his prediction is proved correct, Yohanan is permitted to make a request.]
Two or three days later, news came that Vespasian was emperor.	Give me Yabneh where I may teach Torah and make *sisit* and do the other commandments.
	Behold it is given to you as a gift.

Parts I and II are practically identical in both versions. But parts III and IV are not. In the latter, the prediction comes before the emperor gives any favors, as in b. Git. Likewise, gatekeepers are hostile to the disciples. In general, as we shall see, ARNb combines major elements of ARNa and the Babylonian version; it is a composite of the two, standing between them. The Babylonian and Midrashic accounts compare as follows:

"He often used to say" 209

B. Git. 56b	Lam. R. 1.5.31
I. Abba Sikra was Yohanan's nephew, came to Yohanan. How long will you kill the people by starvation? Abba Sikra cannot help. Then, Yohanan asks, think of a plan to get me out. Perhaps there may be some slight salvation. Pretend to be sick, die, and he did so.	I. Ben Battiah was Yohanan's nephew. When Yohanan heard his nephew had burned the city's supplies, he exclaimed, "woe". Ben Battiah heard, called Yohanan to him, asked why. Yohanan said he had praised the burning of the stores because now the people would have to fight. Three days later, he saw people starving, decided to escape. Asked Ben Battiah to help. Ben Battiah says only dead can leave. Yohanan determined to escape as corpse.
II. Eliezer carried one side, Joshua the other. Guards wanted to push, then stab body. Disciples say it will give you a bad name.	II. Eliezer and Joshua carried him, Ben Battiah accompanied cortege. Guards wanted to stab body, Ben Battiah said it will give us a bad name.
III. When he reached there, he said, Peace be to you, O King. Vespasian says, You are worthy of death. I am not a king, and if I were, why did you not come earlier. I could not come sooner because revolutionaries would not let me.	III. Disciples returned to city. Yohanan wandered among Roman troops, asked where a king was. Yohanan was brought to Vespasian. *Vive domine Imperator.* But you are a king, Yohanan says citing Is. 10:34, Jer. 30:21, Deut. 3:25.

210 *Peripatetic Parallels*

IIIb. Vespasian asks, If you have honey and a reptile is around the cask, would not break the cask to kill the snake?	----- (VI)
Yohanan fell silent.	----- (VI)
R. Joseph/R. Aqiba cites Is. 44:25. He should have answered, One takes tongs.	-----
IV. Meanwhile messenger came from Rome, Vespasian is king.	IV. Yohanan put in room without light, but could tell time because of his study.
V. He had one shoe off, one shoe could do nothing Yohanan says, you have heard good news, cites Prov.15:30. Let someone you dislike pass before you, cites Prov. 17:22.	V. Vespasian bathes at Gophna, but could not get shoes back on, for word came that Nero died and he was king. Yohanan explains, You have heard good news, cites Prov. 15:30 and Prov. 17:22.
VI. If you were so wise, why did you not come sooner? I already told you. So did I.	VI. Then they began to speak in parables. If a snake in a cask, what to do? Yohanan: Charm the snake. Pangar: Break the cask and kill the snake. If a snake in a tower: Yohanan: bring a charmer. Pangar: Burn the tower. Yohanan to Pangar: You hurt us. Pangar: I seek your welfare. So long as Temple exists, heathen kingdoms will attack you, if it is destroyed, they will not. Yohanan: The

"He often used to say" 211

	heart knows what your real intention is.
VII. I, Vespasian continued, will soon leave. What can I give you?	VII. Vespasian: What may I give you?
Vespasian: You endanger my life, for if king hears, he will put me to death.	Yohanan: Abandon this city and depart. Vespasian: I did not become king to abandon Jerusalem.
But you are a king, Is. 10:34.	
Yabneh and its sages, the chain of Gamaliel, and a physician for Sadoq.	Yohanan: Leave the western gate open for refugees.
R. Joseph/R. Aqiba cites Is. 44:25. He should have asked the Romans to leave them alone.	
-----	VIII. After the conquest, Vespasian offered to save Yohanan's friends.
	Yohanan sent Eliezer and Joshua to bring Sadoq.
-----	IX. Vespasian: Why do you stand up before emaciated old man.
	Yohanan: If we had one more like him, you would not have conquered Jerusalem. He lives on a fig, teaches many sessions, fasts a lot.

212 *Peripatetic Parallels*

-----	X. Sadoq's son: Father, give them reward in this world.
	He gave them calculation by fingers and scales for weighing.
-----	XI. After conquest, Vespasian assigned destruction of four ramparts to four generals.
	Pangar had western wall, but did not destroy it.
	Pangar explained to Vespasian, I kept it so people would know what you destroyed.
	Vespasian replied, Well said, but disobeyed, so commit suicide.
	He did so, and thus the curse of Rabban Yohanan ben Zakkai alighted upon him.

Lam R. has been corrected in important details to conform to the criticism of b. Git.; note the comparison of b. Git IIIb and VI with Lam. R. VI and VII. Yet in many other, equally important respects, Lam R. stands by itself. The Abba Sikra account is now expanded into two parts. Lam. R. parts IV, VI, VII, VIII, IX, X, and XI have no close counterpart in the earlier version, though the "physical for Rabbi Sadoq" of Git. part VI becomes the long encounter of Lam. R. part IX and X.

We have no reason to doubt Lam. R. is later than Git. The former is greatly elaborated over the latter. The version appearing in the later document is probably later than the one appearing in the earlier document. Indeed, it is expanded both through details common to both stories, and with completely new materials. The following summarizes the points in common as well as the stories found in one account and not in another:

ARN	B. Git.	Lam. R.
Vespasian asks submission, Yohanan agrees.	-----	-----
Joshua and Eliezer effect the escape of "corpse".	Abba Sikra — "corpse"	Ben Battiah — "corpse"
-----	Starvation.	-----
-----	-----	Burning of stores.
Guards went to stab corpse.	(see *ARN*)	(see *ARN*)
Meets Vespasian	(see *ARN*)	(see *ARN*)
What can I give you?	-----	-----
Yabneh	(see *ARN*)	(see *ARN*)
Prediction, Is. 10:34	(see *ARN*)	(see *ARN*)
News comes.	Honey and reptile.	(see *b. Git.*)
-----	Is. 44:25	(see *b. Git.*)
-----	Feet bloated, Prov.	(see *b. Git.*)

	15:30, 17:22	
-----	Chain of Gamaliel	-----
-----	Heal Sadoq (see b. Git.)	
-----	-----	Yohanan told time miraculously.
-----	-----	Tower and reptile.
-----	-----	Pangar.
-----	-----	Abandon city.
-----	-----	Accept refugees.
-----	-----	Why honor Sadoq?
	-----	Sadoq gives calculation.
	-----	Pangar fails to destroy. Western wall.

All accounts have in common the escape through a ruse, the participation of Joshua and Eliezer, the request for Yabneh, the prediction of Vespasian's coming rise to power on the basis of Is. 10:34, and the arrival of news to verify Yohanan's prediction. Although the order and perspective of ARNa differ from those of the later versions, no important detail in the former is absent in the latter. It seems possible that ARN has served as a source of materials — though as that alone — for the Babylonian and Lam. R. stories. I think it is far more likely, however, that some sort of independent materials circulated widely, and were used by the authors of the several stories independently of one another. Otherwise, I imagine, the relationships between ARN and the other stories would be somewhat more like those between b. Git. and Lam. R. There would be signs of development and augmentation, and we see none. Hence some stories, particularly about the escape and prediction (Is. 10:34) probably antedated the formation of the several accounts. To conclude: ARNA stands by itself, quite apart from b. Git. and its later formulation in Lam. R.; we do not know whether ARNA comes before b. Git. Since the two are not directly related, it hardly matters.

One of the truly original and great minds of Talmudic history, G. Alon (in his *Mehqarim* [Tel Aviv, 1957] I, pp. 238-251) explains the difference between the two escape stories just now surveyed. The sources, Alon says, reveal two traditions concerning Yohanan's escape. According to the first he left the city after the Zealots refused to surrender to Vespasian, because he was opposed to the war and hoped to save the Temple. Vespasian had spies in the city and knew that Yohanan favored his cause. When he came to the Romans, they therefore recognized him, brought him directly to Vespasian, who received him and asked what he could do in his behalf. Yohanan thereupon made his famous request for Yabneh, *then* prophesied Vespasian's rise to power. According to the second view, Yohanan surrendered not because he opposed the *war*, but because he opposed the military *policies* of the Zealots. He favored remaining in the besieged city for a defensive war, rather than making sorties against the Roman lines. The Romans according to this account knew nothing about him, had no special regard for him, and so at his interview with Vespasian he had to justify his actions. Having nothing to his credit, he made a prediction; when it came true, he was granted a small favor.

What is important here in Alon's sensitive analysis is simple. He does not imagine that the two stories tell us about two different happenings. And neither can anyone else — any more. If so, then on the face of it, theories about how "he often used to say," that invoke the same mode of explaining the same phenomenon and parallel phenomena when they occur elsewhere, likewise serve no further purpose. The claim that the sages enjoyed reenacting the scenes of their life, including how they died, for one audience after another, with each statement recorded, each event set down, takes up its lonely vigil alongside the theory of the flat earth and other lost causes of another age. And so we bid adieu, once for all, to the theory of the repetitious rabbis.

What about the problem to which this second edition addresses itself: autonomous versions of the same event? Indeed, that is precisely what we have before us. The two free-standing accounts intersect only tangentially. Alon has left no doubt as to the meaning of the differences. They convey distinct theories of the event and its meaning. What conclusions are we supposed to draw from the fact that the canonical documents contain two (or more) distinct versions of the same happening? The documentary hypothesis requires that we ask whether the document's perspectives or polemics have shaped the details of a given story (as the general theory of Mark, Matthew, Luke, or John shape the stories and sayings preserved in the respective Gospels). The question, once asked, may or may not produce a plausible, let alone a compelling answer. The theory of Goldberg-Schaefer-Becker would have us take the disparate versions as indicators of a different literary situation. It is one in which stories and sayings do more than float freely, hither and yon, a fact that the documentary hypothesis finds entirely familiar within its theory of the literary history of the canonical writings. But then, I cannot myself propose an explanation, within the Goldberg-Schaefer-Becker theory of things, for the present facts; I do not pretend to understand their theory in all its fullness, because they have yet to spell it out within a larger history of the formation of the Rabbinic documents. My larger theory has been articulated in the companion volumes of this project. I do not know where Goldberg, Schaefer and Becker have given theirs. My best sense is, taking an utterly atomistic view of the writing, they cannot account for the documents at all — not for the documents, not for their indicative traits, and not for their striking uniformities.

To state matters simply: the documentary hypothesis proposes a theory of how the documents took shape and also how the non-documentary writing took shape in that same context. The critics of that hypothesis propose no theory at all for the very matter to which, in the end, the claim to provide an account and an explanation.

Chapter Fourteen

In Search of the "Original" "Tradition"

So much for the first explanation of peripatetic parallels. It is that if a given saying occurs in numerous passages, then the person to whom the saying is ascribed is alleged to have said that saying a lot. The second is that, if we have parallel versions, then one of them is the original tradition, the other an amplification.[1] The third is that each version represents a distinct event or occasion, a variation on the first. We deal here with the second, in Chapter Fifteen with the third, of the three explanations.

The second and third explanations of the presence of diverse versions of a single event superficially lay claim to be somewhat more sophisticated. But neither leads to a suitable solution to the problem or even to a theory of how to proceed. The second posits that behind several versions of a saying or story lies (1) an "original", (2) "tradition," handed on in linear fashion. I place quotation marks around both words, not because I wish to impute to the words meanings other than those commonly assigned to them. Rather, the reason is that, in context here, I do not know what they mean. Indeed, that underscores the difficulty faced throughout this project, the problem of understanding the position framed in rejection of the documentary hypothesis concerning the reading of the canonical compilations of Rabbinic Judaism. We have already addressed the problem of

---

[1] The key is, "original tradition." In treating later documents' versions as "variations" of what is in the earlier documents, I lay not claim to "original tradition." If we place the documents into a different order, the phenomena remain stable, though the explanation will change.

making sense, exactly, of what Schaefer has to say.[2] He does not always make a well-articulated statement of his opinions, which presents difficulties in constructing a lucid argument over a common issue.

Let us take up the second of the three explanations, the claim of an "original" "tradition." By "original" one may mean the original version of a *tradition* later on elaborated. But one may also mean the original *saying*, as the person to whom it is attributed really said it. These represent quite different claims.

By "tradition" people commonly mean a story that has been made up *and handed on in linear succession* over a period of time. Hence if we refer to a "tradition" in the Mishnah or in the Bavli, we are properly understood to claim that a saying or story, made up earlier, has reached the Mishnah or the Bavli through a continuous, linear process of handing on, or tradition. But I am not at all sure that that has ever been demonstrated.

Until we know more than we now do about the origins of materials now found in written form in the documents at hand, we cannot claim that they are *traditions,* in the ordinary sense of the word, without quotation-marks. We can only allege that they are stories or sayings now found in the documents at hand. These stories or sayings may in fact prove to be traditions. How so? They may be shown to have undergone a long process of handing on, from one generation to the next, to being written down in the document at hand. But we cannot impute the status of "tradition" to what is in fact only a story or a saying. We have to prove that the pre-history of the story or saying permits us to classify it in that other category, namely, a story of a saying

---

[2] Volume One, Appendix B, "But What If We Have No Documents? The Problem of Establishing the Text and the Solution of Form-Analysis. The Debate with Arnold Goldberg and Peter Schaefer."

that has been handed on for a long time *prior* to reaching written form in the document at hand.

Providing an example of how the "tradition"-theory of the multiplicity of versions demands attention to the thesis that an "original" "tradition" was handed on. Let me explain why, because the present matter underscores the obscurity of the position of the atomistic theory of the Rabbinic documents. That is, without the claim that a given version stands close(st) to an "original" "tradition," the point that a version falls into the classification of tradition is difficult to discern. That is to say, I do not see that we have gained very much if we claim that people have handed a story or saying on over a period of time, but if we do not *also* claim that one version of that "tradition" leads us closer to the "original" than some other. If alongside the theory of "tradition" we do not find a theory of "originality," perhaps even a claim of historicity made in behalf of the "original" "tradition," then the theory of tradition yields trivial observations.

More important, the theory by itself never becomes susceptible to verification or falsification. We never know when we are wrong, therefore we cannot know that we are right. Making up a long "pre-history" of "tradition" back to an "original" version of the tradition therefore leads us deep into the imagination of the scholar who makes up the theory. It is a study of the contemporary imagination, that alone. But not a few have proposed to fabricate their own accounts of "traditions and their histories," in the course of which they create two and three and four steps in a historical sequence, not one of which is sustained by evidence of any kind!

Accordingly, the allegation of "tradition" ordinarily bears in its wake the claim of "original." The claim of the language at hand is this: *something happened or was said or done that* has been *put into permanent verbal formulas through oral formulation and then oral transmission and handed on for some time.*

Then, if we have a number of versions of a given saying or story, these several versions permit us to speculate, as we move backward from the latest tradition to an earlier one and finally to the first, the "original(s)," about the character and wording even of the "original(s)" of the "tradition." In this framework we may speak of the original tradition (now no longer needing quotation-marks).[3]

In order to deal with the present theory on how to interpret thrice-told tales, I wish to lay out the three versions of sayings assigned to lists of recurrent names, or, as these versions are conventionally called, the "chains of Pharisaic tradition." That is to say, in what follows we took for what is original to closely related, yet distinct, versions of a given list. We shall find that, when we have recovered what appears to be the original version of the tradition, hence, the original tradition, we have not gained very much. We know, in point of fact, little more than that there was, at some point, a list that people used for lining up sets of quite diverse sayings about topics in no way related to one another. That is the upshot of the theory at hand when brought to bear on the sources best suited to receive that theory.

We have three "chains of Pharisaic tradition," listing authorities of the party and assigning to them either moral apothegms, purity decrees, or rulings on a minor aspect of the conduct of the sacrificial cult. These chains follow in probable order.

---

[3] Once more I register, comparing different documents' versions of a story or saying common to them all, in the documentary reading of matters yields an account of how each document renders it version; no claim is made to historicity of one version or another, or even priority of one version over another.

1. To Lay on Hands

> A. Yosé b. Yoezer says [on a Festival-day] not to lay [hands on the offering before it is slaughtered]. Yosé b. Yohanan says to lay [hands].
> B. Joshua b. Perahiah says not to lay [hands]. Nittai the Arbelite says to lay [hands].
> C. Judah b. Tabbai says not to lay [hands]. Simeon b. Shetah says to lay [hands].
> D. Shemaiah says to lay [hands]. Ablation says not to lay [hands].
> E. Hillel and Menahem did not differ, but Menahem went forth, and Shammai entered in.
> F. Shammai says not to lay [hands]. Hillel says to lay [hands].
> G. The former were *Nasis*, and the later fathers of the court ('BWT BYT DYN).
>
> M. Hagigah 2:2

The opinions are in indirect discourse, "says to lay," "says not to lay." Normally "says" is followed by direct discourse. Someone has supplied the subscription (G) that the first-named were *Nasis*, the second-named, heads of the court, considerations which do not figure in the body of the pericope and are irrelevant to its contents. But the pattern is not exact; the first-named *always* should say, *not to lay on hands*. Yet while Yosé b. Yoezer, Joshua b. Perahiah, and Judah b. Tabbai, say *not* to do so, Shemaiah has the wrong opinion for his position in the list. The little group at the end, Hillel-Menahem, then Shammai-Hillel, is also difficult. Hillel-Menahem break the pattern; the lemma is a later insertion. In fact, Hillel should say *not to lay on hands*, since he was supposed to have been *Nasi*. We have already seen a story on this very point, in which Hillel is represented as following Shammai's practice.

Clearly, in the pericope before us Hillel is presumed to be *Nasi*, despite the wrong opinion. But if we drop the interpolation of Hillel-Menahem, we find what the form calls for, merely: Shammai/Hillel: not to lay/lay, and that is surely the authentic reading according to the foregoing pattern. Therefore the original list had Shammai as *Nasi* Hillel as Head of the Court. The switch with Menahem (otherwise unknown) permits placing Hillel first, therefore makes him *Nasi*, according to the subscription, so it becomes Hillel-Menahem-Shammai-Hillel. I cannot guess why Shemaiah's opinion has been reversed.

In Tos. Hag., R. Meir provides a far better solution to the problem of making Hillel *Nasi* in traditions which originally have him as Father of the Court. Tos. Hag. 2:8 led. Lieberman, p. 382-3, tines 40-44) is as follows:

> They differed only on the laying of hands.
>
> "They are five pairs. The three of the first pairs who said not to lay on hands, and the two of the last pairs who said to lay on hands were Nasis. The second ones [mentioned] were heads of the court," so R. Meir.
>
> R. Judah said, "Simeon b. Shetah [was] *Nasi*. Judah b. Tabbai [was] Head of the Court."

Meir thus has five pairs:

1. *Nasi* (not to lay) + head of court (to lay)
2. *Nasi* (not to lay) + head of court (to lay)
3. *Nasi* (not to lay) + head of court (to lay)
4. *Nasi* (to lay) + head of court (not to lay)
5. *Nasi* (to lay) + head of court (not to lay)

Meir's list is the same as M. Hag. 2:2 as far as Shemaiah and Abtalion. He presumably had no mention of Hillel-Menahem, for that would have made Hillel-Shammai a <u>sixth</u> pair. But for the last pair he had a "to lay"-Nasi in first place. Was it Shammai or Hillel? Probably Hillel, since the 'not to lay"/"to lay" antithesis is primary to the tradition, and there seems no strong reason for changing the attributions. So we have two forms of the list, one which can be reconstructed from M. Hag. 2:2, the other from Meir's report. They agree for the first four pairs; for the first, the form behind M. Hag. 2:2 had *Shammai not, Hillel to*; while Meir had *Hillel to, Shammai not*. Meir's tradition can be explained as a secondary development from the other, motivated by the desire of the Hillelites to represent Hillel as head of the government, *Nasi*. What was done to the M. Hag. Tradition by inserting the Hillel-Menahem pair before Shammai and Hillel was done in Meir's tradition by simply reversing the customary order and putting Hillel before Shammai. This is neat and may be correct, but it leaves us with a second, unanswered problem: who was Menahem and how did he get in? The possibility that the last of Meir's pairs may have been, <u>Hillel said to lay, Menahem said no to lay</u>, and there may have been no reference at all to Shammai — which would be understandable if we had an old list from the House of Hillel — cannot be wholly excluded. In that event Meir's list would be older and M. Hag. would represent a post-70 revision, when the Shammaites and the Hillelites, for survival's sake, combined their forces, the terms of the compromise (here) being that Shammai's name would have precedence, but the law would in general follow Hillel.

Judah [b. Ilai] differs only with reference to Judah b. Tabbai and Simeon b. Shetah. The latter, he says, was *Nasi*.

The list of M. Hag., excluding Menahem and the subscription, could not have been shaped later than the time of Meir and Judah, since both refer to it. Judah the Patriarch follows Meir, therefore has a *Nasi* Yosé b. Yoezer, Joshua, Judah, Shemaiah, and Hillel. Since he thought he descended from Hillel and referred to the Bené Bathyrans' giving up their position to Hillel and making him *Nasi*, it was natural to explain matters as he did in the subscription. But the subscription in M. Hag. 2:2 cannot come before Meir-Judah, who do not cite it verbatim. It looks like Judah the Patriarch's summary of Meir's comment.

2. *Decrees*

DTNY':

1. Yosé b. Yoezer of Seredah and Yosé b. Yohanan of Jerusalem decreed (GZP,) [the capacity to receive] uncleanness upon the land of the people and on glassware.
2. Simeon b. Shetah obtained (TQN) a marriage-contract for the wife and decreed (GZR) [the capacity to receive] uncleanness upon metal utensils.
3. Shammai and Hillel decreed (GZR) uncleanness on hands.

B. Shab. 14b

Did not R. Zeira b. Abuna in the name of R. Jeremiah say, "Yosef b. Yoezer of Seredah and Yosé b. Yohanan of Jerusalem decreed uncleanness upon the land of the peoples and upon glass utensils."

R. Yonah [Var.: Yuda said, "Rabbi Judah b. Tabbai."
R. Yosé said, "Rabbi Judah b. Tabbai and Simeon b. Shetah decreed uncleanness on metal utensils.
"Hillel and Shammai decreed concerning the cleanness of the hands."

Y. Shab. 1:4 (= Y. Pes. 1:6, Y. Ket. 8:1 1)

The Babylonian *baraita* is a list of decrees. I assume Simeon b. Shetah's saying has been contaminated by the reference to the ordinance (TQN) about the marriage-contract, missing in y., which is out of place here, for all are decrees and concern uncleanness. Judah b. Tabbai is absent — thus following Judah b. Ilai — and the Palestinian version supplies his name, making the list Yosé + Yosé, Judah + Simeon, and Hillel + Shammai, in all three instances with the *Nasi* first, hence following Meir in Tos. Hag., and (of course) placing Hillel in the Nasi's position. The absence of Joshua b. Perahiah-Nittai the Arbelite is curious. The addition of the places of origin of the Yosé's suggests that this might come after M. Hag., so I should also have expected the inclusion of the absent masters. Perhaps no one had traditions on uncleanness-decrees to attribute to the men. That guess depends upon the presumption that without considerable motivation people did not make up what they did not have. But often they did, as we have observed time and again.

The representation of Shammai as *Nasi*, Hillel second to him, is congruent to the stories of the (temporary) predominance of the House of Shammai and of the (later) rise of the House of Hillel to power. It also explains why the Houses-form nearly always puts the Shammaite House ahead of the Hillelite one, in conformity with the order of M. Hag. The later masters, coming long after the Hillelites hegemony had been well established by the patriarchate, appropriately doctored the earlier materials in the ways that have become evident.

This explanation however takes for granted two allegations of the later Tannaim, first, that Yohanan b. Zakkai took over from Shammai and Hillel and was Hillel's heir; second, that the Yavnean patriarch Gamaliel was descended from Hillel. But the allegation that Yohanan b. Zakkai was Hillel's continuator first occurs in M. Abot, which, as we shall see, comes later than the M. Hag.-chain. No Tannaitic or early Amoraic authority refers to Yohanan b. Zakkai as Hillel's disciple, and it is primarily in the highly developed traditions of ARN that Yohanan's discipleship to Hillel plays a considerable role. The *baraitot* of b. Suk. = b. B.B., which make something of the fact, are apt to be later than, and based upon, Abot, therefore do not change matters.

More strikingly still, in all the Gamaliel-traditions — pertaining either to the first or the second one — we find not the slightest allusion to the familiar relationship between Gamaliel and Hillel. To the contrary, Gamaliel II-materials persistently allege that Simeon b. Gamaliel I followed Shammaite rules, certainly an extraordinary state of affairs for the "grandson" (or great-grandson) of Hillel himself. It is moreover remarkable that Simeon b. Gamaliel and Gamaliel I never occur in he Houses-materials. The heirs of Hillel (Yohanan b. Zakkai, Gamaliel) and the House of Hillel on the face of it have nothing whatever to do with one another. It may therefore be anachronistic to suppose that the Hillelites predominated *because* Yohanan b. Zakkai and Gamaliel II were the greatest student and the great-grandson of Hillel, respectively. It looks as if things were the other way around. They were given a relationship to Hillel because they came to power at a point at which the Hillelite House predominated, and the allegation that both were Hillelites was the condition of their leadership at Yabneh. Strikingly, while that allegation later was important, no one took the trouble to invent stories in which either authority ever cited "my master" or "my father" Hillel.

As I said, no named authority from Hillel to Yabneh ever is represented as quoting Hillel. But the predominance of Hillelites at Yabneh is very well attested and may be regarded as an axiom. Nothing in the Tannaitic stratum of Yohanan b. Zakkai-materials places him into relationship with either the House of Shammai or the House of Hillel. Yohanan cites "my teachers" back to Moses, but never mentions Hillel (M. Yad. 4:3). This seems to me probative that the circles of Yohanan's immediate disciples had no traditions relating Yohanan to Hillel. Similarly, Gamaliel II repeatedly is given references to "the house of father," meaning Simeon b. Gamaliel 1, but none to Hillel, directly or inferentially.

3. Moral Apothegms

1. A. Moses received the Torah from Sinai and handed it on to Joshua, Joshua to the Elders, the Elders to the Prophets; and the Prophets handed it on to the men of the Great Assembly (KNST).
   B. They said three things, "Be deliberate in judgment, raise up many disciples, and make a fence around the Torah."
2. Simeon the Just was of the remnants of the Great Assembly. He used to say, "On three things the world stands: on the Torah, on the [Temple-] service, and on deeds of loving kindness."
3. Antigens of Sokho received from Simeon the Just. He used to say, "Be not like slaves that minister to the master for the sake of receiving a reward, but be like slaves that minister to the master not for the sake of receiving a reward; and let the fear of heaven be upon you."
4. Yosé b. Yoezer of Seredah and Yosé b. Yohanan of Jerusalem received from *them* [*sic*].
   Yosé b. Yoezer says, "Let your house be a meeting-house for the Sages, and sit amid the dust of their feet, and thirstily drink in their words."
5. A. Yosé b. Yohanan of Jerusalem says, "Let your house be opened wide; and let the needy be members of your house; and do not talk much with a woman."
   B. They said this of a man's own wife: how much more of his fellow's wife.' Hence the Sages have said, "He that talks much with women brings evil upon himself, and neglects the study of the Law, and at the end he inherits Gehenna."
6. Joshua b. Perahiah and Nittai the Arbelite received from them.
   Joshua b. Perahiah says, "Make for yourself a master (RB), and get a fellow (HBR) [-disciple]; and judge any man with the balance in his favor."
7. Nittai the Arbelite says, "Keep far from an evil neighbor, and do not consort with a wicked neighbor, and do not despair of retribution."

8. Judah b. Tabbai and Simeon b. Shetah received from them. Judah b. Tabbai says, "Make not yourself like them that would influence the judges; and when the suitors stand before you, let them be in your eyes as wicked men; and when they have departed from before you, let them be in your eyes as innocent, as soon as they have accepted the judgment."
9. Simeon b. Shetah says, "Abundantly examine the witnesses; and be cautious in your words, lest from them they learn to swear falsely."
10. Shemaiah and Abtalion received from them. Shemaiah says, "Love work; and hate mastery (RBNWT), and seek not acquaintance with the ruling power (RSWT)."
11. Abtalion says, "Sages, give heed to your words, lest you incur the penalty of exile, and be exulted to a place of evil waters, and the disciples that come after you drink and die, and the name of Heaven be profaned."
12. Hillel and Shammai received from them.
    Hillel says, "Be of the disciples of Aaron, loving peace, and pursuing peace, loving mankind, and bringing them near to the Torah."
13. He used to say, *"A name made great is a name destroyed, and he that increases not decreases, and he that learns not is worthy of death, and he that makes worldly use of the crown perishes."*
14. He used to say, "If I am not for myself who is for me? And being for mine own self, what am I? And if not now, when?"
15. Shammai says, "Make your [study of] Torah [a] fixed [habit]. say little and do much. And receive all men with a cheerful countenance."
16. Rabban Gamaliel says, "Make for yourself a master (RB) [=Joshua b. Perahiah's saying, above and keep distant from doubt; and do not tithe by guesswork."
17. Simeon his son says, "All my days I have grown up among the sages, and I have found nothing better for the person (GWP) than silence; and the expounding is not the principle, but the doing; and he that multiplies words occasions sin."
18. Rabban Simeon b. Gamaliel says, "On three things the world stands: on truth, on judgment, and on peace, as it is written, *Execute the judgment of truth and peace* (Zech. 8:16)."

M. Abot 1:1-18

The form from no. 4 to no. 12 is fixed: the names of the two who received the Torah from the foregoing, then apophthegm assigned to each, in order. The apophthegm are always triplicates; each *says* ('WMR) three things.

The list is heavily glossed. In no. 5, for example, we are given a *qal vehomer*, which then produces a saying of the sages. In no. 8, *as soon as they have accepted* makes specific what has already been presupposed by *when they have departed*. Its purpose is to rule out the possible objection, "What if they have not accepted the judgment?" — a typical sort of Talmudic quibble. Abtalion's saying is not a triplicate, but the three evil consequences make up for the absence of three separate sayings. No. 3 is expanded by the affirmative revision and the gloss, thus three. Nos. 13 and 14 are added to Hillel's saying, not a gloss but a considerable interpolation of materials, some in Aramaic, occurring elsewhere. Now it is *used to say* (HYH 'WMR) as in nos. 2- 3.

Strikingly, with Hillel and Shammai the pairs cease. Also Gamaliel, standing alone, is not said to "receive" from Hillel/Shammai, nor Simeon from Gamaliel. Gamaliel's saying follows the earlier form. Simeon's does not, for it is glossed by *all my days ... I* have found, making an apophthegm, "There is naught better" into an autobiographical comment. But the rest of the saying conforms to the earlier pattern. Then in no. 18, Simeon *his son* becomes *Rabban* Simeon b. *Gamaliel* and is given a statement incongruent to the foregoing form. That saying is a counterpart of Simeon the Just's, though the specification of the "three things" changes, and is glossed with a Scriptural proof-text. What is striking is the persistence of the "three things" form in the sayings that come in-between.

Simeon the Just's saying is parallel to Simeon b. Gamaliel's, which clearly represents a post-I 35 revision of no. 2: the Torah now is truth, a philosophizing tendency; the temple service is now replaced by justice; and deeds of loving kindness are replaced by peace. That this conclusion balances no. 2, and not the saying in no. 1, strongly suggests that no. 2 was originally the first saying in the list, and that the saying in no. 1 is a later addition, putting at the head of the whole list the fundamental principles of the Rabbinic academy as a social form.

But the fact that no. 18 was added to balance no. 2 raises the problem about no. 2 itself: Was it an integral part of the list? We saw that the fixed form characteristic of the list ("A + B received from them; A said [three sayings]; B said [three sayings]") begins only with no. 4. Thus on formal grounds there are strong reasons for thinking that nos. 2 and 3 were secondary accretions, and since the Rabbinic traditions had no substantial legal materials from Simeon the Just and Antigens — indeed, ignored Antigens and treated Simeon primarily through legends — the case is clear. The original list began just as the Rabbinic legal tradition began: with the two Yosé's. The appeal to Simeon the Just, perhaps known from Ben Sira, was motivated by the desire to attach this legal tradition to the last great member of the legitimate Jerusalem priesthood before its fall. Simeon's function is therefore the same as that of Moses etc., — he is part of the biblical (and Ben Sira) stemma of the tradition of the law. Antigens as put in to bridge the temporal gap between Simeon and the Yosé's — a whole century! Whence did they get him? We have no idea.

Another mystery is the beginning of no. 4: the two Yosé's received from *them*, when the solitary Antigens has preceded them. This probably is confirmation of our conjecture that Simeon and Antigens have been added. The original referent of *them* will have been "the men of the great synagogue" — a single mythologumenon which bridged the gap from the prophets to the Pharisees. The original list was thus 1A, 4, 5A, 6, 7, 8, 9, 10, 11, 12, and 15. This elegant structure was broken to insert Simeon and thus claim

In Search of the "Original" "Tradition" 233

connection with the last of the legitimate priesthood, and also to make the representation that the priesthood put the law ahead of the Temple service.

After no. 18, M. Abot 2 begins with the yet later additions from the patriarch's circle, Rabbi, and Rabban Gamaliel III (M. Abot 2:1, 2:2ff), and then a collection of sayings of Hillel, purported ancestor of the patriarchal house, and then in Abot 2:8 comes an earlier addition to the list: Rabban Yohanan b. Zakkai received [the Torah] from Hillel and Shammai. This, which does have the form of the earlier entries, clearly is what has been displaced by the intervening (inserted) patriarchal material. The pre-70 list was therefore expanded by his pupils before it was taken over by the patriarchate. From the material following M. Abot. 2:8 (Yohanan's pupils and their sayings) we can see how it was developed in his school, by contrast to the patriarchal development. The Mishnah combines the two traditions.

The names on the lists compare as follows:

M. Hag.2:2	B. Shab. 14b = y. Shab. 1:4	M. Abot 1:1 1-18
		Moses
		Joshua
		Judah b. Tabbai
		Simeon b. Shetah
		Elders
		Prophets
		Men of the Great Synagogue
		Simeon the Just
		Antigens of Sokho

Yosé b. Yoezer	Yosé b. Yohanan of Jerusalem	Yosé b. Yoezer *of Seredah*
Yosé b. Yohanan	Yosé b. Yoezer *of Seredah*	Yosé b. Yohanan of Jerusalem

234 *The Peripatetic Saying*

Joshua b. Perahiah Nittai the Arbelite		Joshua b. Perahiah Nittai the Arbelite
Judah b. Tabbai Simeon b. Shetah	[y.: Judah b. Tabbai and] Simeon b. Shetah	Judah b. Tabbai Simeon b. Shetah
Shemaiah Abtalion		Shemaiah Abtalion
Hillel-Menahem Shammai-Hillel	Shammai Hillel [y.: Hillel and Shammai]	Hillel Shammai
	----------------------	
		Gamaliel [omits: received] Simeon b. Gamaliel [omits: received]

		[2:8: Yohanan b. Zakkai *received* from Hillel and Shammai]

The second names in the first two pairs, Yosé b. Yohanan and Nittai the Arbelite, elsewhere are given no independent sayings whatever. They occur only in the context of the first-mentioned names, Yosé b. Yoezer and Joshua b. Perahiah. Further, Shemaiah and Abtalion are rarely separated at all, but, except in Abot, normally appear as a pair, with remarkably few independent lemmas attributed to either the one or the other. They are given common ancestry. The first two Yosé's are not supplied with places of origin in M. Hag.

M. Abot corresponds to M. Hag. where the two coincide, except in the additions of the places of origin of Yosé's, and in the reversal of the order to Hillel-Shammai, making Hillel *Nasi;* the subscription of M. Hag. serves the same purpose. The Babylonian version of the cleanness-decree lists does not conform.

The names tacked on to the Abot-list obviously serve to complete the story back to Moses, on the one side, and to A.D. 170, on the other. Gamaliel is made the heir of Hillel's Torah. The Simeon mentioned in the *baraita* in b. Shah. 15a is ignored; perhaps the compiler of the Abot-list did not know that *baraita*.

Since no extant materials have either Simeon b. Gamaliel or Gamaliel I referring to Hillel, we may suppose that the claim of Hillel as an ancestor by the patriarchate came some time after the destruction of the Temple. My guess is that it was first alleged quite a long time later one. Judah the Patriarch's circle probably is responsible for the additions of Gamaliel and Simeon b. Gamaliel to the Abot list. Since that same circle also produced the genealogy linking Hillel to David — presumably because the Babylonian exilarch did the same - the link between Gamaliel I and Hillel may have come some time before Judah the Patriarch, who is the first patriarch to refer to Hillel as his ancestor. The link is to be traced to the point at which the patriarchate made peace with the growing predominance of the Hillelite House, some time soon after the destruction of the Temple. Before then the Shammaites apparently predominated within Pharisaism, and Simeon b. Gamaliel probably was one of them, which accounts for the suppression of virtually all of his legal traditions. The first point at which Hillelite claim would have served the patriarchate therefore was the time of Gamaliel 11. But, since Gamaliel 11 is represented as following Shammaite law (e.g. b. Yeb. 15b), makes no reference to Hillel, plays no role in the Hillel-pericopae or in Hillel's House's materials, as I said, and tells how his father Simeon followed Shammaite rules, the Hillelite ancestry for the patriarchate founded by Gamaliel II may not have been established until ca. 150, by which time it seems to be settled. That is the point at which Meir had to revise the form of the earlier list to make Hillel *Nasi*.

Yosé b. Halafta, Meir's contemporary, knew nothing about b. Shab. 14b, and said the decree about the uncleanness of glassware and the land of the people in fact was in force (with no authority given) eighty years before the destruction of the Temple. The masters certainly recognized that the two Yosé's long antedated Hillel and Shammai. Therefore Yosé b. Halafta's tradition was separate from, and contradicted, b. Shab. He presumably knew no other. It therefore may be that that baraita comes well after ca. 150, as the names of Palestinian Talmud's authorities suggest.

4. *Conclusion*

The "original" "tradition" consisted of the following names:

1. Yosé b. Yoezer
2. Yosé b. Yohanan
3. Joshua b. Perahiah
4. Nittai the Arbelite
5. Judah b. Tabai
6. Simeon b. Shetah
7. Shemaiah
   +
8. Abtalion
9. Shammai
10. Hillel
11. Yohanan b. Zakkai
12. Yohanan's disciples
    Replaced by
13. Gamaliel
14. Simeon b. Gamaliel

Of the foregoing, nos. 2 and 4 exist in the traditions only in association with nos. 1 and 3, nos. 7 and 8 are always connected. As we shall see, furthermore, the relationships between nos. 5 and 6 are extremely complex, and it looks as if separate traditions of the two masters may have been put together for a *post facto* explanation of the union of two originally unrelated circles of disciples. To revert to the point at which we began, if we now have the "original" "tradition," it surely does not amount to much. More important, the theory of the "original" "tradition" proves irrelevant to most of the data at hand. So if the theory is right, then, so what? And the answer is, so nothing.

And nothing has come to mind in the fifteen years since I wrote that sentence that changes that judgment.

Chapter Fifteen

INCREMENTAL HISTORY:

"WHEN HE WAS A STUDENT ... AND WHEN HE GREW UP..."

Sages of ancient times recognized that sayings and stories appeared in diverse versions. They too proposed explanations of how a given saying or story could come down in more than a single statement. The principal approach to the question posited that each detail represented a different stage in the history of the story, or of the life of its hero in particular, with one version characteristic of one such stage, and another version attesting to a different, and later one. So the successive versions of a saying or story supply a kind of incremental history. How so? Each version tells something about concrete events and real lives (biographies) that earlier versions did not reveal.

The classic Talmudic expression of the incremental theory takes up a passage of the Mishnah in which Rabban Yohanan ben Zakkai is called merely "Ben Zakkai:"

> The precedent is as follows: Ben Zakkai examined a witness as to the character of the stalks of figs [under which an incident now subject to court procedure was alleged to have taken place].
> Mishnah Sanhedrin 5:2B

As we shall now see, at paragraph N in the following talmudic analysis, exactly the same story is reported, on Tannaite authority. Now *Rabban Yohanan* ben Zakkai is alleged to have made exactly the same ruling, in exactly the same case. The item is worded in the same way except for the more fitting title. Then, at P-Q, the two versions are readily explained as facts of history. The one of Ben Zakkai was framed when he was a mere disciple. When, later on, he had become a recognized sage, the story was told to take account of that fact. So the theory I call "incremental history" is simple: *each story related to, because it derives from, historical moments in a linear progression.* The Talmudic passage is as follows:

IX
A. Who is this "Ben Zakkai"?
B. If we should proposed that it is R. Yohanan ben Zakkai, did he ever sit in a Sanhedrin [that tried a murder case]?
C. And has it not been taught on Tannaite authority:
D. The lifetime of R. Yohanan ben Zakkai was a hundred and twenty years. For forty years he engaged in trade, for forty years he studied [Torah], and for forty years he taught.
E. And it has been taught on Tannaite authority: Forty years before the destruction of the Temple the Sanhedrin went into exile and conducted its sessions in Hanut.
F. And said R. Isaac bar Abodimi, "That is to say that the Sanhedrin did not judge cases involving penalties."
G. Do you think it was cases involving penalties? [Such cases were not limited to the Sanhedrin but could be tried anywhere in the Land of Israel.]
H. Rather, the Sanhedrin did not try capital cases.
I. And we have learned in the Mishnah:
J. After *the destruction of the house of the sanctuary, Rabban Yohanan b. Zakkai ordained ...* [*M. R.H. 4:1*]. [So the final forty years encompassed the period after the destruction of the Temple, and Yohanan could not, therefore, have served on a Sanhedrin that tried capital cases.]
K. Accordingly, at hand is some other Ben Zakkai [than Yohanan b. Zakkai].
L. That conclusion, moreover, is reasonable, for if you think that it is *Rabban Yohanan* ben Zakkai, would Rabbi [in the Mishnah-passage] have called him merely, "Ben Zakkai"? [Not very likely.]
M. And lo, it has been taught on Tannaite authority:
N. There is the precedent that Rabban Yohanan ben Zakkai conducted an interrogation about the stalks on the figs [so surely this is the same figure as at M. 5:2B].

Incremental History 241

O. But [at the time at which the incident took place, capital cases were tried by the Sanhedrin and] he was a disciple in session before his master. He said something, and the others found his reasoning persuasive, [41B] so they adopted [the ruling] in his name.

P. When he was studying Torah, therefore, he was called Ben Zakkai, as a disciple in session before his master, but when he [later on] taught, he was called Rabban Yohanan ben Zakkai.

Q. When, therefore, he is referred to as Ben Zakkai, it is on account of his being a beginning [student] and when he is called Rabban Yohanan b. Zakkai, it is on account of his status later on.

The relevance of the Talmudic passage is simple, as I shall now explain. Here we find a model for the incremental history that modern and contemporary historians have produced: this version derives from a prior period, when..., and the other version derives from a later period, by which time.... This they do entirely out of their heads, fabricating a theory for the occasion, without a trace of evidence to sustain their concoctions.

Modernist scholars have claimed to explain diverse versions of a single saying or story by much the same thesis as we see before us. That is to say, they alleged that they know why a given detail is added here, dropped there, changed in the third place, built up and augmented in the fourth, and on and on. Accordingly, the modern, critical scholars accomplish a kind of incremental history. This is the history of what happened to account for changes in versions of a story, based on a theory of what *might* have impelled an author to add or revise a given detail. Indeed, practitioners of the incremental approach have not hesitated to declare that they know an entire history for which the text at hand supplies no evidence whatsoever. They then refer to this (entirely undocumented) history in order to explain shifts and changes in versions of a story. Lest readers think I invent, I give a concrete case.

The single best example of the fantasy at hand is supplied by David J. Halperin, *The Merkabah in Rabbinic*

Literature (New Haven, 1980: American Oriental Series 62). Halperin refers to the Merkabah-materials, with which we made our acquaintance in Chapter One. He posits that, prior to the first written version there was an entire cycle of such stories ("presumably oral"!). He knows that one of these stories had a narrative framework, then lost a miraculous element, then got that miracle reinserted later on. This literary history, claiming to explain shifts and changes in the sequence of stories we saw earlier, derives from not a shred of evidence of any kind. There is *no* version of these stories at all. The author just made it up and wrote it down, then the American Oriental Society printed it as "scholarship." [In the concluding footnote to Appendix One, I point to more evidence of what "scholarship" consists of in the hands of the Orientalists at AOS — little more than hack-politics.] True, as we shall note, Halperin introduces appropriate qualifications and caveats. But he pays little attention to them; they are mainly formalities. Here is how he states his conclusions (pp. 138-9):

> 1. I postulate the following development for the *Merkabah* tradition involving R. Johanan b. Zakkai: (1) A cycle of *Merkabah* stories, presumably oral, recounted the miracles that accompanied the expositions of one or another of R. Johanan's disciples; the stories of this cycle contained little beside the miracles. (This stage is purely hypothetical, and is not attested by any literary source.) (2) One of these stories, which involved R. Eleazar b. Arakh, was given a narrative framework, which suggested that R. Eleazar exemplified the "scholar" of M. Hag. 2:1 (*Mek. Rashbi*). (3) The miraculous element was "censored" from the story of R. Eleazar, possibly by the compiler of the mystical collection (Tosefta). (4) Miraculous details were reinserted, and stories of other disciples added, on the basis of the old *Merkabah* stories (PT, BT)....
> 3. If my hypothesis is correct, the Merkabah tradition is rooted in a cycle of miraculous legends. Some historical reality may hide behind these legends, but it is nearly inaccessible. Instead of

trying to recover it, we should focus on what the legends can teach us about (*ma'aseh*) *Merkabah* and the image of those reported to have been expert in it.

Halperin's exposition of his own theories omits all reference to whatever he holds as a fundamental thesis on the character of the literature and its formation, if any. Yet even on the surface, it is clear, he proposes to make up explanations for diverse versions of the Merkabah-story. Each detail has its day. None is spared the ravages of Halperin's imaginative reconstruction of its individual life-history. Everything means something somewhere — and to Halperin it does not matter where. It follows that the theory of "incremental history," assigning a particular event or motive or other explanation for each change in a story as it moves from document to document finds exemplification in Halperin's treatment of the Merkabah-story.

A systematic picture of what Halperin has done and why it is founded on false premises (or on no premises other than an undisciplined imagination) derives from William Scott Green's review of Halperin's book. In his review (*Second Century*, 1983, 3:113-115) Green observes:

> For reasons never specified, Halperin tends to construe each literary unit, each manuscript variant, and each textual version as a discrete historical moment. he then constructs his history by arranging these textual moments into chronological sequence. By adopting this strategy, Halperin forces himself into the grueling exercise of determining the relative dates of decontextualized literary segments. Much is at stake in these demonstrations; the very possibility of Halperin's history depends on their rigor and cogency. Halperin uses a wide range of criteria to date his materials, and he sometimes deploys these inconsistently. That is, he established his chronologies on the basis of the differences among versions of a passage. But the variables he deems decisive are not systematically applied. Rather, they seem to shift from case to case. This sort of unevenness undermines Halperin's demonstrations of chronology and makes at least some of them appear arbitrary. The problems of

particular chronologies aside, Halperin's method limits the kind of history of Rabbinic, *Merkabah* speculation he can write. His catenae of textual events result in schematic accounts that flip and flop, sparse chronicles of unexpected reversals and inversions in which discrete passages undergo marked, sometimes radical shifts of meaning. He argues, for instance, that the Mishnaic rule that the *Merkabah* may not be expounded "by an individual [variant: *to* an individual], unless he is a scholar, understanding on his own" (M. Hagigah 2:1) had three distinct meanings before the time of Tosefta's redaction (ca. A.D. 250). When the passage circulated independently, it allowed the sage, but not the disciple, "to undertake on his own an exegesis of Ezekiel's vision" (p. 35). When it was redacted into the Mishnah and incorporated into a list of other biblical passages whose exposition is restricted, "the effect was to reverse the other biblical passages whose exposition is restricted, "the effect was to reverse the meaning of the Merkabah ruling; solitary study of the Merkabah was no longer the object of the restriction, but a concession granted to certain exceptional individuals" (p. 36). Still later, the meaning of the rule was changed again to make it "refer to instruction" (p. 36), an alteration reflected in the variant reading. This final meaning is apparent in a story about Yohanan b. Zakkai and Eleazar b. Arakh at T. Hagigah 2:1, which, ironically, preserves the earliest version of the Mishnaic rule.

This kind of lean and linear history disappoints because it does not account for the changes it describes. Even if Halperin's textual sequences are correct, they leave too much unexplained. For instance, to whom within Rabbinism were these changes important? Did the different meanings supersede one another or exist simultaneously? Are these changes literary, or do they reflect deeper theological, religious, and social diversions within Rabbinism? Are such changes, particularly the reversal of meaning, accidental or deliberate, the result of misunderstanding or of manipulation? Without some theory of Rabbinic culture and society, of textual transmission and tradition, and of literary tendencies, Halperin's textual sequences lead nowhere. They are merely chronologies masquerading as history.

[Halperin went on to do more compelling scholarship. This was his early work indeed.] In singling

Halperin out, my intent is only to show what people are doing now. I do not want anyone to suppose that I have taken a particularly weak example of an otherwise vital theory. On the contrary, Halperin presents us with as capable an exercise of the incremental-historical theory as is in print — alas! For it seems he is talking to himself, in the privacy of his study. He clearly is not engaging in reasoned arguments with the generality of interested participants in the inquiry. Only by that theory can I explain how anyone can make up a "cycle" of Merkabah-stories ("presumably oral"), tell us what was in them, then what was removed from them — and only then relate the whole to the actual sources at hand. The theory that details in successive versions of a saying or story bears historical meanings deserves better than it has gotten to date.

The approach that seeks to account for shifts and changes by reference to the interests of later authors, tradents, and redactors, remains entirely open. Indeed, in due course we may took forward to the rehabilitation of the theory at hand. My criticism, like Green's, is that, so far as Halperin exemplifies the theory, he provides yet another instance of the dreary approach of made-up explanations, never subjected to tests of falsification or validation. That approach, suitable for talmudic exegesis, does not serve for historical and literary work in our day. While both the theory that "he often used to say..." and the claim that there is an "original" "tradition," promise little for the future, the one at hand awaits rigorous attention.

IV

TOWARD A GENERAL THEORY OF THE RABBINICAL LITERATURE: THE DOCUMENTARY PICTURE OF THE FORMATIVE AGE

Chapter Sixteen

A Documentary-Historical Theory

The Goldberg-Schaefer-Becker school takes a position of extreme, academic nihilism: no history, no Judaism, only random occurrences of we know not what. The members of the German school of the study of Judaism offer no constructive theory of how they think the Rabbinic literature took shape, no account of the nature of the writing down of stories and sayings, the conglomeration of compositions into composites, the formation of documents — even those represented by the singleton-manuscripts of this or of that that the Goldberg-Schaefer-Becker school conceives to constitutes the literary record of that (to them, fissiparous) Judaism. By contrast, I do set forth a theory, based on the facts of literary analysis of compilations (my "documents") and their indicative traits, of the way in which the writing before us reached the form in which we now know it.

Let us now revert to the results of our comparison of the successive documents' versions of sayings and stories. These show the persistence of a stable tradition on what was said or done, a tradition that varies in details but preserves the main lines of a consistent account of matters. The reader will not find surprising the allegation that the authors of later documents in the canon of Judaism in a fairly consistent way fill holes in stories and sayings received from earlier ones. When, therefore, we wish to explain why details are added or dropped, the first appeal will carry us to the matter of rhetoric. We ask whether we are able to explain why a detail makes a first appearance by asking about the relative relationship of the document in which it surfaces to other documents in which it is absent. If we can show that the document bearing the fresh fact comes later in the formation of the canon than the one lacking it, we may appeal first of all to the claim that the later authors' sense of rhetoric, their larger aesthetic theory, precipitated their making up and including that detail. That hypothesis wilt gain substantial credibility if we can show that, in general, authors of the document at hand did pretty much the same thing with whatever they received.

Yet the theory at hand, which I call the documentary hypothesis, marks the beginning, not the ending, of the matter. For aesthetics, including rhetoric, in the system at hand brings to expression the fundamental and generative character of the system as a whole. Aesthetics constitutes a cultural indicator and relates in a contingent way to the culture — in this case, the textual community — at hand. To invoke a theory of aesthetics by itself as explanation of why rhetoric takes one form rather than some other simply is to beg the question. Why so? Because in a truly integrated community of culture, such as the canon of Judaism attests to the sages of late antiquity, each detail addresses the whole. Each one in some small way expresses the character of the entire system. The sages' own convictions about the utter harmony of the hole, the congruity of law to theology, of meal-time to bed-time and of conduct in the toilet to behavior in the synagogue, reinforce the claim at hand. Indeed these commonplace allegations bring it to explicit expression. It must follow that, when we appeal to a rhetorical explanation for the facts at hand and therefore treat the matter as an essentially literary problem, we have only succeeded in restating the question, not resolving it. Aesthetics, including rhetoric, adds up to little more than making something out of interesting arrangements of words into patterns. By itself it constitutes a formalist inquiry into formalism, a quest for trivial explanations of small things.

The fact that later sages rewrote in their own way what earlier sages had handed on to them looms as an enormous presence in the interpretation of the formative age of Judaism. As I said at the end of Chapter One and underscore in Appendix Two of this edition, the sages at hand surely do not conform to the definition of traditionalism ordinarily imputed to their culture. For white they faithfully handed on what they had received, it never was never intact, if in their view it always was unimpaired. Why so? Because they saw for themselves a role in the process of formation of what would be "the tradition." That role proved inventive, therefore creative. It must follow that the facts of rhetorical preference and the configuration of a larger sense of aesthetics in important ways convey definitive traits of the system at hand. But describing and analyzing those traits, interpreting them in context for what they reveal about the larger system — these labors only now begin.

What I have done here is to dismiss some silly notions and to ask in an urgent way for the reconsideration of the significance of facts hitherto explained away and never explained. The task accomplished here proved pressing because the old modes of thought — "He often used to say..." "When he was a student... and when he grew up..." not to mention the theory of an "original" "tradition" — continue to flourish, and not only in stagnant backwaters of the eastern Mediterranean. Not only so, but exaggerating the diversity of variant readings of parallel versions of stories and sayings, or variant manuscript readings, yields no insight whatsoever. I have now shown at some length how vastly the Goldberg-Schaefer-Becker school overstates the matter. That that school collects and arranges variant MS *readings without a word of comment or interpretation* underscores the nihilism that characterizes them.

Still more ominous, the theory of a linear development of a single "tradition," leading to the whole and harmonious completion in the Bavli, itself obscures far more than it illuminates. For the documents at hand seen one by one exhibit only limited harmony and cogency. It must follow that the documents first have to testify to their own context and setting. Only then can they tell us anything about the relationships between each of them and the next and among them all. To such an exercise the theory of a single and linear movement from one place to the next presents a barrier. To the contrary, I at the outset insisted that the Bavli stands at the end only to make a simple point. it is that the *beginning* of all inquiry into the meanings of the diversity of versions of a given saying or story carries us to traits of documents, what they generally do, how they ordinarily hand on what they have received. Aesthetic theory communicates inner concerns, points of tension, generative and definitive characteristics, of the authors of the documents, who write in one way, not in another. In their aesthetic choices, these authors express the deepest convictions of their system — their culture, their textual community and its context. So, as I cannot overemphasize, aesthetics marks the beginning. But aesthetics does supply an indicator and present a starting-point.

To move forward, the theory I have called "incremental history" fails not because it lacks merit, but because it lacks successful exemplars. If we are to move on, the route must carry us not from one detail to the next, but to a height affording a perspective overall. Once we have a theory of how to proceed and a thesis worth testing, then, but only then, we move to the details, from large to small, in proper and proportionate succession. Beginning from the outside and systematically working our way within, we first seek large and definitive traits. These then will tell us what to discern in the small field of an individual story.

The incremental-historical theory then undergoes an appropriately rigorous exercise of falsification. How so? We must ask whether details conform to the main point. The alternative is that we make things up as we go along, text by text and detail by detail like Halperin. But a useful theory will prove its worth if we are able to explain and even predict the course of matters in a consistent and cogent way. The ultimately useless result of Halperin's work, surveyed just now, derives not from the rather private and subjective character of the results, his meditations on this and that. Even though it is easy to dismiss as mere subjectivity Halperin's power of making up version after version of a tradition no one has ever seen, then appealing to hypothetical version A to explain what is lost in imaginary version C, that is not the main point. It is the methodological inconsistency, the made-up character of the whole approach, not merely the manufactured quality of the individual parts that requires us to dismiss Halperin's work as hopeless. A useful and plausible theory works wholesale, not retail. It cannot come tailor-made but has to come right off the plain pipe rack, so to speak. Halperin's exemplification of all that can go wrong with the incremental theory therefore should not lead to the dismissal of the theory. What we have to do is more thoughtfully consider how to proceed from the documentary facts, awaiting discovery, to the explanation of the documents' preferences, overall, and then *also* to details of a given story (such as the Merkabah-one), in proper sequence.

Fifteen years ago I attempted such a program in *Development of a Legend. Studies on the Traditions Concerning Yohanan ben Zakkai*' (Leiden, 1970: E. J. Brill). What I proposed to do was explain why a story appeared with one set of details in one document, and with a different set of details in another. I used two methods. First, I compared versions of the same story as they appeared in successive texts. Second, I asked about the larger tendencies of the framers of the texts, viewed one by one. So the two approaches I advocate here to the problem of sorting out and making sense of diverse versions of a saying or a story — documentary, then incremental-historical — find ample illustration in *Development of a Legend*. The main point is that I appealed to the then-established facts that one document came from one school among the Talmudic sages, another and parallel document from a different school. I took the view that traits (at that time) pretty well known to characterize one school might also guide me to explain why that same school would tell a story in one way and not in some other. This I did for the entire corpus of sayings and stories concerning Yohanan ben Zakkai.

The book failed for a host of reasons. In that naive period of my life, I assumed books get read; authors' theories get taken up. I did not know that people could dismiss a book by looking for some minor detail and determining that they did not agree with it (hence: an error), or that the fact was a fact but had already been seen to be a fact before a claim made without reference to the service said fact had earlier contributed to some other book (hence: ho-hum). The one serious review the book got — by Morton Smith *in Conservative Judaism*, 1971 — recognized its contribution to the study of Yohanan ben Zakkai, but did not take up the larger methodological theory I had tried to define. The fault lay not with the audience but with the author. In that book I never made explicit the methodological experiment I proposed to carry out. I left matters inarticulate and inchoate. My guilt lay, I admit, in the assumption that things were ineffably obvious. What came to me as self-evident and beyond need for articulation I imagined would prove equally commonplace to everyone else in the world. It has taken me many years to accept the fact that the world is not made up of mind-readers, any more than, in the field in which I work, it is made up of book-readers. It is what it is. if it is to be made better, the work will have to be done one day at a time, and on one book at a time.

Yet these lessons of age, requiring me now to restate in clear and simple terms things I feared I said in an all-too-obvious way fifteen years ago, do not lead me to dismiss the project. On the contrary, *Development of a Legend* and the books that carried forward its basic inquiry, *Rabbinic Traditions about the Pharisees* before 70 and *Eliezer ben Hyrcanus. The Tradition and the Man*, did invoke the two modes I advocate here for explaining why sayings and stories change as they move. That is to say, I did ask systematically whether the authors of a document made changes in received sayings and stories for reasons characteristic of their document as a whole, that is the documentary theory. And I did ask systematically what we learn about the historical context and viewpoint of the authors of a document that revealed in received sayings and stories that is, the incremental-history-theory.

Let me therefore provide a reprise of how I originally exemplified these two quite distinct approaches to our problem, and then explain what I think is wrong, and remains right, with each of them.

First let me show how one might ask about the tendencies of documents' authors. Specifically will what is established overall allow us to account for shifts and changes in versions of discrete sayings and stories? For this purpose we deal with two collections of scriptural exegeses on the book of Exodus, one attributed to the school of Ishmael, the other to the school of Aqiba. I reproduce both passages, together with my discussion of them, as they originally appeared in *Development of a Legend*. In what follows as a comment, I.i.2 refers to Ishmael's version, I.ii.1 to Aqiba's. That is, the former derives from the Mekhilta of R. Ishmael, the latter from the Mekhilta of R. Simeon b. Yohai, who is supposed to have been a disciple of the school of Aqiba. With these facts in hand, the passages will be reasonably accessible.

2 (a) For If *Thou Lift Up Thy Sword upon it* (Ex. 20:25). In this connection R. Simon b. Eleazar used to say, "The altar is made to prolong the years of man and iron is made to shorten the years of man. It is riot right for that which shortens life to be lifted up against that which prolongs life."

(b) R. Yohanan b. Zakkai says, "Behold it says: *Thou shalt build... of whole stones* (Deut. 27:6). They are to be stones that establish peace.

(c) "Now, by using the method of *qal vehomer*, you reason: The stones for the altar do not see nor hear nor speak. Yet because they serve to establish peace between Israel and their Father in heaven, the Holy One, blessed by he, said, *Thou shalt lift up no iron tool upon them* (ibid., v.5). How much the more then should he who establishes peace between man and his fellow-man, between husband and wife, between city and city, between nation and nation, between family and family, between government and government, be protected so that no harm should come to him."

(Mekhilta of R. Ishmael, Bahodesh 11, ed. and trans. J. Lauterbach, 11, p. 290)

On this passage I commented:

I.ii.1, the Aqiban version given presently, substitutes sons of Torah for *peacemakers* who escape punishment; it omits the *altar*, and the sword *shortens life* becomes the sword *as a sign of punishment*. The *altar* does not prolong life but *atones* for Israel. I.ii.1 thus shows what the Aqiban party made of this Midrash, which was none too palatable to them. The essential element was the exegesis on whole stones/peace. The function of the altar was that of making peace. Therefore peace-makers in this world perform the function of the altar — and more so! This is Yohanan's essential idea; the functions performed by the Temple and its instruments can be replaced by human virtues. So the *qal vehomer* preserved in the Ishmaelean tradition 1.1.2 and I.ii.5 is also originally from Yohanan, and the saying of Simeon b. Eleazar in I.i.2 shows an early development of Yohanan's idea in its original spirit: war is bad, peace is good. The Aqibans therefore omitted the exegesis of peace/whole stones; revised the *qal vehomer* to make the essential virtue *not* peace-making but study of the Torah; revised Simeon's saying to make both the sword and the altar symbols of the attributes of the divine nature — judgment and mercy, thus making the sword a good thing too; and attributed all of their revised complex to Yohanan. And they did an amazingly good job — their revised version looks so much like the original that the careless reader would think them nearly identical. it is only when one looks closely that he sees the reversal of the implications.

We proceed to the version of the same saying as presented in what I then thought was the Mekhilta to be attributed to the school of Aqiba:

This is what Rabban Yohanan ben Zakkai says, "What was the reason iron was prohibited more than all [other] metals [for use in building the tabernacle (Ex. 20:25)]? Because the sword is made from it, and the sword is a sign of punishment, but the altar is a sign of atonement. A sign [means] of atonement.

"And is this not a matter of *qal vehomer?* Stones, which neither see nor hear nor speak — because they bring atonement between Israel and their father in heaven, the Holy One blessed be he said [concerning them] *Thou shalt lift upon them no iron tool* (Deut. 27:5). Sons of Torah, who are an atonement for the world, how much the more so that none of all the harmful forces in the world should ever touch them!"

(Mekhilta of R. Simeon b. Yohai, Yitro 20:22, ed. Epstein-Melamed pp. 157-8, 1.29-3 1, 1-4)

On this passage I said:

We have two separate sayings. The first is Yohanan's, that metal is prohibited because the sword is made of metal and is a sign of punishment, while the altar is a sign of atonement. The second saying is the *qal vehomer*, that as stones should not be injured because they bring atonement, so sons of Torah should all the more so be fee of injury from harmful forces. The *qal vehomer* has nothing to do with Yohanan's observation, and need not be directly attributed to him, though it occurs in all formulations of this passage. It seems to be a later development.

By way of amplifying the same matter, let me give a further instance of invoking what I then imagined was a trait of Aqiban tradents to explain diverse versions of similarly connected materials:

> Rabban Yohanan ben Zakkai says, "Behold it says, [*With*] *whole stones* [*avanim shelemot*] *will you build the altar of the Lord your God* (Deut. 27:5) — Stones which make peace [*shalom*], and behold it is a matter of *qal vehomer*. Stones which do not see and do not hear and do not speak, because they bring peace between Israel and their father in heaven, Scripture says *You shall not lift up iron over them* (Deut. 27:6). A man who brings peace between a man and his wife, between one family and another, between one city and another, between one province and another, between one nation and another — how much the more so that punishment should not come near him!"

I then commented:

> The exegesis is practically identical with I.ii.1. The Scriptures are different. There it is "why is iron prohibited" and here it concerns the play on words: "whole stones — stones which make peace." *Atonement* becomes *peace, sons of Torah become peacemakers*. The structure is otherwise the same; the thought is the same ("Peacemakers or those who atone for the world should come to not harm"). The details are somewhat different. Yet the differences are not very considerable. I suspect that Yohanan would have said something about the altar/altar-stones in the form of a *qal vehomer*. The context was Deut. 27:5 and 27:6. The play on words concerning the "whole stones" was dropped in I.ii.1, the stress on "iron" of all metals was omitted here. Strikingly, the Ishmaelean version, I.i.2, follows I.ii.5; both versions elide the whole stones play on words and the *qal vehomer* involving an iron tool. I should thus suppose that I.i.2 = I.ii.5. I.ii.1 differs, as I said, in omitting "whole stones" and

A Documentary-Historical Theory 259

stressing "iron." Both schools preserved an account exhibiting formal parallels (I.i.2 + I.ii.5), but the Aqibans alone preserved the other (I.ii.1), probably because they invented it. Some anterior version was available to both schools, and that anterior version derived from circles close to Yohanan himself. In a period of less than a few decades between Yohanan's death and the formation of the schools of Ishmael and Aqiba, a group of Yohanan's disciples must have put into final form materials which were subsequently made use of by *both* schools. This supposition is likely to be valid if the following conditions are also valid: (1) if both documents actually come from the schools to which they are attributed; (2) if the present form was edited ca. 200, if not somewhat earlier; and most important (3) if they were *not* expanded since that time. Then the story stands in both by A.D. 200 and was known to teachers in both schools. The common source of the story would have come substantially earlier than the founding of the two schools, ca. 100-120. In that case, as I said, the story is certainly part of the corpus of Yohanan-sayings edited by the time of Yabneh. We may safely go a step further and designate as Yavnean, *all* materials occurring in substantially similar form in materials ascribed to the two schools; as Ishmaelean, materials unique to that school, hence not necessarily later that Yabneh but probably from a circle at Yabneh riot known or acceptable to the Aqibans; as Aqiban, materials unique to that school, within the same limitation. It would be tempting to suppose that materials unique to one or the other school were later than materials common to both, but the obvious imponderables prevent it. It is consequential, since we have no documents edited at Yabneh, to recognize that within documents edited later on are materials which probably did come from Yabneh. But it is equally noteworthy that even the materials in the earliest collections have already undergone substantial development. Primitive loggia, in which stories or sayings about Yohanan are transcribed close to when they happened or were actually stated, are unavailable. In general, the closest we can come to the man himself is through secondary materials based on Yavnean traditions.

In conclusion I stated these results:

> The condemnation of war and reproaches in its aftermath may likewise have been acceptable in the school whose master did not encourage the holy war of Bar Kokhba, but in any event ought to

have been quite obnoxious to the one whose master did. Service of the Lord in love would have preserved the prosperity of the people, and the implied condemnation of war is present in the Ishmaelean stories about the Israelite girl.

In all I think it has been proven that no *tendenz* concerning Yohanan *himself* characterized either school. Both preserved favorable, and more important, authoritative sayings and precedents. His legal role is, if anything, slightly greater among the Aqibans than among the Ishmaeleans, but the data are too sparse for the to matter much. Most important: *where the two schools differ in the sorts of stories they preserve about Yohanan, the reason for the difference is certainly found in the interests of the schools themselves, and not in their attitudes to Yohanan.*

As I took back on the exercise at hand, I take comfort that, despite the obvious fundamentalism throughout, I did have the presence of mind to specify the premises. Accordingly, I emphasize that, even then, I stated as a condition that both documents had to come from the schools to which they were attributed and represent matters in a final way as they emerged from those schools at that time. Of course, those conditions were not met and cannot be shown ever to have been met. So the whole in retrospect stands as what I believe to be a good example of method and a bad example of result. But at least I did not make things up as I went along. And the concluding, underlined judgment is one by which I should firmly stand today.

Besides paying attention to the definitive traits of a document, we ask about how the context of documents explains, and is explained by, alterations in received versions of sayings and stories.

To illustrate the experiment at appealing to the context of a given document for explanation of what the authors of that document do to peripatetic sayings, I turn to my discussion of the later Talmudic ("Amoraic") treatment of stories about Yohanan ben Zakkai and the conclusions I drew from the topics included in the corpus of those stories

A Documentary-Historical Theory 261

and sayings. Admittedly, what follows focuses not upon why a given story gets or loses a detail, or why a saying is reworded. Rather, I pay attention to the selections, out of the larger repertoire of sayings and stories, made by a given group of tradents. The method is the same, however, and so is the premise. That is, I claim to explain not what the authorities did not choose, for I do not know what they did not use, but only the points of emphasis revealed by the topics they did choose to discuss. These topical choices are signified, over all, by their interventions into the formulation of the sayings or stories at hand. So we know that authorities of the generation at hand took an interest in an item because of a comment in their names made on it or because of evidence that they have dealt with some detail or other of it. Accordingly, the approach designated incremental-historical finds exemplification in what follows.

What is said here rests on claims as to the facts of the history of the fourth-century sages described in my *History of the Jews in Babylonia. IV. The Age of Shapur II* (Leiden, 1968).

> The Yohanan of Pumbedita was, therefore, primarily a political figure, a judge and administrator, rather than a mystic, moralist, or legislator. What interested the Pumbeditans was, specifically, Yohanan's relationships with the Hillelite house and the priesthood, his discipleship at Hillel's school, his subsequent position of equality with Gamaliel I and dominance over Gamaliel II. If we did not know that the Pumbeditans were involved in a bitter struggle with the Davidic scion of Babylonia, the exilarch, we might have supposed some such difficulty lay at the root of the Pumbeditan's interest in Yohanan. But, in fact, what is known about Pumbedita is precisely this: its half-century effort to raise its own funds and to preserve its independence from the exilarchate. The stories and references to Yohanan conform to that effort and serve its cause. Simply translating Gamaliel, Hillel, and the like to the Davidic exilarch, we find that the rabbi, or collegium of rabbis, is here alleged in times past to have been superior to the exilarch; to have even been selected disciple of the Davidic to the exclusion of the

exilarch; to have proved equal to the high priests of old; to have judged at the best court of the day; to be worthy precedent in murder trials (and the only known murder trial of Babylonian Jewish history came toward the end of this period). The prince-exilarch is to be praised if he confesses his unwitting sin and brings a sin-offering, and happy the generation whose prince does so (— would that ours did.). Torah and good deeds avert the curse of the house of Eli — that and not the blessing of the priest or king-messiah. The rabbi, not the exilarch, decrees what is to be done about troublesome priests. In other words, Yohanan-sayings and stories served the Pumbeditans as important precedents in their struggle with the exilarch, for it is clear that his relationships to Hillel and the Hillelites provided a vital example of what ought even now to be the case in Babylonia. It seems to me that the disproportionate interest in Yohanan at Pumbedita had no equivalent provocation in Palestine, or, if it did, the issues were argued in a different way. In any event, it is a fact that Pumbedita bears by far the largest — practically sole — responsibility for the Yohanan-references in the Babylonian Talmud, and Pumbeditans may even have formed some of the *beraitot* as we now have them. So far as I can tell, no similar interest in Yohanan was localized at any other Babylonian or Palestinian academy.

The results just now represented mark the age in which they were composed, just as much as I claim the same for the sources under discussion. The focus of interest — the historical Yohanan ben Zakkai — to begin with limited matters. More important, the things taken for granted as facts comprise a long and disheartening list. But even then I asked what if the Mekhilta of Ishmael does not in fact represent the historical Ishmael and his disciples? What if Simeon did not really study with Aqiba, and what if the Mekhilta of Simeon is not "Aqiban"? what if both Mekhiltas are made up in medieval times? Then every word I wrote is not wrong but beside the point.

And, of course, I now grasp the obvious fact that the entire exercise at hand in its original formulation rested on premises that I can now call mere fundamentalism. How so?

At every point I took for granted that whatever is imputed to a sage really was said about him, with only one exception: Yohanan ben Zakkai. I further assumed that whatever story was told really represented the state of affairs in the time and place to which the story referred, except for the historical setting of Yohanan ben Zakkai himself. On those bases the study at hand rested. But the premises scarcely escape the simple criticism that, at each point, they share those traits of gullibility and credulity that then, as now, I have attempted to overcome. Asking how we know what Yohanan ben Zakkai really said and did, I failed to inquire into how we know that anything imputed to anyone claiming to know what Yohanan ben Zakkai really said and did also demands answers to exactly the same question. It took me a long time — several more books — to understand that fact and also to confront it and draw the consequences dictated by it. Others assuredly recognized the same problem. But I was the only one to try to solve it. And by redefining the foci of inquiry, I did solve it.

The reason that *Development of a Legend* made so little impression in its day, however, is not because it was insufficiently critical. By the standards not only of that day but also of the present age, a decade and a half and many books later, *Development* remains too radical in its methods, in its points of fundamental insistence, for the generality of scholars in the field to confront. If they respond to the book at all, it is by pointing out misprints. This means they cannot take up the challenge of the book and all that followed it. Why the avoidance? Because if *Development of a Legend* points to what work must be done, then the sort of scholarly work people want to do cannot be done. It is one thing to recognize the utter obsolescence of everything accomplished in the critical study of the history of the Jews and of Judaism in late antiquity, so far as the Rabbinic canon constitutes the principal literary source. It is quite another to insist, as I did and do insist, that everything people now propose as a scholarly program rests on the same false premises.

The way lies open to inquiry into the relationship of text to context, of detail to main point of insistence. Results of the inquiry will tell us something about why a given set of ideas became self-evident and remained manifestly "right" for a very long time. Then we also may find a clue on why those same ideas, that same system of a world-view and a way of life characteristic of a single social group for a long span of history, lost the trait of self-evidence and became manifestly irrelevant. That is to say, at stake is how to interpret the history of Judaism: its formation and persistence, change and renewal. The first task is to describe, analyze, and interpret the facts in hand. Among these facts, the obvious ones concern how, to the naked eye, a story will change as it is told and retold, a saying will undergo revision when it is repeated.

Let me close by placing into the correct, appropriately large, context the humble facts that have occupied us for so long. Why, specifically, do I regard as indicative the persistence and transformation of sayings and stories? And what do I hope will be indicated? The answer lies in the three basic dimensions by which we take the measure of every document of the canon of Judaism, from the Mishnah through the Bavli. (I elaborate on this matter in the appendix that follows.)

Every book of the canon stands by itself. Each is *autonomous*.

Except for the Mishnah and Scripture, every book in the canon refers back to some other book. Some of the books relate as a whole to the Mishnah. They serve as exegeses and amplifications of the Mishnah. Others depend upon Scripture. So every book in the canon, except for the

Mishnah and Scripture, is not only autonomous but also *connected to* some other book. *The autonomy is limited by connection.*

And, finally, comes the relationship of continuity, one with all, all with one. That is, all of the books together, Scripture and the Mishnah, Tosefta and the Talmuds, Sifra, the two Sifrés, Genesis Rabbah, Leviticus Rabbah, and the rest of the compositions, viewed whole, all at once, and in their entirety, constitute the "one whole Torah of Moses, our rabbi." That continuity is not merely the *post facto* assertion of the believing community. It also constitutes a fact to be induced from evidence by detailed inquiry into the shared conceptions and values, alleged at the end of the process of the formation of the canon as a whole, to characterize all documents of the canon. Looking backward, I should not be prepared to make an exception, in that characterization, even of Scriptures. That is so even though sages, in the manner of their age and all ages before and since, read into Scripture whatever they wished to see there. That qualification should not present an exception to this simple claim: the documents all together do constitute a canon. So they establish a continuity from one to the next and among them all.

Two of the three dimensions of the canon — autonomy, connection, continuity — obviously appear to the naked eye: autonomy and connection. How so? A document, by definition, stands alone and autonomous. The Tosefta, the Mishnah, the two Sifrés each will afford examination on its own. The connection of all of the compositions of the canon to either Scripture or the Mishnah comes to vivid expression in the fundamental redactional preferences of each document. The Tosefta is organized in accord with the order of passages of the Mishnah, the two Talmuds with the same structure, and all compilations of scriptural exegeses ("Midrashim") follow the order of verses in the book of Scripture they allegedly explain. The variations in degree of explicit dependence, for redactional order and structure, on one or the other of the two base-documents make little difference.

But when we ask whether and how the documents form a continuity from one to the next and, among all of them together constitute a canon, where shall we look for relevant data? I see only two sources of facts for the assessment of where and how documents relate as a whole to one another, not only back to a single shared source of structure supplied by Scripture or the Mishnah. One source flows from shared conceptions, symbols, fundamental and everywhere-definitive values. The other source derives from shared sayings and stories. The contrast speaks for itself.

The former source — shared symbols — flows at random and aimlessly, much as at floodtide the sea overcomes the shore, and the river its banks. We never know the limits. We form impressions of where the boundaries lie, only to discover, as water recedes and advances, that, short of going out and wading around, we have missed the mark dividing dry shore from ocean or river. But if we wade out in the shifting tide, we may drown. So too if we aimlessly seize upon one ubiquitous value or another and allege that one congeries defines what is shared, uniform, continuous, and another does not, we shall drown in facts. We shall never have a clear criterion for knowing when we are right, and when we are wrong. Once need not dismiss as impressionistic the great and valiant efforts of such exemplary scholars as George Foot Moore and Max Kadushin to recognize the failures they left behind. The field of learning in the nineteenth and twentieth century is strewn with the carcasses of abandoned definitions of "Judaism," including the system of Judaism revealed by the canon concluded in late antiquity.

But there endures that other source of information — shared sayings and stories — on what moves in continuity from one document to another. What *in fact* travels from the Mishnah to the Tosefta to the Yerushalmi to the Bavli, or from a Mekhilta to the Tosefta, to the Fathers according to Rabbi Nathan, or hither and yon or here and there? The peripatetic saying and the thrice-told tale constitute concrete, material proofs of the actualities. They define facts of continuity that to begin with make possible the claim that autonomous documents relate not in general but very particularly. Then we may see, in the character of detail, that main point that we seek. The shape of the whole, the measure of the dimension of continuity — these to begin with emerge from the simple fact that the same saying or story will be shared among two or more documents of the canon. That validates the claim of continuity, though obviously not exhausting what is meant by the claim. But, in the details of what is like and what is unlike in the traveling tale and the peripatetic saying we see clearly, without distortion, what is common to important components of the canon of Judaism. True, all we have at the moment is detail. But of canonical Judaism we cannot speak just now, except to say that, after all, God really does live in the details.[1]

---

[1] Only later on, from the early 1990s forward, did I realize that issues of continuity require attention to theology, specifically, the description and analysis of the cogency of the theological conceptions attested in one Rabbinic document or another. In a number of experimental works, I formed some basic notions, which came to fruition in *The Theology of the Oral Torah. Revealing the Justice of God.* Kingston and Montreal, 1999: McGill-Queens University Press and Ithaca, 1999: Cornell University Press, and in *The Theology of the Halakhah* (in press).

APPENDICES

Appendix

Autonomy, Connection, Continuity: The Three Dimensions of a Text of Formative Judaism

[Plenary presentation in the series, "How My Mind Has Changed," Society of Biblical Literature, Chicago, December 10, 1984.]

When we take up a book that speaks of a single document in the canon of Judaism — I refer to *Judaism: The Evidence of the Mishnah*[1] — and propose to describe, analyze, and interpret that book in particular, we violate the lines of order and system that have characterized earlier studies of these same documents. Until now, people have tended to treat all of the canonical texts as testimonies to a single system and structure, that is, to Judaism. What sort of testimonies texts provide varies according to the interest of the scholars, students, and saints who study them. Scholars look for meanings of words and phrases, better versions of a text. For them all canonical documents equally serve as a treasury of philological facts and variant readings. Students also took for the sense of words and phrases and follow a given phrase hither and yon, as their teachers direct them on their treasure hunt. Saints study all texts equally, looking for

---

[1] *Judaism. The Evidence of the Mishnah.* Chicago, 1981: University of Chicago Press. *Choice,* "Outstanding academic book list" 1982-3. Paperback edition: 1984. Second printing, 1985. Third printing, 1986. Second edition, augmented: Atlanta, 1987: Scholars Press for Brown Judaic Studies. *Hayyahadut le'edut hammishnah.* Hebrew translation of *Judaism. The Evidence of the Mishnah.* Tel Aviv, 1987: Sifriat Poalim. *Il Giudaismo nella testimonianza della Mishnah.* Italian translation by Giorgio Volpe. Bologna, 1995: Centro editoriale Dehoniane.

God's wilt and finding testimonies to God in each component of the Torah of Moses our Rabbi.

Among none of these circles will the discrete description, analysis, and interpretation of a single text make sense. Why not? Because all texts ordinarily are taken to form a common statement, "Torah" in the mythic setting, "Judaism" in the theological one. Since I spent the first half of my scholarly life trying to use all of the texts in the canon, more or less without differentiation and equally, to answer historical questions, I participated in the approach now rejected. I thought that what was definitive, what laid forth lines of structure and order, was not the text at hand but the problem I had defined. So I did not tease out of the texts the threads of context, looking for the fabric's coherence in its small details, in the interstices of warp and woof. I set up my own loom. I pulled the texts apart and made them into mere threads, then rewove them my way. On that, as is clear, I have changed my mind, and, I would claim, my field.

Let me spell out the change at hand and then briefly address *Judaism: The Evidence of the Mishnah* and *Judaism in Society: The Evidence of the Yerushalmi*, the principal documents of the day. To begin with, however, I emphasize that nothing I say will surprise scholars in the biblical fields of Old and New Testament, Israel in ancient times and earliest Christianity. They understand that the work of the hour does not demand more harmonies of the Gospels. They rigorously debate issues of orthodoxy and heterodoxy in earliest Christianity and whether and where, among the diverse Christianities, they may find patterns of Christian truth. In the nineteenth century they abandoned any notion of using all of the (canonical) texts equally and for a single purpose. In the twentieth, such giants as H.E.W. Turner and Walter Bauer ended for all time the simple notions that you can open a book, thumb the pages and pull out a Christianity. When my mind changed, under the influence of the examples of my colleagues in other areas of history, the history and comparison of religion, and, obviously, in the biblical areas and those of earliest Christianity, I had to relive two hundred years of scholarship in twenty years. Permit me, then, to report in my field what are methodological commonplaces of other fields.

We begin with theology and move to texts. For the hermeneutical issue defines the result of description, analysis, and interpretation. From today's perspective the entire canon of Judaism — "the one whole Torah of Moses, our rabbi" — equally and at every point testifies to the entirety of Judaism. Why so? Because all documents in the end form components of a single system. Each makes its contribution to the whole. If, therefore, we wish to know what "Judaism" or, more accurately, "the Torah," teaches on any subject, we are able to draw freely on sayings relevant to that subject wherever they occur in the entire canon of Judaism. Guided only by the taste and judgment of the great sages of the Torah, as they have addressed the question at hand, we thereby describe "Judaism."

Composites of sayings drawn from diverse books in no way violate the frontiers and boundaries that distinguish one part of the canon from some other part of the same canon. Why not? It is a theological conviction that defines the hermeneutic. Viewed as serving the Torah, which is a single and continuous revelation, all frontiers, all boundaries stand only at the outer limits of the whole. Within, as the saying has it, "There is neither earlier nor later," that is to say, temporal considerations do not apply. But if temporal distinctions make no difference, no others do either.

Accordingly, as Judaism comes to informed expression in the Judaic pulpit, in the Judaic classroom, above all in the lives and hearts and minds of Jews loyal to Judaism, all parts of the canon of Judaism speak equally authoritatively. All parts, all together, present us with one harmonious worldview and homogenous way of life, one Torah ("Judaism") for all Israel. That view of "the Torah," that is to say, of the canon of Judaism, characterizes every organized movement within Judaism as we now know it, whether Reform or Orthodox, whether Reconstructionist or Conservative, whether in the "Exile" (Diaspora) or in the State of Israel. How so? Among circles of Judaism indifferent to considerations of time and place, anachronism and context, every document, whenever brought to closure, testifies equally to that single system. For those circles Judaism emerges at a single moment ("Sinai"), but comes to expression in diverse times and places, so that any composition that falls into the category of Torah serves, without further differentiation, to tell us about the substance of Judaism, its theology and law.

An important qualification, however, has now to make its mark. Among those circles of Judaism to whom historical facts do make a difference, for example, Orthodoxy in the West, Reconstructionist, Conservative and Reform Judaism and the like, considerations of what was completed earlier as against what came to closure only later on, for instance, in the second century as against the eighteenth century, do make some difference. Earlier documents provide more compelling and authoritative evidence than later ones. But even in the view of this other sector of Judaism, all documents, if not everywhere equally authoritative, still form part of a continuous whole, Judaism. The distinction between the two positions makes no material difference. Why not? Because both circles hold as self-evident that the numerous components of the canon of Judaism form a continuity, beginning, middle, and end. That is why considerations of priority and of closure, should these considerations find their way into discourse at all, change little and affect nothing. Torah is Torah, early, middle, and late. And so it is — except from the perspective of one outside the magic circle of the faith. Here we ask exactly *how* various documents became "Torah," *what* each document added to the whole, in *which* ways do the several documents relate to one another and to the larger system, and so, in all, reverting to mythic language, what makes Torah Torah.

For a person engaged in such an inquiry into the formation of Judaism studied through the analysis of the literary evidence of the canon, documents stand in three relationships to one another and to the system of which they form part, that is, to Judaism, as a whole. The specification of these relationships constitutes the principal premise of my work. It is a premise since, to begin with, the relationships I perceive derive not inductively, from the documents at hand, but from the mind of the one who turns to analyze the documents. So at this point I cannot claim to approach matters inductively.

1. Each document, as a matter of theory, is to be seen all by itself, that is, as autonomous of all others.

2. Each document, again as a matter of theory, is to be examined for its relationships with other documents universally regarded as falling into the same classification, as Torah. So each text is *connected* to others.

3. And, finally, each document is to be allowed to take its place as part of the undifferentiated aggregation of documents that, all together, constitute the canon of Judaism, that is to say, "Torah." So each text stands in *continuity* with others.

1. Simple logic makes self-evident the proposition that, if a document comes down to us within its own framework, as a complete book with a beginning, middle, and end, in preserving that book, the canon presents us with a

document on its own and not solely as part of a larger composition or construct. So we too see the document as it reaches us, that is, as autonomous.

2. If, second, a document contains materials shared verbatim or in substantial content with other documents of its classification, or if one document refers to the contents of other documents, then the several documents that clearly wish to engage in conversation with one another have to address one another. That is to say, we have to seek for the marks of connectedness, asking for the meaning of those connections.

3. Finally, since, as I said at the outset, the community of the faithful of Judaism, in all of the contemporary expressions of Judaism, concur that documents held to be authoritative constitute one whole, seamless "Torah," that is, a complete and exhaustive statement of God's will for Israel and humanity, we take as our further task the description of the whole out of the undifferentiated testimony of all of its parts. These components in the theological context are viewed, as is clear, as equally authoritative for the composition of the whole: one, continuous system. In taking up such a question, we address a problem not of theology alone, though it is a correct theological conviction, but one of description, analysis, and interpretation of an entirely historical order.

In this way we may hope to trace the literary evidence — which for Rabbinic Judaism in particular is the only evidence we have — for the formation of Judaism, what it is, how it works. By seeing the several components of the canon of Judaism in sequence, first, one by one, then, one after the other, and finally, all together all at once, we may trace the literary side of the history of Judaism. We may see how a document came into being on its own, in its context (so far as we may posit the character of that context). We interpret the document at its site. As a matter of fact, moreover, all documents of the Rabbinic canon except for the Hebrew Scriptures relate to prior ones, on the one side, and all, especially the Scriptures, stand before those to follow, on the other. The Mishnah normally is understood to rest upon the written Torah, and, later in its history in Judaism, came to be called the oral Torah. So even the Mishnah stands not distinct and autonomous, but contingent and dependent. The two Talmuds rest upon the Mishnah, and the several compilations of exegeses of Scripture, called "Midrashim", rest upon Scripture. So, in all, like the bones of the body, each book is connected to others (with Scripture and the Mishnah the backbone). All together they -form a whole, a frame that transcends the parts and imparts proportion, meaning, and harmony to them.

The bones of the body develop more or less in shared stages, however, while the documents of the Torah, the canon of Judaism, developed in a sequence. The order, if not so linear as it seems on the surface, is mostly clear. First came Scripture, then the Mishnah, then the Talmud of the Land of Israel and earlier compilations of biblical exegeses, then the Talmud of Babylonia and the later compilations of biblical exegeses. In that sequence of the important texts we shall find whatever evidence of growth, development, and change, as we shall ever have available to tell us the history of Judaism. To complete the matter, what do we hope to learn as we relate growth, development, and change in the history of Judaism, traced through the formation and character of its canon, to the growth, development, and change in the history of the Jewish people? It is not only to describe and analyze, but also to explain, the history of the formation of Judaism. That is to say, we may frame theories not only on the formative history of the world-view and way of life we call Judaism, but on the reasons that the history went the route it took, rather than some other route. How so? We may ask why people thought what they thought and did what they did, rather than thinking other thoughts and doing other things. When we can relate the ideas people held and the way they lived their life to the context in which they found themselves, we shall have reached that level of interpretation at which present and past come together in the setting of shared human existence: the meeting of text and context. But we stand at a distance from that elusive goal.

What I have said in general makes sense in particular of Judaism: The Evidence of the Mishnah and Judaism in Society: The Evidence of the Yerushalmi. I mention two other titles, Judaism and Scripture: The Evidence of Leviticus Rabbah and Judaism in Conclusion: The Evidence of the Bavli.[2] These four works yield yet a final one, on which I now work, The Oral Torah: An Introduction. What each item proposes is two exercises which are one. First, I wish to describe a single document. Second, I also want to address to a given document one important question. My premise is that a document ordinarily is about something. Except for

---

[2] *Judaism in Society: The Evidence of the Yerushalmi. Toward the Natural History of a Religion.* Chicago, 1983: The University of Chicago Press. *Choice*, "Outstanding Academic Book List, 1984-1985." Second printing, with a new preface: Atlanta, 1991: Scholars Press for South Florida Studies in the History of Judaism. *Judaism and Scripture: The Evidence of Leviticus Rabbah.* Chicago, 1986: The University of Chicago Press. [Fresh translation of Margulies' text and systematic analysis of problems of composition and redaction.] Jewish Book Club Selection, 1986. *Judaism: The Classical Statement. The Evidence of the Bavli.* Chicago, 1986: University of Chicago Press. *Choice*, "Outstanding Academic Book List, 1987." *Judaism and Story: The Evidence of The Fathers According to Rabbi Nathan.* Chicago, 1992: University of Chicago Press. The final item in the list was much postponed, until I was ready to do the entire work. It emerged as *Introduction to Rabbinic Literature.* N.Y., 1994: Doubleday. The Doubleday Anchor Reference Library. Religious Book Club Selection, 1994. Paperback edition: 1999.

Appendix One: Autonomy, Connection, Continuity

anthologies of information, people write books to make points, to answer questions, to say something important. In the ancient world people copied and preserved books at great expense, so books had to matter. The premise, then, that a given document tells us something important to those who wrote it and their successors, seems to me self-evident.

It follows that we have to find out what polemic, what point of insistence, what aspect of self-evidence a given text reveals. As I have stressed in every work of mine, we begin the search with the smallest details, we then ask what the details of the text repeatedly stress. This commonly emerges not from what the text says, but from how it says what it says. In the main beams of rhetoric, in the repeated details, ubiquitous, implicit, self-evident, and therefore definitive, I claim to find that principal message that speaks for the work as a whole. The deepest structures of syntax may convey the principles of order. The techniques of rhetoric, broadly construed, properly understood, may speak also to us. They accordingly may deliver a text's substantive message through the forms of proportion and of intelligible, therefore logical, speech.

About what main point do the texts at hand then speak? I see the Mishnah as a complete statement of an entire system. I see the documents of succession, typified by the Yerushalmi, as large-scale efforts to translate the Mishnah's philosophical system into social order. I see counterpart documents of Scripture-exegesis, which treat Scripture as the two Talmuds treat the Mishnah, as exercises in the construction of dialogue between Scripture and the Mishnah. And I see the final document of the canon, the Bavli, as a synthetic work of restatement and completion. The Bavli joins the two main lines of order and systemic structure, the Mishnah and Scripture, and makes them the basis for its proportions and the foundations of its social order.

In my view the various documents of the canon of Judaism produced in late antiquity demand a different hermeneutic altogether from the one of homogenization and harmonization, the ahistorical and anti-contextual one I have outlined. It is one that does not harmonize but that differentiates. It is a hermeneutic shaped to teach us how to read the texts at hand one by one and in a particular context, exactly in the way in which we read any other text bearing cultural and social insight. The texts stand not as self-evidently important but only as examples, sources of insight for a quite neutral inquiry. Let me spell out what I think is at issue between the established hermeneutic and the one I propose.

The three key-words of the inherited hermeneutic are *continuity*, *uniqueness*, and *survival*. Scholars who view the texts as continuous with one another seek what is unique in the system formed by the texts as a whole. With the answer to what is unique, they propose to explain the survival of Israel, the Jewish people. Hence: continuity, uniqueness, survival.

The words to encapsulate the hermeneutic I espouse are these: *description, analysis,* and *interpretation*. I am trying to learn how to describe the constituents of the canon, viewed individually, each in its distinctive context. I wish to discover appropriate *analytical* tools, questions to lead me from description of one text to comparison and contrast between two or more texts of the canon. Only at the end do I address the question of *interpretation*: how do all of the texts of the canon at hand flow together into a single continuous statement, a "Judaism."

Within the inherited hermeneutic of continuity, survival, and uniqueness, the existence of the group defines the principal concern, an inner-facing one, hence the emphasis on uniqueness in quest, in continuities, for the explanation of survival. Within the proposed hermeneutic of

Appendix One: Autonomy, Connection, Continuity 281

description, analysis, and interpretation, by contrast, the continued survival of a "unique" group does not frame the issue. For my purposes, it is taken for granted, for the group is not the main thing at all. The problematic emerges from without. What I want to know is not how and why the group survived so as to help it survive some more. It is how to describe the society and culture contained within, taken as a given, how to interpret an enduring world-view and way of life, expressed by the artifacts in hand. How did, and does, the group work?

So I claimed that the results of the literary inquiry will prove illuminating for the study of society and culture. I have now to explain why I think so. The answer ties in our will and capacity to generalize, out of details, a judgment on a broad issue of culture, as it is exemplified in the small problem at hand. The issue here is secular. True, I too ask how the components of the canon as a whole form a continuity. I wonder why this document in particular survived to speak for the whole. But for me the answers to these questions generate theories, promise insight for the study of other canonical religions. So far as I shall succeed, it will be because I can learn from these other canonical religions. I have tried to learn from, and also to teach something to, those who study the history, the thought, the social reality, of religions that, like Judaism, form enduring monuments to the power of humanity to endure and to prevail so far.[3]

---

[3] [The occasion of this plenary address at the Society of Biblical Literature's national meeting was made memorable not by what I said there, but by what happened after I gave my lecture. The chairman of the occasion, Professor W. D. Davies, called for questions. Morton Smith raised his hand. Instead of asking a question, however, he came to the podium and read prepared remarks, denouncing me, and thereupon distributed copies of Saul Lieberman's review of a volume of my Yerushalmi translation, which had been published in *the Journal of the American Oriental Society* the preceding July. It was part of a campaign of

character-assassination, in which various rabbis, Reform and Conservative, participated. He effort was not to criticize and correct errors, generally trivial, but to discredit me as a scholar. For example, William Braude, Providence, rabbi of Temple Beth El, distributed the same review to every rabbi in the state of Rhode Island, where I was then living as a professor at Brown University; and Eugene Mihaly sent the same review to every member of the faculty of the Hebrew Union College-Jewish Institute of Religion in Cincinnati, New York, Los Angeles, and elsewhere. Lest anyone not see the screed, *Biblical Archaeology Review* reprinted most of it in an admiring article. When I asked the editor of JAOS a professor at University of Pennsylvania whose name I forget, for permission to reply to the review, he did not answer my letter. When I called, he said, No, and hung up on me. That Lieberman's criticisms were marginal is shown in my *In the Margins of the Yerushalmi. Notes on the English Translation*. Chico, 1985: Scholars Press for Brown Judaic Studies. After he disrupted the plenary session of the Society of Biblical Literature called to honor me, Smith never again was invited to give a plenary address at an academic society meeting. He had discredited not me but himself and had marked himself as disreputable. I was subjected to that treatment on his part because I rejected the anti-Christian part of his *Jesus the Magician* and dismissed it as propagandistic, not academic argument. This I did in footnote 18 of the published version of my prior SBL plenary address, given in 1979 and printed in 1980-1. Only after Smith died, however, did scholarly opinion surface that rejected his Clement fragment as a forgery of an obsessive, Christianity-hating, tormented man. I do not regret repudiating anti-Christian bigotry, even on the part of the man with whom I wrote my doctoral dissertation, and to whom I had been devoted for nearly two decades. Many Christians have done no less for Judaism, particularly in this century.]

Appendix Two

The Bavli at the End:
The Judgment of Menachem Fish

In connection with the argument of Chapter One, that on formal grounds the Bavli may be shown the work of critical minds, I here include an account of the contrary view. I see the Bavli's authors and compilers as independent, entirely prepared to impose their judgment on the received heritage of tradition. The opposite view is taken by Menachem Fish. It is that the earlier generations of the Rabbinic sages, in the first century C.E., exercised critical judgment, while the later ones, in the time of the Bavli, proved uncritical, servile, and "traditional." That judgment contradicts the conclusions reached here, and my criticism of the presentation of that judgment therefore demands a hearing. For that purpose, I reproduce my review of Dr. Fish's statement of his views, *Rational Rabbis. Science and Talmudic Culture*. Bloomington, IN, 1997: Indiana University Press. 360 pp.

Fish has written an intellectually ambitious book, and the high aspiration implicit on every page to make a considerable mark on Talmud studies in the academy deserves the response of serious and sustained attention. He has succeeded in establishing that the Talmud of Babylonia contains some sayings and stories that he classifies, quite persuasively, as traditional, and others, as anti-traditional. Not an experienced book-writer and scholar of Judaism, however, Fish sets forth this perfectly good idea in an intellectually prolix and confused manner. His idea has merit, his execution thereof none. Fish ends up flogging his observation to death.

His book is fundamentally flawed through errors of confusion of distinct modes of thought and analysis. Perfectly valid and, in the hands of others, well-formulated modes of description, analysis, and interpretation — theology, hermeneutics, and exegesis, not to say, historical and literary criticism — come and go in these pages, so that we never can be entirely certain where we stand in the argument, or what is at stake. Specifically a task in religious thought has been assigned to secular modes of inquiry. I think Fish has made every mistake one can make in confusing theological hermeneutics with historical and literary analysis. He wants mere facts to prove religious convictions, but even if all his facts were factual — and many are not — he still should not have proved his theological proposition. And his presentation proves verbose, pretentious, prolix, and in the end, boring.

A mathematician, physicist, historian and philosopher of science at Tel Aviv University and at the Shalom Hartman Institute, Jerusalem, Fish claims to wish to address to the Talmud, broadly construed the ontological and epistemic questions of philosophy. He does so in response to two essays. The first is Harold Fish's *Poetry with a Purpose*, where Qohelet ("Ecclesiastes") is read as irony, and the second is this writer's lecture at Tulane University, "Why No Science in Judaism?" (published in *The Making of the Mind of Judaism*. Atlanta, 1987: Scholars Press for Brown Judaic Studies). Professor Harold Fish, Professor Menachem Fish's father, reads Qohelet "as an ironic reductio ad absurdum of the very possibility of an anthropocentric, self-sufficient notion of rationality." I maintained that the modes of thought that produce coherent discourse in the Talmud make scientific learning improbable. Fish proposes the following argument:

> Contrary to the claim attributed by my father to Qohelet, science...provides a living example of a self-sufficient, humanly attainable, rational undertaking that is well aware of its own shortcomings. And, contrary to Neusner, the Talmud's manner of Halakhic reasoning

seemed to me to resemble quite closely the type of discourse I had learnt to associate with the scientific method of trial and error.

Here Fish deals with scientific rationality, with a reconstruction of talmudic epistemology along those lines. That is what he tells us he is going to do.

But this book is not about philosophy of science and it does not deal with Harold Fish's or my proposals at all. *Rational Rabbis* sets forth a theological argument about traditionalism and anti-traditionalism in the documents of the Oral Torah as these trends are revealed in various talmudic stories and sayings. Affirmed on one page, denied on the next, Fish's theory of the historical unfolding of these trends and the temporally determinate points of conflict between them then invokes historical "facts" to validate the presence of an anti-traditionalist "voice." Faced with a barrage of signals about the critical spirit that is supposed to animate the whole, we in the end are asked to accept as fact a mass of attributions of sayings to named masters and descriptions of events, temporal sequences of opinion, and all of the other panoply of the uncritical and gullible pseudo-history that with diminishing success Israeli scholarship asks the rest of the academic world to accept.

The source of energy in the arguments of Fish's book makes manifest that he is engaged in an altogether different enterprise, one to which both his father's and my essays prove of only marginal interest and in which they play no important role. We provide not the reason but only the excuse for what we shall see is a rather clumsy, intellectually unrefined, demonstration, through naked historicism, of a theological proposition never argued in its own terms at all. Not only so, but while the prose in some of the sections — those involving philosophy of science — is spare, dynamic, and purposeful, when he comes to Talmudic subjects, Fish turns verbose and prolix. Readers can test that proposition by counting the number of adjectives per page in the opening section, on philosophy of science, with the number on any page chosen at random in the shank of the book. The book then shows itself unfocused and uneconomical and amateurish because, as I shall explain, beyond the opening pages on philosophy of science, the writing only occasionally exhibits the rigor that philosophy of science is supposed to inculcate.

Something Fish calls "Talmudic culture" (then not defined carefully) then is characterized along the specified lines. The work is in two unequal parts, about a fifth on philosophy of science, and the rest on Rabbinic Judaism. First comes Science as an exemplar of rational inquiry, and, second, the Jewish covenant of learning. This latter section, the bulk of the book, is in these parts and topics:

Chapter I. The great Tannaitic dispute: The Jabne Legends and their context: traditionalism and its discontents, the Jabne reforms, the testimony of Eduyyot, "It is Not in Heaven," Jabne's anti-traditionalist manifesto, a traditionalist response: Hillel and b'nai Beteira;

Chapter II. The changing of the guard: Amoraic texts and Tannaitic legacies: discerning the Bavli's point of view, a schematic overview; introducing the Bavli's paradigm: Berakhot 19b, the logic and rhetoric of transgenerational negotiation, Yerushalmi and Bavli compared, anti-traditionalism for the advanced, and giving away the game or the gentle art of inaudible instruction; and

III. Understanding the Bavli: problem one: explaining the Bavli's double-talk, problem two: discerning the rule of the Mishnah for the Bavli, the Mishnah as a formative code, rational rabbis, or the Mishnah as textbook, "Turn thee around" (Bavli Menahot 29b) or Back to the future."

If this summary of the chapters and their divisions leaves us wondering what has become of "rational rabbis," and their science, at the outset Fisch organizes his statement in response to my view, which he quotes,

> that the paramount of documents...inculcated a particular way f forming propositions and also a particular mode of joining these propositions together into sizable compositions of thought. The very means by which these modes of thought were transmitted and held together, the extraordinary power of analysis and argument characteristic of the normative documents — these explain also the incapacity of those same modes of thought to frame philosophy, including natural philosophy.

Now my stress is on *"means by which these modes of thought were transmitted..."* since I emphasize on how the system formulated by the sages was put together and transmitted by the Talmud of Babylonia, which is a highly systematic mode of thought and argument set forth as commentary, that is, in traditional form. I characterized the Bavli as a system in the form of a tradition ("a traditional system," "a systematic tradition"), and that defined the center of my argument.

The refocusing of matters makes a difference. I have argued in subsequent works that the system itself took shape in profoundly philosophical ways and appealed to philosophical modes of argument. The method corresponded to that of the natural history in the manner of Aristotle, the modes of analysis to the dialectical analysis in the manner of Plato's Socrates. These propositions I show in *Judaism as Philosophy. The Method and Message of the Mishnah.* Columbia, 1991: University of South Carolina Press, and in *Jerusalem and Athens: The Congruity of Talmudic and Classical Philosophy.* Leiden,

1997: E. J. Brill. *Supplements to the Journal for the Study of Judaism*, respectively.[1]

To meet the challenge, Fish maintains, "one must...compare the ontological and epistemological assumptions behind each of the two great intellectual endeavors, Torah study...and Western science." And that is what he proposes to do. The focus of his analysis is supposed to be, quite properly, the character of science. But Fish can have formulated his argument in its own terms, for none of this plays any role in his book; it is window-dressing. In fact, at stake in this book, prominent in nearly every discussion in Part II, approximately 80% of the whole, is an acutely contemporary issue pertaining to the politics of Israeli religious life.

It follows that Fish has composed, in the guise of an academic work of history and hermeneutics, an actively theological polemic against Israeli Orthodox Judaism, which is traditional while he wishes it were otherwise. He wants to set aside the triumphalism — not to mention the obscurantism — of its traditionalism, and this he will do by explaining "the frequently tacit, meditative discourse about the nature of humanly possible intellectual achievement that shaped the thinking of the framers of the Talmudic canon." His main argument is "to substantiate...the presence in the Jewish texts of a major voice, or school of talmudic thought, whose views of human knowledge, learning, and intellectual accomplishment bear a striking resemblance to the latter-day theory of rationality argued for in Part One...anti-traditionalist

---

[1]Fisch knew neither of these works when he wrote the book before us, the latter appearing simultaneously with his monograph; but if he kept up on the scholarly literature, he ought to have known the former. It is the fact that Israeli scholarship on Judaism simply does not read overseas work or pay much mind to it. Israeli mathematicians, physicists, historians and philosophers of science, certainly do.

by virtue of its commitment to the critical appraisal, rather than to the unquestioned reception of its inherited teachings." Part Two proposes to locate and retrieve this anti-traditionalist voice. And here is the theological charge:

> It is a voice that shares with the modern constructive skeptic the idea that no knowledge is set forever, that all knowledge needs to be questioned for its deficiencies, that former rulings and sensibilities have to be constantly reinterrogated. It is a voice that shares with this school of thought a fundamental skepticism towards all first-order knowledge claims, yet premises standards and criteria for deciding between rival conjectures...the view of rationality I argue for and the view of Torah-study I aspire to expose and analyze share a basic openness, an intellectual modesty and a genuine pluralism, that...render the retrieval of the latter especially timely.

Now this formulation on the face of it focuses Fish's interest on an immediate and practical question facing the practice of Judaism in the state of Israel; it can have been formulated without introducing Harold Fish's reading of Qohelet or my *Making of the Mind of Judaism*.

For Fish has given us a theological thesis in the form of a philosophical analysis of a literary problem in historical terms — a massive and needless complication of an issue best argued in its own terms and by appeal to the authoritative documents themselves. He has turned a perfectly valid observation about diverse viewpoints in the Talmud into a problem of hermeneutics, beginning in theology and ending in exegesis, that he is engaged in solving. But he has framed matters in historical and literary terms. So as we move through the book, we can never be sure to whom he wishes to speak and for what purpose; that is what I mean when I term the work prolix and unfocussed, amateurish as book-writing goes. When he speaks of "a steadfast, reactionary traditionalism that preaches rigid and dogmatic adherence to a set of inherited norms for no more reason than that they are inherited," he has turned to a different audience from the one that an academic monograph comprises for the purpose of learning. He has made a tendentious theological argument (as he admitted in so many words)[2] but given it the form of mere secular scholarship. It is a theological argument constructed out of data he deems the mere this-worldly facts of cultural precedent.[3] That confuses matters not only for readers but for the author himself, and it also marks the work within its own limits as political and in the end not pure in its academic vocation.

In fact Fish implicitly comes to that same judgment when he centers the shank of the book on the texts that he deems pertinent. Since he wants to recover that "voice" that he wishes spoke for Judaism in his own country, in quest of his cultural precedent in the documents the other side values, he frames matters in literary terms: "Whatever second-order considerations informed these texts are to a large extent embedded in the editorial policies and narrative frameworks employed by their framers and redactors." He then thinks that we can take the texts apart "at their appropriate stratified

---

[2] In so stating, he admits he paraphrases Daniel Boyarin. He says his work is consciously modeled after Boyarin's "constant intellectual self-reflection." What, in ordinary language, this can possibly mean — do we have Spinoza's God in academic garb? — I cannot say. But, as we shall see, the massive confusion between theological and historical and literary categories, the dismissal of standard critical considerations, the framing of matters in a self-indulgent way, the casual and capricious dismissal of massive components of the scholarly canon, such as characterize Boyarin's opus to date, also mar Fisch's.

[3] The role of "Talmudic culture" in this book is never explained and only occasionally active. My sense is that he has borrowed the category from the rather odd title of Daniel Boyarin's chair at University of California, Berkeley.

seams" and "reconstruct...each subtext in relation to its proper place, time, and context...." These form on their very surface claims as to not hermeneutics and exegesis in the service of theology, but (mere) historical and literary fact. Those whom he criticizes rightly reject these critical considerations, reading the documents within an altogether different hermeneutics.

But then Fish shifts ground. He promises only an account for "theories of knowledge...that directed and motivated those responsible for the texts in their finished form." When he speaks of Jabne (a.k.a. Yabneh, Jamnia) or the debates of the Houses of Hillel and Shammai, he means to use "short-hand for the talmudic redactor's views of these matters." In so stating he prays ritual obeisance to the critical program that I have advanced, as those familiar with that program will recognize in every sentence of his presentation. But as we shall see, it is only a formality. For Fish does make numerous claims that are historical, not merely phenomenological, about the order in which ideas unfolded and the context in which they took shape. He uses the historical past tense; he thinks he is presenting precedents out of determinate time, embodied by great sages, and not merely stories that illustrate attitudes he wished would prevail. The methodological upshot is everything and its opposite: stories and history, descriptions of facts and normative judgments.

To prove his announced proposition about science in Judaism, Fish did not have to make any judgments of a determinate, temporal and contextual character at all. But, as matters turn out, whether Fish to accomplish his goal had to give us an account of science as we know it seems to me subject to doubt. The doubt is this: had he not responded to his father's essay and to one of my books that caught his eye, would the issue of science have been required at all for an essay on the two voices, traditionalist and anti-traditionalist, that he wishes to identify in the Talmudic writings? I think not. The history and philosophy of science that he lays out link up to Talmudic theology only because Fish has so set forth his theological argument as to invoke them. That responds to his professional situation in those fields. Only a mathematician and physicist, of enlightened, integrationist Orthodox convictions, who has turned to philosophy and history of science would have found necessary this quite idiosyncratic framing of the theological question.[4] But one must wonder why his publisher has denied him the advantage of a critical reading, and, further, one must find puzzling the professional qualifications of those with whom, at the Hartman Institute, Fish engages in academic dialogue. Not experienced in book-writing, he has been poorly served by both referees and colleagues.

More to the point, the shank of the book can have been written, and now can be read, pretty much in its own terms. For the rest, "the same notion of rational action...is not only implicit in the modus operandi of the rabbis...but can be shown to have been explicitly and self-consciously adhered to by many of the framers of these documents." Had matters been packaged simply as "anti-traditionalism" and "traditionalism," the point would have been entirely clear. He wants to show that the texts "are framed...as long and sustained arguments against blindly following tradition...

---

[4]At the end of this exposition, what emerges is, "The existence of theories of rationality...will not suffice to sustain rational discourse. What are needed are well-established institutions geared to value, stimulate, promote, and reward debate, criticism and reform." But that is the very point I thought I was making about the transformation of a system — Aristotelian method, neo-Platonic message, Socratic medium of analysis — into a tradition, namely, the Talmud's Judaism of the dual Torah, in *The Making of the Mind of Judaism,* which concludes on that very point: Bible and Bavli, tradition in the form of a system, system in the form of a tradition.

Anti-traditionalists take the teachings of their forebears in utmost seriousness, but do so...with a view not to following them indiscriminately so much as to seriously putting them to the test...to reason rationally about the content of their legacies in the same way open-minded and self doubting agents were shown [in the section on science] to act rationally when strivingly knowing to improve upon the systems on which they work."

Not only so, but despite his protestations about not doing history, Fish thinks he has identified "in at least one major Tannaitic corpus" anti-traditionalism not as merely "one viable option among many" but the normative one. "The anti-traditionalist... is a voice that is central to any understanding of how the founder-fathers of Torah Judaism conceived of themselves and of their great intellectual undertaking." Now that statement unabashedly claims to speak of a determinate past, on the one side, and a specific "corpus," on the other — marks of historical and literary judgment. We no longer speak of what documents say but what the named fathers of Torah Judaism actually thought. So at stake in the end is not a viewpoint that the author wishes to espouse and sustain with appropriate proof-texts, but rather a specific judgment of a historical- and literary-critical character upon the texts that are studied. This work did not have to take the academic form that it did, but since it has, it must be read in the explicit context the author has invoked in judgment of his work: history.

This historical and literary critical claim — denied on one page, embodied in actual words on the next — too is (alas!) explicit: "it is at the Tannaitic level, where the question of the proper attitude towards the teachings of one's forebears hardly effects the redactory and narratory [sic!] level of the text, that the anti-traditionalist voice can be heard most audibly, while in Amoraic treatments of Tannaitic writings, where one would expect the anti-traditionalist approach to be felt most conspicuous, it is present, but curiously and vexingly muted, especially in the Bavli." But most (though not all) of the stories that Fish labels "Tannaitic" receive the label because of the names in the stories — therefore assumed to have said what is assigned to them, at the time and place that the story-teller has determined — and not because of the point of origination, the document in which the story first appears. He devotes much attention to stories in the Talmud of Babylonia that bear the sign of Tannaite status but first occur only in the final document of the corpus. Indeed, most of his most explicit evidence in fact originates in the final document of the Oral Torah in its formative age, the Talmud of Babylonia, rather than in the first documents to reach closure. On that basis, one might form exactly the opposite hypothesis as to the history of traditionalism and anti-traditionalism in Rabbinic Judaism in the formative age: the earliest documents were traditionalist, the final one the most sustainedly anti-traditionalist of all.

Fish claims to characterize the "Amoraic" stratum as traditionalist. But that allegation is simply false in light of the persistent critical spirit toward received opinions exhibited by the Talmud and its authorities both named and anonymous; the regnant voice of the document is dialectical and critical of every factual allegation and proposed probative argument — it is what makes the Talmud talmudic. The dialectical argument that imparts to the Bavli its dynamism and systemic character in no way gives comfort to what Fish would call traditionalism. It is fundamental, negative, persistent, tough-minded, systematic, and fresh. Not only so, but the Amoraic materials encompass a vast range of stories about the indeterminacy of specific propositions, the priority of *Auseinandersetzungen* in the processes of learning, the determinative power of reason — all of the traits of Fish's "anti-traditionalism."[5] So a vast corpus of Amoraic materials, which Fish knows full well, contradicts his ordering of matters, and, readers may stipulate, a considerable corpus of Tannaitic materials bears the marks of deep traditionalism — beginning, after all, with the opening chapter of tractate Abot! At this point one is tempted to cry out in despair, *iqqar haser min hassefer* — the book misses its point.

So grand a mistake in the characterization of layers of writing ("Tannaitic" and "Amoraic" read as historical notwithstanding) is possible only because Fish has at once denied the historicist hermeneutic and adopted it. That is, while Fish repeatedly denies intending a historical account and means by "Tannaitic" "that which is presented by the rabbis as Tannaitic," that is mere dust in the eyes of the scholars. In fact he has a diachronic logic which should give him early anti-traditionalism and late traditionalism, and he says so in so many words; he cannot then take away what he has given with an open hand. Not only so, but when he wishes to explain the data, he invokes nothing less than historical *context*, — not philosophical *logic* — time and again. Fish not only confuses theological with literary and historical discourse but simply ignores the boundaries between literary analysis and historical narrative.

A single, craftily worded formulation, suffices to show the confusion (I italicize the qualifying language to underscore its substantive irrelevance): "*It is possible that* the Halakhic discussions and the legends recorded by the talmudic literature attest to the fact that *at least some of the* rabbis *may have* regarded, *if even in retrospect*, the shifting of the

---

[5]The really interesting question is how such a sustainedly-critical mode of thought as the Talmud inculcates has produced so subservient and amiable a spirit of traditionalism as characterizes the yeshiva-world that Fisch denounces. That is a question of culture, of Talmudic culture, awaiting his attention.

prime focus of religious performance from the Temple to the academy, from the altar to the synagogue, as a welcome development, as a step forward more than as a necessary evil." With or without the italicized language, the statement concerns what happened, and that is history, not hermeneutics, let alone exegesis of texts. Fish honestly believes that the texts tell him what was happening beyond their limits, at the time of which the speak, in the place of which they speak. But surely a viable alternative would direct our attention to the time in which the texts take shape, and the issues alive in that day and age and venue. It is possible that the Halakhic discussions attest to the fact that at least some of the rabbis who fabricated these discussions....

And again, in the same context, "...with the fall of Jerusalem Rabbinic Judaism...was in fact significantly transformed from a largely ritualistic religion dominated and regulated by the Temple rituals to a 'community of learners' whose religious life was both structured and informed by the talmudic academy." He cannot have written this sentence and many like it if he really thought that "Tannaitic" means merely, "that which is presented by the rabbis as Tannaitic." Within the very same context he has shaded over into an account of how things were, which (lest we misunderstand) he explains by reference to the historical circumstances that defined Rabbinic Judaism.

Lest readers doubt the inferences I draw, the following language is Fish's, not mine, in the context of the sentences just now quoted:

> The high point of the talmudic revolution...was undoubtedly the establishment of the Jabne center...by Rabban Yohanan b. Zakkai.

This, I maintain, is a blatantly historical statement in a diachronic context, not a mere synchronic and analytical characterization of what some stories allege about this and that; historical facts, e.g., the destruction of the Temple, are invoked to explain other facts, which, by consequence, cannot be represented as mere traits of writings but as things that really happened.[6] What Fish does not realize is that merely alleging a critical position does not suffice; one has also to frame questions within the premises of criticism. That explains why Fish formulates his presentation as essentially historical, temporally determinate, with the sources attesting to the period of which they speak, not of those for whom they speak, even while claiming time and again that that is not what he thinks. The very framing of matters betrays him as a highly sophisticated fundamentalist. Once again, hear Fish:

> We shall focus attention in the first instance on the rabbis' own description...of one crucial moment in the course of one crucial phase of the process. The crucial phase begins with the destruction of the Second Temple and the foundation of the new center of Jewish life and learning at Jabne...From this point on, according to talmudic lore, hampered no longer by the Sadducees and Boethusians, who had virtually vanished after losing their Jerusalem Temple-centered power base, the rabbis set about in earnest to define and deliberate the order of the day among themselves.

Now the qualifying language once more notwithstanding, Fish has organized his discourse, has framed his questions, has formulated his dialectic, within the premise that he deals

---

[6]Not only so, but without explaining how late sources tell us what really happened four or five hundred years prior to their redaction, he takes as fact a variety of late allegations, e.., "This is...the widely accepted interpretation of the Talmuds account of Rabban Yohanan b Zakkai's decision to abandon and surrender the besieged Jerusalem on condition that Jabne...be saved."

with historical facts.[7] Many times as I read his book I regretted he did not know or absorb the explicit lessons of my *Reading and Believing: Ancient Judaism and Contemporary Gullibility*. Atlanta, 1986: Scholars Press for Brown Judaic Studies, where I point to numerous cases in which the premise of the sources' historicity alone can explain the framing of historical questions to the sources.

Had he really believed that all we have is the claim of "talmudic lore," he would have placed this "revolution" of his not in the aftermath of the destruction of the Temple but at that point at which the Talmudic lore took shape and made its statement, in pseudo-historical terms of a determinate point in the past, of what amounted to its theology of the Torah and the proper way in which it should be studied. Narrative theology, after all, defines the mode of discourse of the written Torah; theology in the form of a story constituting the medium of the prophetic message in Genesis through Kings. But in the context in which Fish wishes to formulate his thesis about traditionalism and anti-traditionalism, to the audience that he wishes to persuade, arguments from historical precedent as set forth in the holy books will carry weight and compel conviction. Not only so, but within integrationist, Western Orthodox Judaism, to be able to show a correspondence between theories of knowledge (epistemology) and a prestigious school in the philosophy of science marks a proposition as weighty and legitimate.

And, once more, Fish himself supplies the evidence

---

[7]Worse still, the footnotes for the section under discussion refer only to sources and to articles that take those sources at face value. Fisch really does not grasp how matters change when critical-historical issues of method register. It would be easy to cite note after note that cites a source to sustain a historical fact. But Fisch has promised us that that is not his view of matters.

for what is at stake in his presenting his data in one way, rather than in some other:

> In the course of these revolutionary developments, the texts comprising the talmudic canon were written, collated, anthologized and edited.

But if he really believes that the texts are all we have and speak only for themselves, not for what lies beyond their margins, then how does he know that the texts were written at a determinate point, "in the course of revolutionary developments," of which, after all, we are informed only by the very texts that Fish maintains took shape at that particular moment.

In light of these observations, the shank of the book, noted above, enjoys considerably less interest than at the outset one might have hoped. Once we perceive what actually is going on, we understand the reality. The work is a mass of fundamental contradictions between a critical and a fundamentally gullible spirit. He has given us Yabneh as the turning point, but then tells us "in the Bavli...the anti-traditionalist voice of talmudic Judaism receives its clearest articulation as well as its most effective stifling." These are simply not the same things, they are statements of two distinct orders. Quite what this reference to a metaphor of an anti-traditionalist voice" means is difficult to say. But let me try. I think Fish means, the Bavli contains stories that convey both viewpoints. Then why not say matters in a clear and simple way and be done with it? And why spend the first fifth of the book on an account of philosophy of science, which then plays no weighty part in the exposition of the Talmudic stories?

But the book sometimes comes alive and overcomes the dread weight of dreary, pseudo-critical argument about pseudo-historical facts. Where Fish really lives, there he transcends the empty pretense to which I have called attention and sets forth powerful arguments, and I think quite profound analysis. Here he shows what he could have done, had clear thinking and careful, analytical differentiation dictated his strategy of exposition and argument in behalf of his ideas. His discussion of "traditionalism and its discontents" — involving a systematic exposition of the realist position in hermeneutics — shows that of which Fish is capable. Here he engages in no pseudo-historical reflection but undertakes a systematic argument, a clear and carefully crafted analysis of two contradictory *positions*. And, it pays to notice, when he reaches what he has mastered and knows well, he also writes in unadorned and vigorous prose, without all the heavy burden of prolixity and verbosity, needless and pointless qualification and an excess of wordage, that slows up the reader's progress in much of the rest of the book. Here he shines:

> one would expect thoroughly traditionalist centers of learning...to be [a] unflinchingly dogmatic in preserving their legacies; [b[highly selective; [c] genuinely critical only of the credentials and authenticity of the bearers of tradition but never of the content of their teachings; and [d] to view themselves as fighting a hopelessly loosing battle to preserve and transmit an inevitably dwindling body of revealed truth. All four features are explicitly associated with the traditionalist opposition envisaged by the Jabne stories, and all four are reputed to have been markedly reversed by the triumphant anti-traditionalist Jabne reformers.

The elegant passage goes on for some pages, and here we do not have to wonder whether he is paid by the word.

Alas, from this point, we plunge back into the paraphrase as history of a variety of stories, deriving from a variety of documents of various periods and venues, and the old pseudo-history and paraphrase of fables take over and put an end to analytical discourse, such as Fish shows himself entirely able to mount (if not to sustain). To address the remainder of the shank of the book would require saying the same thing about many things, and it suffices to say that the book as a whole suffers from the deep flaws indicated by this survey: a confusion of types of discourse, a claim to criticism that is denied in the very formulation of matters, and a profound misunderstanding of the requirements of theological discourse. Fish is a victim of the historicism that he clearly hoped to sidestep. This is because he has evaded the critical issues — differentiating theological from historical discourse, devising an accurate and reliable way of characterizing "the Talmudic position(s)," and dealing with the whole and only then the parts.

Any serious worker, motivated by curiosity, will test his mode of explaining data by devising other explanations and asking whether his is the best, the most plausible, way of interpreting the facts. This Fish does not commonly do, as even the snippets I have given show. That is why it is obvious that he undertook the work to make a point important in his circles of contemporary Orthodox Judaism, and he wants "Talmudic culture" to prove his point by providing a probative precedent. So he has set out to find precedents for the kind of Orthodox Judaism that he wishes would prevail in the state of Israel. He has found those demonstrative facts among the anti-traditionalists for whom his book forms a protracted cheer. That, and not "talmudic culture," is, sum and substance, is what this book is about.

How to explain this disappointing outcome of what is obviously a sincere effort? It is the enthusiasm of the autodidact, the specialist in one thing who wishes to invoke what he knows in the service of what he wants, in some other context altogether, to prove. Clearly, what Fish knows in a professional, not an impressionistic or merely political, way is philosophy of science, his academic vocation. He also has the power to compose a beautiful treatise of abstract comparison and contrast, as I just showed. But he has worked much harder at philosophy of science than at study, in a professional way, through systematic reading of the academic literature, of the subject at hand. And he is surrounded by amateurs like himself. I state flatly that Fish simply does not know most of the critical literature produced in the past three decades concerning the sources with which he purports to deal. It is a work, then, of surpassing ignorance of the field in which it claims its place. In his enthusiasm for his position Fish does not formulate a null hypothesis, such as social and natural sciences routinely set forth; he does not attempt to produce diverse explanations of the same phenomenon and show why his explanation is the most plausible, he does not conduct a critical argument with himself. With lavish spreads of chirpy words he papers over enormous holes in his argument. Time and again he marks himself as a thorough-going amateur.

  I do not think he would dare to present to philosophers of science a proposition set forth in the shoddy and ill-informed manner in which he sets forth that of the shank of the book: an effort not to analyze a problem but to prove a point by reading the evidence in one way only. And I do not think he would publish in philosophy of science a work that ignores a sizable sector of the literature on the problem of his monograph. I doubt that a professional monograph series in history and philosophy of science would have permitted so bald a disaster to take place in its pages: a failure simply to consult the pertinent academic literature and to conduct a systematic *Auseinandersetzung* therewith. As between his unwinning enthusiasm and his massive ignorance of much of the scholarly literature, which he has not read, and, worse still, the implications of which he has not absorbed into the fabric of his argument and its formulation, I am inclined to blame the failure of the book on the latter. Fish really does not know the territory, he has not read the critical discussion of several decades, and that is why he could formulate his proposition — the theological one, I mean — in so goofy a manner.

So a good intention has come to poor execution. The failure of intellect that characterizes the very framing of matters here, I am inclined to think, finds its explanation in the difference between vocation and avocation. It is what must happen when a scholar of Jewish origin and commitment who has achieved distinction in a secular field of learning presents himself as a voice in the sacred sciences. There he decides to use what he has learned in secular learning for advancing a bright idea in the service of the sacred sciences of Judaism that he knows but has mastered only superficially. Scholars from the periphery bring to the center of those sacred sciences important learning only when those scholars at the margins of matters devote to the sacred sciences the same rigorous thought and disinterested learning that have distinguished them in their secular studies. And first of all they must do their homework in the same disinterested and conscientious way in the Judaic area that they do in the secular one. Absent that same seriousness about the Torah that the secular sciences demand, the result can only prove immature and enthusiastic: theology made easy, criticism evaded, only the immediate requirements of local theological politics well served.

BIBLIOGRAPHY

Bibliography

These are the titles of mine that contribute to the arguments of the present book.

The Talmud of the Land of Israel. A Preliminary Translation and Explanation. Chicago: The University of Chicago Press: 1983. XXXV. *Introduction. Taxonomy.*

The Integrity of Leviticus Rabbah. The Problem of the Autonomy of a Rabbinic Document. Chico, 1985: Scholars Press for Brown Judaic Studies.

Comparative Midrash: The Plan and Program of Genesis Rabbah and Leviticus Rabbah. Atlanta, 1986: Scholars Press for Brown Judaic Studies.

From Tradition to Imitation. The Plan and Program of Pesiqta deRab Kahana and Pesiqta Rabbati. Atlanta, 1987: Scholars Press for Brown Judaic Studies. [With a fresh translation of Pesiqta Rabbati *Pisqaot* 1-5, 15.]

Canon and Connection: Intertextuality in Judaism. Lanham, 1986: University Press of America. *Studies in Judaism* Series.

Midrash as Literature: The Primacy of Documentary Discourse. Lanham, 1987: University Press of America *Studies in Judaism* series.

The Bavli and its Sources: The Question of Tradition in the Case of Tractate Sukkah. Atlanta, 1987: Scholars Press for Brown Judaic Studies.

Sifré to Deuteronomy. An Introduction to the Rhetorical, Logical, and Topical Program. Atlanta, 1987: Scholars Press for Brown Judaic Studies.

Uniting the Dual Torah: Sifra and the Problem of the Mishnah. Cambridge and New York, 1989: Cambridge University Press.

Sifra in Perspective: The Documentary Comparison of the Midrashim of Ancient Judaism Atlanta, 1988: Scholars Press for Brown Judaic Studies.

Mekhilta Attributed to R. Ishmael. An Introduction to Judaism's First Scriptural Encyclopaedia. Atlanta, 1988: Scholars Press for Brown Judaic Studies.

The Midrash Compilations of the Sixth and Seventh Centuries. An Introduction to the Rhetorical Logical, and Topical Program. I. Lamentations Rabbah. Atlanta, 1990: Scholars Press for Brown Judaic Studies

The Midrash Compilations of the Sixth and Seventh Centuries: An Introduction to the Rhetorical Logical, and Topical Program. II. Esther Rabbah I. Atlanta, 1990: Scholars Press for Brown Judaic Studies

The Midrash Compilations of the Sixth and Seventh Centuries: An Introduction to the Rhetorical Logical, and Topical Program. III. Ruth Rabbah. Atlanta, 1990: Scholars Press for Brown Judaic Studies

The Midrash Compilations of the Sixth and Seventh Centuries: An Introduction to the Rhetorical Logical, and Topical Program. IV. Song of Songs Rabbah. Atlanta, 1990: Scholars Press for Brown Judaic Studies

Making the Classics in Judaism: The Three Stages of Literary Formation. Atlanta, 1990: Scholars Press for Brown Judaic Studies.

The Canonical History of Ideas. The Place of the So-called Tannaite Midrashim, Mekhilta Attributed to R. Ishmael, Sifra, Sifré to Numbers, and Sifré to Deuteronomy. Atlanta, 1990: Scholars Press for South Florida Studies in the History of Judaism.

Tradition as Selectivity: Scripture, Mishnah, Tosefta, and Midrash in the Talmud of Babylonia. The Case of Tractate Arakhin. Atlanta, 1990: Scholars Press for South Florida Studies in the History of Judaism.

Language as Taxonomy. The Rules for Using Hebrew and Aramaic in the Babylonian Talmud. Atlanta, 1990: Scholars Press for South Florida Studies in the History of Judaism.

The Bavli That Might Have Been: The Tosefta's Theory of Mishnah-Commentary Compared with That of the Babylonian Talmud. Atlanta, 1990: Scholars Press for South Florida Studies in the History of Judaism.

The Rules of Composition of the Talmud of Babylonia. The Cogency of the Bavli's Composite. Atlanta, 1991: Scholars Press for South Florida Studies in the History of Judaism.

The Bavli's One Voice: Types and Forms of Analytical Discourse and their Fixed Order of Appearance. Atlanta, 1991: Scholars Press for South Florida Studies in the History of Judaism.

The Bavli's One Statement. The Metapropositional Program of Babylonian Talmud Tractate Zebahim Chapters One and Five. Atlanta, 1991: Scholars Press for South Florida Studies in the History of Judaism.

How the Bavli Shaped Rabbinic Discourse. Atlanta, 1991: Scholars Press for South Florida Studies in the History of Judaism.

The Bavli's Massive Miscellanies. The Problem of Agglutinative Discourse in the Talmud of Babylonia. Atlanta, 1992: Scholars Press for South Florida Studies in the History of Judaism.

Sources and Traditions. Types of Composition in the Talmud of Babylonia. Atlanta, 1992: Scholars Press for South Florida Studies in the History of Judaism.

The Law Behind the Laws. The Bavli's Essential Discourse. Atlanta, 1992: Scholars Press for South Florida Studies in the History of Judaism.

The Bavli's Primary Discourse. Mishnah Commentary, its Rhetorical Paradigms and their Theological Implications in the Talmud of Babylonia Tractate Moed Qatan. Atlanta, 1992: Scholars

Press for South Florida Studies in the History of Judaism.

The Discourse of the Bavli: Language, Literature, and Symbolism. Five Recent Findings. Atlanta, 1991: Scholars Press for South Florida Studies in the History of Judaism.

How to Study the Bavli: The Languages, Literatures, and Lessons of the Talmud of Babylonia. Atlanta, 1992: Scholars Press for South Florida Studies in the History of Judaism.

Form-Analytical Comparison in Rabbinic Judaism. Structure and Form in The Fathers *and* The Fathers According to Rabbi Nathan. Atlanta, 1992: Scholars Press for South Florida Studies in the History of Judaism.

The Bavli's Intellectual Character. The Generative Problematic in Bavli Baba Qamma Chapter One and Bavli Shabbat Chapter One. Atlanta, 1992: Scholars Press for South Florida Studies in the History of Judaism.

Decoding the Talmud's Exegetical Program: From Detail to Principle in the Bavli's Quest for Generalization. Tractate Shabbat. Atlanta, 1992: Scholars Press for South Florida Studies in the History of Judaism.

The Principal Parts of the Bavli's Discourse: A Final Taxonomy. Mishnah-Commentary, Sources, Traditions, and Agglutinative Miscellanies. Atlanta, 1992: Scholars Press for South Florida Studies in the History of Judaism.

The Bavli's Unique Voice. A Systematic Comparison of the Talmud of Babylonia and the Talmud of the Land of Israel. Volume One. *Bavli and Yerushalmi Qiddushin Chapter One Compared and Contrasted.* Atlanta, 1993: Scholars Press for South Florida Studies in the History of Judaism.

The Bavli's Unique Voice. A Systematic Comparison of the Talmud of Babylonia and the Talmud of the Land of Israel. Volume Two. *Yerushalmi's, Bavli's, and Other Canonical Documents' Treatment of the Program of Mishnah-Tractate Sukkah Chapters One, Two, and Four Compared and*

Contrasted. *A Reprise and Revision of* The Bavli and its Sources. Atlanta, 1993: Scholars Press for South Florida Studies in the History of Judaism.

The Bavli's Unique Voice. A Systematic Comparison of the Talmud of Babylonia and the Talmud of the Land of Israel. Volume Three. *Bavli and Yerushalmi to Selected Mishnah-Chapters in the Division of Moed. Erubin Chapter One, and Moed Qatan Chapter Three.* Atlanta, 1993: Scholars Press for South Florida Studies in the History of Judaism.

The Bavli's Unique Voice. A Systematic Comparison of the Talmud of Babylonia and the Talmud of the Land of Israel. Volume Four. *Bavli and Yerushalmi to Selected Mishnah-Chapters in the Division of Nashim. Gittin Chapter Five and Nedarim Chapter One. And Niddah Chapter One.* Atlanta, 1993: Scholars Press for South Florida Studies in the History of Judaism.

The Bavli's Unique Voice. A Systematic Comparison of the Talmud of Babylonia and the Talmud of the Land of Israel. Volume Five. *Bavli and Yerushalmi to Selected Mishnah-Chapters in the Division of Neziqin. Baba Mesia Chapter One and Makkot Chapters One and Two.* Atlanta, 1993: Scholars Press for South Florida Studies in the History of Judaism.

The Bavli's Unique Voice. A Systematic Comparison of the Talmud of Babylonia and the Talmud of the Land of Israel. Volume Six. *Bavli and Yerushalmi to a Miscellany of Mishnah-Chapters. Gittin Chapter One, Qiddushin Chapter Two, and Hagigah Chapter Three.* Atlanta, 1993: Scholars Press for South Florida Studies in the History of Judaism.

The Bavli's Unique Voice. Volume Seven. *What Is Unique about the Bavli in Context? An Answer Based on Inductive Description, Analysis, and Comparison.* Atlanta, 1993: Scholars Press for South Florida Studies in the History of Judaism.

312 *Peripatetic Parallels*

Introduction to Rabbinic Literature. N.Y., 1994: Doubleday. The Doubleday Anchor Reference Library. Religious Book Club Selection, 1994. Paperback edition: 1999.

Talmudic Dialectics: Types and Forms. Atlanta, 1995: Scholars Press for South Florida Studies in the History of Judaism. I. *Introduction. Tractate Berakhot and the Divisions of Appointed Times and Women.*

Talmudic Dialectics: Types and Forms. Atlanta, 1995: Scholars Press for South Florida Studies in the History of Judaism. II. *The Divisions of Damages and Holy Things and Tractate Niddah.*

Rationality and Structure: The Bavli's Anomalous Juxtapositions. Atlanta, 1997: Scholars Press for South Florida Studies in the History of Judaism.

Judaism. The Evidence of the Mishnah. Chicago, 1981: University of Chicago Press. *Choice*, "Outstanding academic book list" 1982-3. Paperback edition: 1984. Second printing, 1985. Third printing, 1986. Second edition, augmented: Atlanta, 1987: Scholars Press for Brown Judaic Studies.

Hayyahadut le'edut hammishnah. Hebrew translation of *Judaism. The Evidence of the Mishnah.* Tel Aviv, 1987: Sifriat Poalim.

Il Giudaismo nella testimonianza della Mishnah. Italian translation by Giogio Volpe. Bologna, 1995: Centro editoriale Dehoniane.

Judaism in Society: The Evidence of the Yerushalmi. Toward the Natural History of a Religion. Chicago, 1983: The University of Chicago Press. *Choice*, "Outstanding Academic Book List, 1984-1985." Second printing, with a new preface: Atlanta, 1991: Scholars Press for South Florida Studies in the History of Judaism.

Judaism and Scripture: The Evidence of Leviticus Rabbah. Chicago, 1986: The University of Chicago Press. [Fresh translation of Margulies' text and systematic analysis of problems of composition and redaction.] Jewish Book Club Selection, 1986.

Judaism: The Classical Statement. The Evidence of the Bavli. Chicago, 1986: University of Chicago Press. *Choice,* "Outstanding Academic Book List, 1987."

Judaism and Story: The Evidence of The Fathers According to Rabbi Nathan. Chicago, 1992: University of Chicago Press.

The Making of the Mind of Judaism. Atlanta, 1987: Scholars Press for Brown Judaic Studies.

The Formation of the Jewish Intellect. Making Connections and Drawing Conclusions in the Traditional System of Judaism. Atlanta, 1988: Scholars Press for Brown Judaic Studies.

The Four Stages of Rabbinic Judaism. London, 2000: Routledge.

What, Exactly, Did the Rabbinic Sages Mean by "the Oral Torah"? An Inductive Answer to the Question of Rabbinic Judaism. Atlanta, 1999: Scholars Press for South Florida Studies in the History of Judaism.

A Theological Commentary to the Midrash: I. *Pesiqta deRab Kahana.* Lanham, 2001: University Press of America. STUDIES IN ANCIENT JUDAISM SERIES.

A Theological Commentary to the Midrash: II. *Genesis Rabbah.* Lanham, 2001: University Press of America. STUDIES IN ANCIENT JUDAISM SERIES.

A Theological Commentary to the Midrash: III. *Song of Songs Rabbah.* Lanham, 2001: University Press of America. STUDIES IN ANCIENT JUDAISM SERIES.

A Theological Commentary to the Midrash. IV. *Leviticus Rabbah*

A Theological Commentary to the Midrash: V. *Lamentations Rabbati*

A Theological Commentary to the Midrash VI. *Esther Rabbah I and Ruth Rabbah*

A Theological Commentary to the Midrash VII. *Sifra*

A Theological Commentary to the Midrash VIII. *Sifré to Numbers*

A Theological Commentary to the Midrash IX. *Sifré to Deuteronomy*
A Theological Commentary to the Midrash X. *The Theological Foundations of Rabbinic Midrash*
The Talmud of Babylonia. A Complete Outline. Atlanta, 1995-6: Scholars Press for *USF Academic Commentary Series.*
- I.A Tractate Berakhot and the Division of Appointed Times. Berakhot, Shabbat, and Erubin.
- I.B Tractate Berakhot and the Division of Appointed Times. Pesahim through Hagigah.
- II.A. The Division of Women. Yebamot through Ketubot
- II.B. The Division of Women. Nedarim through Qiddushin
- III.A The Division of Damages. Baba Qamma through Baba Batra
- III.B The Division of Damages. Sanhedrin through Horayot
- IV.A The Division of Holy Things and Tractate Niddah. Zebahim through Hullin
- IV.B The Division of Holy Things and Tractate Niddah. Bekhorot through Niddah

The Talmud of The Land of Israel. An Outline of the Second, Third, and Fourth Divisions. Atlanta, 1995-6: Scholars Press for USF Academic Commentary Series.
- I.A Tractate Berakhot and the Division of Appointed Times. Berakhot and Shabbat
- I.B Tractate Berakhot and the Division of Appointed Times. Erubin, Yoma, and Besah
- I.C Tractate Berakhot and the Division of Appointed Times. Pesahim and Sukkah
- I.D Tractate Berakhot and the Division of Appointed Times. Taanit, Megillah, Rosh Hashanah, Hagigah, and Moed Qatan
- II.A. The Division of Women. Yebamot to Nedarim
- II.B. The Division of Women. Nazir to Sotah

III.A The Division of Damages and Tractate Niddah. Baba Qamma, Baba Mesia, Baba Batra, Horayot, and Niddah

III.B The Division of Damages and Tractate Niddah. Sanhedrin, Makkot, Shebuot, and Abodah Zarah

The Two Talmuds Compared. Atlanta, 1995-6: Scholars Press for USF Academic Commentary Series.

I.A Tractate Berakhot and the Division of Appointed Times in the Talmud of the Land of Israel and the Talmud of Babylonia. Yerushalmi Tractate Berakhot

I.B Tractate Berakhot and the Division of Appointed Times in the Talmud of the Land of Israel and the Talmud of Babylonia. Tractate Shabbat.

I.C Tractate Berakhot and the Division of Appointed Times in the Talmud of the Land of Israel and the Talmud of Babylonia. Tractate Erubin

I.D Tractate Berakhot and the Division of Appointed Times in the Talmud of the Land of Israel and the Talmud of Babylonia. Tractates Yoma and Sukkah

I.E Tractate Berakhot and the Division of Appointed Times in the Talmud of the Land of Israel and the Talmud of Babylonia. Tractate Pesahim

I.F Tractate Berakhot and the Division of Appointed Times in the Talmud of the Land of Israel and the Talmud of Babylonia. Tractates Besah, Taanit, and Megillah

I.G Tractate Berakhot and the Division of Appointed Times in the Talmud of the Land of Israel and the Talmud of Babylonia. Tractates Rosh Hashanah, Hagigah, and Moed Qatan

II.A The Division of Women in the Talmud of the Land of Israel and the Talmud of Babylonia. Tractates Yebamot and Ketubot.

II.B   *The Division of Women in the Talmud of the Land of Israel and the Talmud of Babylonia. Tractates Nedarim, Nazir, and Sotah.*

II.C   *The Division of Women in the Talmud of the Land of Israel and the Talmud of Babylonia. Tractates Qiddushin and Gittin.*

III.A   *The Division of Damages and Tractate Niddah in the Talmud of the Land of Israel and the Talmud of Babylonia. Tractates Baba Qamma and Baba Mesia*

III.B   *The Division of Damages and Tractate Niddah in the Talmud of the Land of Israel and the Talmud of Babylonia. Baba Batra and Niddah.*

III.C   *The Division of Damages and Tractate Niddah. Sanhedrin and Makkot.*

III.D   *The Division of Damages and Tractate Niddah. Shebuot, Abodah Zarah, and Horayot.*

The Components of the Rabbinic Documents: From the Whole to the Parts. Volume I. *Sifra.* Atlanta, 1997: Scholars Press for USF Academic Commentary Series.

Part i.   *Introduction. And Parts One through Three, Chapters One through Ninety-Eight*

Part ii. *Parts Four through Nine. Chapters Ninety-Nine through One Hundred Ninety-Four*

Part iii. *Parts Ten through Thirteen. Chapters One Hundred Ninety-Five through Two Hundred Seventy-Seven*

Part iv. *A Topical and Methodical Outline of Sifra*

The Components of the Rabbinic Documents: From the Whole to the Parts. Volume II. *Esther Rabbah I.* Atlanta, 1997: Scholars Press for USF Academic Commentary Series.

The Components of the Rabbinic Documents: From the Whole to the Parts. Volume III. *Ruth Rabbah.* Atlanta, 1997: Scholars Press for USF Academic Commentary Series.

The Components of the Rabbinic Documents: From the Whole to the Parts. Volume IV. *Lamentations Rabbati.* Atlanta, 1997: Scholars Press for USF Academic Commentary Series.

The Components of the Rabbinic Documents: From the Whole to the Parts. Volume V. *Song of Songs Rabbah.* Atlanta, 1997: Scholars Press for USF Academic Commentary Series.

    Part i. *Introduction. And Parashiyyot One through Four*

    Part ii. *Parashiyyot Five through Eight. And a Topical and Methodical Outline of Song of Songs Rabbah*

The Components of the Rabbinic Documents: From the Whole to the Parts. VI. *The Fathers Attributed to Rabbi Nathan.* Atlanta, 1997: Scholars Press for USF Academic Commentary Series.

The Components of the Rabbinic Documents: From the Whole to the Parts. VII. *Sifré to Deuteronomy.* Atlanta, 1997: Scholars Press for USF Academic Commentary Series.

    Part i. *Introduction. And Parts One through Four*

    Part ii. *Parts Five through Ten*

    Part iii. *A Topical and Methodical Outline of Sifré to Deuteronomy*

The Components of the Rabbinic Documents: From the Whole to the Parts. VIII. *Mekhilta Attributed to R. Ishmael.* Atlanta, 1997: Scholars Press for USF Academic Commentary Series.

    Part i. *Introduction. Pisha, Beshallah and Shirata*

    Part ii *Vayassa, Amalek, Bahodesh, Neziqin, Kaspa and Shabbata*

    Part iii. *A Topical and Methodical Outline of Mekhilta Attributed to R. Ishmael.*

The Components of the Rabbinic Documents: From the Whole to the Parts. IX. *Genesis Rabbah.* Atlanta, 1998: Scholars Press for USF Academic Commentary Series.

Part i. *Introduction. Genesis Rabbah Chapters One through Twenty-One*

Part ii. *Genesis Rabbah Chapters Twenty-Two through Forty-Eight*

Part iii. *Genesis Rabbah Chapters Forty-Nine through Seventy-Three*

Part iv. *Genesis Rabbah Chapters Seventy-Four through One Hundred*

Part v. *A Topical and Methodical Outline of Genesis Rabbah. Bereshit throughVaere, Chapters One through Fifty-Seven*

Part vi. *A Topical and Methodical Outline of Genesis Rabbah. Hayye Sarah through Miqqes. Chapters Fifty-Eight through One Hundred*

The Components of the Rabbinic Documents: From the Whole to the Parts. X. *Leviticus Rabbah.* Atlanta, 1998: Scholars Press for USF Academic Commentary Series.

Part i. *Introduction. Leviticus Rabbah Parashiyyot One through Seventeen*

Part ii. *Leviticus Rabbah Parashiyyot Eighteen through Thirty-Seven*

Part iii. *Leviticus Rabbah. A Topical and Methodical Outline*

The Components of the Rabbinic Documents: From the Whole to the Parts. XI. *Pesiqta deRab Kahana.* Atlanta, 1998: Scholars Press for USF Academic Commentary Series.

Part i. *Introduction. Pesiqta deRab Kahana Pisqaot One through Eleven*

Part ii. *Pesiqta deRab Kahana Pisqaot Twelve through Twenty-Eight*

Part iii. *Pesiqta deRab Kahana. A Topical and Methodical Outline*

The Components of the Rabbinic Documents: From the Whole to the Parts. XII. *Sifré to Numbers.* Atlanta, 1998: Scholars Press for USF Academic Commentary Series.
Part i. *Introduction. Pisqaot One through Eighty-Four*
Part ii *Pisqaot Eighty-Five through One Hundred Twenty-Two*
Part iii *Pisqaot One Hundred Twenty-Three through One Hundred Sixty-One*
Part iv *Sifré to Numbers. A Topical and Methodical Outline*

The Documentary Form-History of Rabbinic Literature. I. *The Documentary Forms of the Mishnah.* Atlanta, 1998: Scholars Press for USF Academic Commentary Series.

The Documentary Form-History of Rabbinic Literature II. *The Aggadic Sector: Tractate Abot, Abot deRabbi Natan, Sifra, Sifré to Numbers, and Sifré to Deuteronomy.* Atlanta, 1998: Scholars Press for USF Academic Commentary Series.

The Documentary Form-History of Rabbinic Literature III. *The Aggadic Sector Mekhilta Attributed to R. Ishmael and Genesis Rabbah.* Atlanta, 1998: Scholars Press for USF Academic Commentary Series.

The Documentary Form-History of Rabbinic Literature IV. *The Aggadic Sector Leviticus Rabbah, and Pesiqta deRab Kahana.* Atlanta, 1998: Scholars Press for USF Academic Commentary Series.

The Documentary Form-History of Rabbinic Literature V. *The Aggadic Sector: Song of Songs Rabbah, Ruth Rabbah, Lamentations Rabbati, and Esther Rabbah I.* Atlanta, 1998: Scholars Press for USF Academic Commentary Series.

The Documentary Form-History of Rabbinic Literature. VI. *The Halakhic Sector. The Talmud of the Land of Israel.* A. *Berakhot and Shabbat through Taanit.* Atlanta, 1998:

Scholars Press for USF Academic Commentary Series.

The Documentary Form-History of Rabbinic Literature. VI. *The Halakhic Sector. The Talmud of the Land of Israel.* B. *Megillah through Qiddushin.* Atlanta, 1998: Scholars Press for USF Academic Commentary Series.

The Documentary Form-History of Rabbinic Literature. VI. *The Halakhic Sector. The Talmud of the Land of Israel.* C. *Sotah through Horayot and Niddah.* Atlanta, 1998: Scholars Press for USF Academic Commentary Series.

The Documentary Form-History of Rabbinic Literature. VII. *The Halakhic Sector. The Talmud of Babylonia.* A. *Tractates Berakhot and Shabbat through Pesahim.* Atlanta, 1998: Scholars Press for USF Academic Commentary Series.

The Documentary Form-History of Rabbinic Literature. VII. *The Halakhic Sector. The Talmud of Babylonia.* B. *Tractates Yoma through Ketubot.* Atlanta, 1998: Scholars Press for USF Academic Commentary Series.

The Documentary Form-History of Rabbinic Literature. VII. *The Halakhic Sector. The Talmud of Babylonia.* C. *Tractates Nedarim through Baba Mesia.* Atlanta, 1998: Scholars Press for USF Academic Commentary Series.

The Documentary Form-History of Rabbinic Literature. VII. *The Halakhic Sector. The Talmud of Babylonia.* D. *Tractates Baba Batra through Horayot.* Atlanta, 1998: Scholars Press for USF Academic Commentary Series.

The Documentary Form-History of Rabbinic Literature. VII. *The Halakhic Sector. The Talmud of Babylonia.* E. *Tractates Zebahim through Bekhorot.* Atlanta, 1998: Scholars Press for USF Academic Commentary Series.

The Documentary Form-History of Rabbinic Literature. VII. *The Halakhic Sector. The Talmud of Babylonia.* F. *Tractates Arakhin through Niddah. And Conclusions.* Atlanta, 1998:

Scholars Press for USF Academic Commentary Series.

WITHDRAWN